BUS

3/5/03

The Handbook of
Alternative Investments

The Handbook of
Alternative Investments

Edited by
Darrell Jobman

John Wiley & Sons, Inc.

Darrell Jobman is a writer and editorial consultant in Deerfield, Illinois. He is an acknowledged authority on derivative markets and has spent his career writing and publishing about them. He was the editor-in-chief of *Futures Magazine* and is currently a contributing editor. He has edited and written a number of training courses and books, the most recent of which was *The Complete Guide to Electronic Futures Trad*ing published by McGraw-Hill.

Tremont Advisers is an Oppenheimer Funds Company. Tremont is a global source for alternative investment solutions focused on three specific areas: advisory services, information, and investment services. TASS Research is the Tremont's industry-leading information and research unit specializing in alternative investments. HedgeWorld provides news and features about hedge funds. CSFB/Tremont Hedge Fund Index provides the financial industry with the most precise tool to measure returns experienced by the hedge fund investor. Visit Tremont at tremontadvisers.com or call 914-925-1140.

Martin S. Fridson, CFA, is the chief high-yield securities strategist for Merrill Lynch. He is a member of *Institutional Investor's* All-America Fixed Income Research Team. He is a board member of The Association for Investment Management and Research. He is the author of three books, each of which are published by John Wiley & Sons, Inc.: *It Was a Very Good Year*, *Investment Illusions*, and *Financial Statement Analysis*.

Thomas E. Galuhn is a senior managing director of Mesirow Financial's private equity division. He has had a number of senior management positions with investment management and investment banking firms, including First Chicago Investment Advisors. He is a director of a number or publicly owned companies including Azteca Foods, Inc., SMS Technology, Inc., Jungle Laboratories, Corporation, Meridian Financial Corporation, and Swingles Furniture Rental, Inc. He received his B. S. degree from the University of Notre Dame and an MBA from the University of Chicago.

Geoffrey A. Hirt is the Mesirow Fellow in finance at DePaul University, and an advisor to Mesirow Financial Services. He is a frequent speaker at academic and professional conferences, and is a member of the Pacific Pension Institute. He is the author of two leading textbooks in investments and corporate finance. He received his Ph. D. from Texas Christian University.

John Lefebvre is president of Shareholder Relations, an investor relations firm in Denver, Colorado. He is an acknowledged authority on employing direct-marketing strategies in investor relations programs. He speaks and writes about the most recent developments in stock trading and market making, and the impact of electronic communications networks on stock valuations. He is the co-author of the forthcoming book, *Investor Relations for the Emerging Company*, (John Wiley & Sons, Inc.)

Jeffrey E. Modesitt is chief financial officer of Kern County Resources, Ltd., a private exploration and development company in Littleton, Colorado. He has been founding principal of two investment banking boutiques, and was the editor of a highly regarded newsletter on private investments. He is a graduate of Williams College and The New York Institute of Finance.

Paul E. Rice is a senior managing director of Mesirow Financial's private banking division. Prior to joining Mesirow, Mr. Rice managed the Alternative Investments Division for the State of Michigan Retirement System, (SMRS). He was also a member of The University of Michigan's Technology Advisory Group. He is a member of the executive committee of the Illinois Venture Capital Association and the advisory boards of Accel Partners, Arlington Capital Partners, Wind Point Partners, IV, L.P. and The Peninsula Fund II, L. P.

Mark G. Roberts is the director of research at INVESCO Realty Advisors, Inc. and is a member of their portfolio/investment committee. Mr. Roberts has more than 18 years of real estate experience, including 11 years in real estate development with a national hospitality firm. He has a M.S. degree from the Massachusetts Institute of Technology.

Thomas Schneeweis is a professor of finance at the CISDM/Isenberg School of Management at the University of Massachusetts and the Director of its Center for International Securities and Derivatives Markets. His research on managed futures performance was commissioned by the Alternative Investment Management Association in 1996 and has been updated frequently.

Richard Scott-Ram is chief portfolio strategist for the World Gold Council. Prior to joining the Council, he held senior positions with a number of financial institutions. He was deputy chief economist with Chemical Bank and with Merrill Lynch, and was the chief economist of the Conference Board of Canada.

Ben Warwick is the chief investment officer of Sovereign Wealth Management, Inc., a registered investment advisor for institutional investors and high-net-worth families. He is the author of several books including the acclaimed *Searching for Alpha* (John Wiley & Sons, Inc.). He received his B. S. degree in chemical engineering from the University of Florida and his MBA from the University of North Carolina at Chapel Hill.

contents

preface

This book is intended as a guide for investment professionals, accredited investors, fiduciaries, and trustees to assist them in developing asset allocation strategies. We have provided information on the most common investment alternatives employed for diversification and for protection from cyclical dips in the equities and debt markets. The contributors to this book are acknowledged authorities in their respective areas, and all have had extensive experience in developing alternative investing strategies.

Each chapter focuses on the unique attributes of its respective vehicle or strategy: historical returns, risk characteristics, valuation issues, transaction costs, custodial issues, and taxes.

Trillions of dollars are invested throughout the world for retirement plans, endowments, foundations, family offices, and corporations. The preservation of this wealth is critical to the welfare of the citizens of developed and emerging countries. The theme of this book is wealth preservation. Alternative investments are strategic wealth preservation vehicles and strategies. They are not necessarily speculative. They afford hedging protection and return enhancement when prudently employed. Being informed about the structure and nature of these alternatives is the first step in prudent employment. This book was developed as a point of departure in the reader's quest for authoritative and responsible information about alternative investments.

CHAPTER 1

Alpha Generating Strategies: A Consideration

By Ben Warwick

Investment pros have tried numerous methods to protect their clients against the occasionally vicious whims of market volatility. They all lead to one rather unconventional conclusion: Hedge funds and other alternative investments are better suited to generate exceptional returns than their more traditional mutual fund progenitors.

Having trouble adding value to the investment process? Take heart. Even Smokey Bear had his problems.

In 1942, Americans were in the midst of the largest world war in history. Many were fearful that an enemy of the United States would attempt to burn down the nation's woodlands, an act of terrorism that would have done considerable damage to the war effort. In response to this threat, the War Advertising Council heavily promoted fire prevention in the nation's forests. Even naturally occurring fires were to be extinguished "by 10 o'clock the following morning."

The advertising campaign took on a face in 1945, when a black bear cub was rescued from a fire at the Lincoln National Forest in Capitan, New Mexico. Later dubbed Smokey, the animal became the symbol for fire safety and prevention.

There was only one problem with the campaign: No one seemed cognizant that fire is a natural part of the ecological cycle.

That all changed in 1998, a year that witnessed the greatest drought in nearly a century. Catalyzed by the accumulation of five decades of excess underbrush, pine needles, and other organic material that make up a forest's "fuel load," fires devastated millions of acres of forest and timberland.

The Forest Service suddenly became infatuated with the idea of pre-scribed burns. What a great way to preserve the nation's natural places for future generations! All that was necessary were a few controlled fires, and the woods would once again be safe for all to enjoy.

There was only one problem with this new approach: Land management policies, based on commercial logging and cattle grazing, removed sur-rounding prairie grasses. Such grasses encourage moderate fires that tend to burn out quickly. As a result, prescribed burns were hotter, deadlier, and spread much faster than anyone had anticipated. All of a sudden, the term "controlled fire" took on less and less meaning.

Take the Cerro Grande Fire, for example, which was started at Bandelier National Monument on May 4, 2000. It was supposed to burn 968 acres but was fanned by winds of 50 miles per hour in drought conditions. It burned more than 47,000 acres and engulfed 235 homes. About 25,000 peo-ple were forced to evacuate.

THE ULTIMATE INVESTMENT

The current state of investment management has a lot more in common with the prescribed burns than most professionals would care to admit. In an effort to curtail naturally occurring disasters, such as the 1998 Russian ruble-inspired stock market meltdown or the equally vicious Nasdaq carnage of late 2000, investment pros have tried numerous methods of protecting their clients against the occasionally vicious whims of market volatility. Much like the Forest Service, it remains questionable whether these attempts have resulted in any positive consequences.

Sadly, investment managers have been as unsuccessful in adding value during bull markets as they had during bear market periods. As a result, actively managed funds have become increasingly correlated to passive indices. What solutions are available to those truly committed to producing excellent risk-adjusted returns?

The purpose of this chapter is to describe the components necessary to build an actively managed fund capable of generating consistent, market-beating returns. In this context, the term "market beating" is defined in two ways:

1. A return in excess of a broad representation of the U.S. equity market.
2. A return on par with the U.S. stock market but achieved with less volatility.

The previous requirements assume that the fund is considered in lieu of an investment in the stock market. If the fund is to be used as a diversifier in a traditional portfolio, it must be non-correlated with the return of either the stock or bond market. The fund should also generate an absolute return that is large enough to keep from dragging down the performance of the overall portfolio.

As we shall see, the requirements for building such a fund are vexing. Factors at the root of this difficulty include dealing with the issue of idea generation, the problems of asset size versus performance, and the question of determining which parts of the investment landscape are best suited for that most illusive of quarry—tradable market inefficiencies.

This exercise will lead us to a rather unconventional conclusion: Hedge funds and other alternative investments are better suited to generate exceptional returns than their more traditional mutual fund progenitors.

A DUBIOUS TRACK RECORD

Financial gurus have a term for adding value to the investment process: alpha (α). If the underlying market gains 10 percent for the year and an active manager is able to generate a 12 percent return, the alpha is +2 percent. This example is much more the exception than the rule: Over the last decade, there has been only one year when more than 25 percent of actively managed mutual funds beat the S&P 500 Index.

Of course, this period coincided with the most spectacular bull market in history—a point not missed by proponents of active management. Fans of the approach claim that it is during periods of tumult that investment pros add the most value, perhaps by holding a larger cash position or avoiding certain stocks that have such deteriorating fundamentals that the only direction possible for their stock's price is south.

The year 1998 was the perfect year for evaluating the promise of active management to produce attractive returns during periods of declining stock prices and increased market volatility. Instead of the broad market advances that made indexed funds the investment of choice in the last decade, 1998 proved to be a year in which a select handful of stocks performed spectacularly enough to take the market indices to new highs. According to Morgan Stanley equity analyst Leah Modigliani, 14 companies accounted for 99 percent of the S&P 500 Index's returns for the first three-quarters of the year. Moreover, just a handful of stocks made up the gains in the S&P in the fourth quarter of 1998, and two stocks alone—high-fliers Microsoft and Dell Computer—produced one-third of the year's gains.

Thus, 1998 should have been a stock picker's dream—an environment where a portfolio consisting of a selected few issues would have trounced the returns of the overall market. So how did active managers fare?

Unfortunately for the throngs of individuals invested in such funds, 1998 will be remembered as one of the worst years for actively managed mutual funds in history. One-third of all actively managed domestic equity funds trailed the S&P 500 Index by 10 percentage points or more, and one-third of them actually lost money—a seemingly impossible result in a year when the index gained nearly 29 percent. The recent carnage was far more severe than the industry experienced in 1990, when the S&P 500 Index lost 3.12 percent (the average fund lost 5.90 percent), and in 1994, when the S&P 500 Index was essentially flat (and nearly one-third of funds beat the index).

Still, investment managers seem to be obsessed with beating the market, even though they often end up defeating themselves in the process. As we shall see, the problem is more with the latter than with the former.

FULLY REFLECTED

Investment managers use a variety of methods in their attempt to generate outsized returns. The most common method is the use of company fundamentals in discerning the fair value of a firm. This style of investing was inaugurated in 1934, when the landmark text *Security Analysis*, by Benjamin Graham and David Dodd, was published. According to this text, securities that trade below their fair value can be purchased and later sold for a profit as prices are eventually corrected by the marketplace to reflect a company's true financial performance.

Like many great ideas, fundamental analysis is much easier to perform on paper than it is in the real world. This is partly due to the large herd of investment professionals who use the method to manage billions of dollars in client assets. The resulting plethora of suspender-clad fund pros chasing the few incorrectly priced stocks that boast enough trading volume to buy and sell in large chunks makes a difficult game nearly impossible to win.

This simple fact has not stopped the throngs of Ivy League MBAs from trying. There are some winners, but so few have generated consistently outstanding results that the term "random walk" starts to rear its ugly head.

Curiously, the group most enamored with fundamental analysis is its biggest customer. Institutional investors seem absolutely giddy about discussing various fundamentally-based methodologies with investment management candidates. Yet, it seems that this fundamental fetish shared by many big-time consumers of investment advice is a response to the bad reputation of the other school of investment philosophy: technical analysis.

Market technicians believe that all of the information necessary to make a valid buy or sell decision is contained in the price of the security in question. As a result, an examination of sales growth, profit margins, or other company-specific metrics is deemed to be unnecessary for predicting stock price movement. A cursory examination of price trends, trading volume, and other market indicators is all that is necessary, proponents of the approach argue.

Even though security prices have an occasional tendency to move in trends, the financial witchcraft associated with technical analysis is anathema to the gatekeepers of pension assets and other sizable pools of money. *Perhaps my investment manager is not keeping up with the market indices*, these investors seem to be thinking, *but at least they are not reading price charts.*

Fortunately for technicians, there is about as much academic evidence supporting the use of price charts as there is touting the scrutiny of a firm's financial statements. Unfortunately, this evidence amounts to a molehill compared to the mountains of data that suggest the market-beating potential of human intervention in the capital markets—regardless of the approach used —is close to nil.

A COSTLY CONUNDRUM

Traditional active management essentially relies on in-depth research to supply insights that are good enough to overcome the tenacious efficiency of the capital markets. When one examines just how good his or her forecasting ability must be, the difficulty in generating market-beating returns takes on a particularly astringent taste.

Figure 1.1 plots the combination of accuracy (depth) and repetition (breadth) that is required to generate an exceptional level of investment performance. As shown on the extreme left portion of the curve, one could become a market beater by being "bang on" just a few times per year. Market calls, such as "Buy IBM today" or "Sell Amazon now," are nearly impossible to repeat without making a few gaffes.

On the flip side, one could make a large number of prescient but less accurate predictions. Note that the depth requirement dips dramatically as the number of useful insights approaches 100. The curve only begins to flatten out as the number of good ideas passes 400.

A natural conclusion after examining Figure 1.1 would be to hire a mass of analysts. After all, how can one generate such a large number of investable ideas without a cadre of highly trained professionals?

Judging by the vast increase in hiring by securities firms, this line of thinking is hardly original. MBA graduates keen on maximizing their after-tax net worth have honed in on the trend; as a result, first-year associates

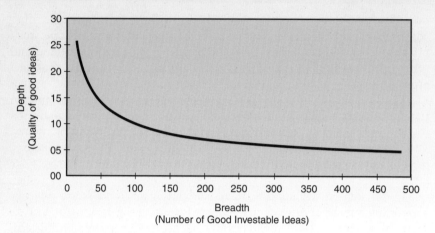

FIGURE 1.1   Combination of breadth (number) of insights and depth (quality) of insights needed to produce a given investment return/risk profile.

often make $150,000 on Wall Street. After three years, the figure rises to $400,000.

The numbers become even more staggering for experienced players. Analysts who reach *Institutional Investor* magazine's coveted "first-team" status typically earn $2 million to $5 million annually. The next lower tier is paid about $1 million per year. Veteran telecommunications analyst Jack Grubman became the first of his ilk to achieve pop-star status when he signed a one-year, $25 million package with Salomon Smith Barney.

Some forward-thinking firms with the need to decrease their per-thought costs have sequestered at least part of their decision-making needs to computers. Quantitative models are excellent at sifting through mountains of economic and company-specific data, of course, but human intervention (in the form of programmers) is necessary to make this possible. The investment managers who have employed computers as number crunchers always filter the machine's output with a human's. As a result, computers have minimized —but not completely eliminated—the cost problems associated with generating the next great investing idea.

In addition to the obvious quantity/quality issues, another problem with producing high-quality investment ideas is the level of costs incurred in their implementation.

Much has been written about the decreasing levy charged by brokerage firms in the past few years, which has served to vastly increase the volume of trading on domestic exchanges. However, it is the other costs associated with buying and selling securities that is most troubling among market professionals.

One of the most egregious is market impact, which is defined as the difference between the execution price and the posted price for a stock. Market impact can be substantial and is often quite large at the worst possible moment. For example, after the release of a negative earnings report, a company's stock can be quoted "49–50" ($49 per share to sell; $50 per share to buy) by a specialist on the floor of the New York Stock Exchange. If the portfolio manager for a large fund wants to sell a large block of this stock—say, 100,000 shares—the bid/ask spread might widen to "47–50" ($47 per share to sell; $50 per share to buy). In fact, the spread could widen so much that the manager may decide that, based solely on market impact, the trade is simply not economically feasible. Managers are thus forced to hold a position they do not want, which prevents them from using the cash gained from the transaction to buy a stock they do want to own. The profit potential lost from the manager's not owning the stock of choice can be equally onerous and is commonly referred to as *opportunity cost*.

According to Charles Ellis, author of the classic tome *Investment Policy*, active managers would have to be correct, on average, more than 80 percent of the time to make up for the implementation costs incurred in active trading. Unless market pros can get a grip on the onerous effects of such costs, the odds of generating market-beating returns appear quite slim.

This one fact explains why so many investment managers are called to greatness . . . and why so few are chosen.

THE REAL PROBLEM

Unfortunately, there are few ways for investment managers to minimize transaction costs. The most effective solution—limiting the amount of client assets that they are willing to accept—seems an abomination to many. However, by directing a relatively modest-sized portfolio, there is no doubt that advisors are able to implement their market strategies in a more effective manner.

Investment firms are barking up the right tree when they obsess about minimizing their transaction costs. The term that best captures their inherent desires is "economic rent," which was developed by one of the founders of the Classical School of Economics, David Ricardo (1772–1823). According to him,

Economic rent on land is the value of the difference in productivity between a given piece of land and the poorest, most costly piece of land producing the same goods under the same conditions.

According to Ricardo's thinking, rational agents would naturally seek to maximize the economic rents derived from their trading activities. If managers think that they have truly found a way to generate market-beating returns—be it through fundamental analysis, technical analysis, or a combination of the two—the trick is to maximize their fee revenue per unit of client assets under management.

This solution can take many forms. Some market pros may want to manage a much larger pool of client monies. In this view, managers assume that their revenue (which would consist solely of an asset-based fee in this model) is as dependent on their marketing acumen as it is on their breadth of market knowledge.

Managers with a bit more ingenuity might decide to cap the amount of client assets they are willing to oversee. In return, they demand higher fees per dollar under advisement. This usually takes the form of a performance fee, which enables managers to profit from the success of their trading activities.

This latter course of action is commonly packaged in an unregulated pool of client assets referred to as a hedge fund. Such vehicles have the additional advantage of giving managers the freedom to express themselves in any way they deem most prudent in the capital markets. This lack of regulatory constraint is lauded by some and derided by others.

It should be noted that the hedge fund alternative is only rational if the investment pro is truly generating positive alpha. Unfortunately, a plethora of non-rational money managers have decided on this approach.

It seems that David Ricardo tilled the soil of his intellect quite well indeed. He left school at the tender age of 14 to pursue his career as a speculator. By his mid-20s, he had amassed a fortune on the stock market. He retired from business at the age of 42 and spent the remainder of his life as a member of Parliament.

Ricardo's other great contribution to economics is the law of comparative cost, which demonstrated the benefits of international specialization in international trade. This law became the foundation of the free-trade movement, which set Great Britain on the course of exporting manufactured goods and importing raw materials.

As we will see, this idea forms another important topic for alpha-producing investment managers—whether to specialize in a given style or sector of the market or branch out to include other strategies.

THE DANGERS OF CONCENTRATION

Let us assume that a savvy, intelligent market professional has engineered a way to extract a sizeable amount of alpha from the securities markets. How will this talented manager's future be affected by frequent appearances on Louis Rukeyser's *Wall $treet Week* and the ever-increasing throngs looking to replicate the manager's success?

Andrew Lo and A. Craig Mackinlay put a unique spin on this issue in their book, *A Non-Random Walk Down Wall Street*. When they began examining stock price changes in 1985, they were shocked to find a substantial degree of auto-correlative behavior—evidence that previous price changes could have been used to forecast changes in the next period. Their findings were sufficiently overwhelming to refute the Random Walk Hypothesis, which states that asset price changes are totally unpredictable.

The most important insight from their work occurred when they repeated the study 11 years later, using prices from 1986 to 1996. In stark contrast to their earlier finding, the newer data conformed more closely with the random walk model than the original sample period. Upon further investigation, they learned that over the past decade several investment firms—most notably, Morgan Stanley and D.E. Shaw—were engaged in a type of stock trading specifically designed to take advantage of the kinds of patterns uncovered in their earlier study. Known at the time as "pairs trading"—and now referred to as statistical arbitrage—these strategies fared quite well until recently but are now regarded as a very competitive and thin-margin business because of the proliferation of hedge funds engaged in this type of market activity. In their Ricardan view, Lo and Mackinlay believe that the profits earned by the early statistical arbitrageurs can be viewed as "economic rents" that accrued via their innovation, creativity, and risk tolerance.

David Shaw, a former computer science professor cum investment manager, reported similar market exploits. When he founded D.E. Shaw and Company in the early 1980s, a number of easily identifiable market inefficiencies could be exploited. According to him, increased competition caused many strategies to disappear. However, as an early adopter, he was able to use the profits earned from this prior trading to subsidize the costly research required to find more market eccentricities.

There lies the rub. Specialists who limit themselves to one particular market anomaly may soon find themselves out of a job *if they do their job correctly in the first place*—that is, if they mine a market inefficiency to its extinction. It is much better to use profits from such a discovery to underwrite further financial expeditions in other areas of the investment universe.

Of course, some of the holes in market efficiency are deeper than others. One such grotto may be the universe of small cap stocks. Wall Street analysts generally do not follow many stocks that are significantly below $1 billion in market capitalization, probably because the opportunities for brokerages to earn significant investment banking revenues from such tiny firms is so low. As a result, an opportunity appears for savvy buy-side analysts to pick the next diamond in the rough.

Some evidence supports this view, as nearly one-half of all small-cap domestic mutual funds have exceeded the return of the Russell 2000 Index over the last five years. Perhaps this is one rip in the efficient market veil that will take a while to mend.

A QUESTION OF AGENCY COSTS

Much has been said in the popular press regarding the performance of buy recommendations from the major brokerage firms. The failure of analysts to keep up with the major market indices has been widely explained by the conflicts of interests inherent in such an environment.

Many believe that the dramatic underperformance of analyst recommendations is due to the conflicts of interest that arise when the Wall Street firms act as investment bankers to the companies their analysts cover. That certainly explains part of the problem; another issue less commonly raised is the tendency for analysts to act in herd-like fashion, recommending one stock in near unison. The thinking that perpetuates such actions is simple: A mistake, even a serious one, will only injure one's career if your peers at other firms disagreed with you and made the right call.

That same thinking is rife in the investment management business. Job security is preserved if the returns of mutual funds are sufficiently close to the market indices and tightly clustered so that mistakes cannot be easily discerned.

I believe that these behavioral biases explain why traditional mutual funds with asset-based fees have produced mediocre results over the years. Simply put, the managers of these funds are not motivated to generate the best possible return; they are paid to follow the indices and not rock the boat.

As Ricardan thinkers, alternative investment managers have an entirely different view of their role in the investment process. Hedge fund managers are a good example. Hedge fund fees encourage exceptional performance, while the commonly high amount of manager investment in the fund serves as a stopgap measure against excessive speculation. A further incentive to performance is the widespread practice of limiting the amount of funds under management.

Alternative investment strategies aren't perfect, of course. Transparency issues, liquidity issues, and the tendency of convergence strategies to correlate highly during tumultuous market periods are all important topics worthy of discussion. However, in our experience, they fulfill an important objective in client portfolios—the generation of market-beating returns.

CHAPTER 2

Hedge Funds

By Tremont Advisers and TASS Investment Research Ltd.

Aside from the spectacular successes—and failures—that have made headlines, the 10 categories of hedge funds offer ways to produce superior risk-adjusted returns by capitalizing on the managers' skills in using the widest possible range of financial instruments to be either short or long and getting compensation based on performance.

Since 1949, when Alfred Jones established the first hedge fund, the hedge fund industry continues to be one of the most misrepresented and misunderstood areas of finance. The often trumpeted spectacular successes of the likes of George Soros and Julian Robertson over the last two decades, contrasted with the dramatic losses of Long Term Capital Management and others in 1998, have done little to advance understanding of an industry frequently shrouded in mystery.

Indeed, these examples have only fueled wild speculation and misconceptions, much of it press-driven, that hedge funds represent the ultimate roulette table for a chosen few. This perception, however, is inconsistent with the reality that hedge funds have remained one of the fastest growing financial sectors, experiencing unprecedented growth throughout the 1990s.

This chapter will show that hedge funds can produce superior risk-adjusted returns. We recognize that statistical results are routinely discounted by cynics who attribute these results to convenient curve-fitting or optimization. However, we contend that the results are not a statistical aberration but rather the result of the inherent source of return in the asset class. The inherent return of hedge funds is the excess profit that can be earned from consistently dealing in the world's capital and derivative markets on superior terms. These terms are augmented by the positive selection of alpha intrinsic in the structure of all hedge funds. Hedge funds are paid to trade —and have the incentive to do so—when others cannot, will not, or need to be on the other side.

Further, this chapter offers a summary of the current size of the industry, explains the 10 primary categories of hedge funds, and analyzes key industry issues including fees, transparency, and capacity.

INTRODUCTION

Hedge funds comprise one of the fastest growing sectors of investment management. With rare exception, their distinguishing characteristics today are (1) an absolute return investment objective, (2) the ability to be long and/or short, (3) the freedom to use the widest possible range of financial instruments needed to implement the investment strategy, and (4) performance-related compensation. Typically, Tremont and TASS do not classify long-only funds as hedge funds. However, we recognize certain exceptions in niche markets and where it is difficult to implement a short position—for example, specialist distressed securities and high yield managers.

In 1949, when Alfred Jones established the first hedge fund in the United States, the defining characteristic of a hedge fund was that it hedged against the likelihood of a declining market. Hedging was employed by businesses as far back as the 17th century, mainly in the commodity industries where producers and merchants hedged against adverse price changes. In his original hedge fund model, Jones merged two speculative tools—short sales and leverage—into a conservative form of investing. At the time of the fund's inception, leverage was used to obtain higher profits by assuming more risk. Short selling was employed to take advantage of opportunities. Jones used leverage to obtain profits and short selling through baskets of stocks to control risk.

Jones' model was devised from the premise that performance depends more on stock selection than market direction. He believed that during a rising market, good stock selection would identify stocks that rise more than the market, while good short stock selection would identify stocks that rise less than the market. However, in a declining market, good long selections will fall less than the market, and good short stock selection will fall more than the market, yielding a net profit in all markets.

Jones' model performed better than the market. He set up a general partnership in 1949 and converted it to a limited partnership in 1952. Although his fund used leverage and short selling, it also employed performance-based fee compensation. Each of the previous characteristics was not unique in itself. What was unique, however, was that Jones operated in complete secrecy for 17 years. By the time his secret was revealed, it had already become the model for the hedge fund industry.

Jones kept all of his own money in the fund, realizing early that he could not expect his investors to take risks with their money that he would not be willing to assume with his own capital. Curiously, Jones became uncomfortable with his own ability to pick stocks and, as a result, employed stock pickers to supplement his own stock-picking ability. In 1954, Jones hired another stock picker to run a portion of the fund. Soon, he had as many as eight stock pickers, autonomously managing portions of the fund. By 1984, at the age of 82, he had created the first fund of funds by amending his partnership agreement to reflect a formal fund of funds structure.

Although mutual funds were the darlings of Wall Street in the 1960s, Jones' hedge fund was outperforming the best mutual funds, even after the 20 percent incentive fee deduction. The news of Jones' performance created excitement; by 1968, approximately 200 hedge funds were in existence, most notably those managed by George Soros and Michael Steinhardt.

During the 1960s' bull market, many of the new hedge fund managers found that selling short impaired absolute performance while leveraging the long positions created exceptional returns. The so-called hedgers were, in fact, long leveraged and totally exposed as they went into the bear market of the early 1970s. During this time, many of the new hedge fund managers were put out of business. As Jones pointed out, few managers have the ability to short the market because most equity managers have a long-only mentality.

During the next decade, only a modest number of hedge funds were established. In 1984, when Tremont began tracking hedge fund managers, it was able to identify a mere 68 funds. Fifteen years later, TASS, the investment research subsidiary of Tremont, was tracking 2,600 funds and managers (including commodity trading advisers). Most of these funds had raised assets to manage on a word-of-mouth basis from wealthy individuals. Julian Robertson's Jaguar Fund, Steinhardt Partners, and Soros' Quantum Fund were compounding at 40-percent levels. Not only were they outperforming in bull markets but in bear market environments as well. For example, in 1990, Quantum was up 30 percent and Jaguar was up 20 percent while the Standard & Poor's 500 Index was down 3 percent and the MSCI $ World Index was down 16 percent. The press began to write articles and profiles drawing attention to these remarkable funds and their extraordinary managers.

During the 1980s, most of the hedge fund managers in the United States were not registered with the Securities and Exchange Commission (SEC). Because of this, they were prohibited from advertising, relying on word-of-mouth references to grow their assets. The majority of funds were organized as limited partnerships, allowing only 99 investors; the hedge fund managers, therefore, required high minimum investments. European investors were quick to see the advantages of this new breed of manager, which fueled the development of the more tax-efficient offshore funds. In the United States and Europe, the hedge fund industry of the 1980s was an exclusive club of wealthy individuals and their private bankers.

Hedge funds currently represent one of the fastest growing segments of the investment management community. During the 1990s, the number of funds increased at an average rate of 25.74 percent per year, showing a total growth of 648 percent (including funds of funds). The reason for the unprecedented growth is simple: Money follows talent. Having attained significant personal wealth as fund managers or proprietary traders, the talented managers are leaving large companies to manage their own money. They are establishing simple, corporate structures with limited employees and forming funds with absolute and risk-adjusted return objectives. These funds typically charge performance fees, usually 20 percent of the profits. By limiting the size of assets under management, these companies can react quickly to events in the financial community, trading without impacting share prices. With fees earned as a percentage of profits, a company can earn as much money on a $100 million asset base as a traditional money manager earns on $1 billion.

During the 1990s, the flight of money managers from large institutions accelerated, with a resulting surge in the number of hedge funds (see Figure 2.1). Their fledgling operations were funded, increasingly, by the new

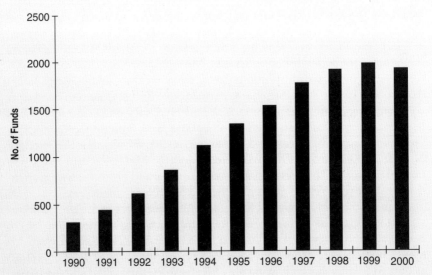

FIGURE 2.1 Growth in hedge funds (includes fund of funds; does not include commodity-trading advisors).

wealth that had been created by the unprecedented bull run in the equity markets. The managers' objective was not purely financial; many established their own businesses for lifestyle and control reasons. Almost all invest a substantial portion of their net worth in the fund alongside their investors.

The 1990s saw another interesting phenomena: A number of the established money managers stopped accepting new money to manage; some even returned money to their investors. Limiting assets in many investment styles is one of the most basic tenets of hedge fund investing if the performance expectations are going to continue to be met. This reflects the fact that managers make much more money from performance fees and investment income than they do from management fees. Due to increasing investor demand in the 1990s, many funds established higher minimum investment levels ($50 million) and set up long lock-up periods (five years).

Lack of access to certain established funds created a large funds of funds business. A fund of funds offers a wide array of managers for a lower minimum investment while providing oversight and monitoring of the investment. As in the mutual fund industry, where more funds than stocks exist on the New York Stock Exchange, one day there may be more funds of funds than individual hedge funds. Although many of the original and truly great hedge fund managers may no longer be available to investors, the market continues to be well supplied with newcomers.

SIZE OF THE INDUSTRY

Much confusion exists within the industry about the total number of hedge funds. We estimate that there are more than 5,000 funds in the whole industry. However, in excess of 90 percent of the U.S. $400 billion under management in the industry is managed by some 2,600 funds.

About one-third of the funds but more than 90 percent of the fund managers are domiciled in the United States (see Figure 2.2 and Figure 2.3).

It is often observed that the overall size of the industry differs, depending upon one's source of information. There are a number of reasons for this:

1. The hedge fund industry has evolved in a culture of secrecy. This secrecy was mandated in the United States for statutory reasons, and hedge funds are neither allowed to advertise nor to hold themselves out as investment opportunities to the public. Further, the culture of secrecy stemmed from the fact that most hedge funds either carry short positions or operate in unlisted securities. In either case, general knowledge by the marketplace of a hedge fund manager's position carries consequences.

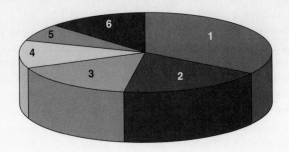

Key
1. United States (33.9%)
2. Cayman Islands (18.9%)
3. British Virgin Islands (16.5%)
4. Bermuda (11%)
5. Bahamas (7.2%)
6. Other (12.5%)

[1] The makeup of the domiciles in 'Other' is as follows: Australia 0.2%, Austria 0.2%, British West Indies 0.07%, Canada 0.2%, Channel Islands 2%, France 1.6%, Ireland 2.1%, Isle of Man 0.2%, Luxembourg 2.53%, Mauritius 0.2%. Mexico 0.07%, Netherlands Antilles 1.0%, Netherlands 0.2%, Nevis 0.07%, Sweden 0.8%, Switzerland 0.3%, United Kingdom 1.2%

FIGURE 2.2   Domicile of funds.

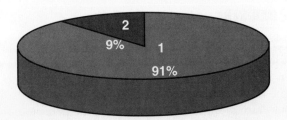

Key:
1. Fund managers domiciled in the United States
2. Fund managers domiciled outside the United States

FIGURE 2.3   Domicile of fund managers.

2. Hedge funds in the United States are almost always structured as private limited partnerships. So are many other forms of non-public investment designed for the sophisticated investor. It is not unusual for private, non-SEC-registered funds to be included, accidentally or otherwise, in the overall hedge fund count.

3. Opinions differ regarding the definition of the words "hedge fund." The most commonly accepted definition is that a hedge fund must
   - Have an absolute return performance objective
   - Allow the manager to be active on both the long and short sides of the markets
   - Compensate the manager with performance-related fees
   - Allow the manager tremendous flexibility in investment style and approach

   However, some analysts include all absolute return funds within the hedge fund definition, even if these funds do not typically go short.

PRIMARY INVESTMENT CATEGORIES OF HEDGE FUNDS

Hedge funds are not homogeneous. Although more than 80 percent of the total assets under management in the industry are invested in the equity markets, the investment disciplines used are diverse and distinct. Tremont and TASS have defined 10 primary investment categories in the hedge fund industry:

1. Long/short equity
2. Equity market neutral
3. Event-driven
4. Convertible arbitrage
5. Fixed-income relative value/arbitrage
6. Global macro
7. Short sellers
8. Emerging markets
9. Managed futures
10. Funds of funds

(*Note: All asset figures in the sections below are as of December 2000.*)

Long/Short Equity

This directional strategy involves equity-oriented investing on both the long and short side of the market. The objective is not to be market-neutral. The manager has the ability to shift from value to growth; from among small-, medium-, and large-capitalization stocks; and from a net long position to a net short position. The strategy may hedge with options and futures. The focus may be regional—long/short a U.S. equity or long/short a European equity—or sector-specific, such as long/short technology stocks, long/short financial stocks, and long/short healthcare stocks. Long/short equity funds tend to construct and hold portfolios that are significantly more concentrated than traditional fund managers.

Long/short equity represents 49 percent of all assets under management.

Convertible Arbitrage

This strategy is identified by hedged investing in the convertible securities of a company. A typical investment position is long the convertible and short the common stock of the company issuing the convertible. Positions are designed to generate profits from the bond and the short sale while protecting principal from directional market moves. Hedge funds may limit their activities to a single market (such as the United States) or they may invest globally.

There are two components to the overall return from a convertible arbitrage position: static return and volatility return. The static return is comprised of the coupon from the convertible bond plus the interest rebate on the cash from the short sale minus the dividend on the underlying short stock. The volatility return is comprised of profits generated by short-term position adjustments of the short stock position. Adjustments are necessary to account for the changing ratio of stock needed to hedge the underlying convertible bonds as prices fluctuate. Leverage may be employed to augment both the static and volatility return.

Convertible arbitrage represents 5.5 percent of all assets under management.

Event-Driven

This strategy is categorized by equity-oriented investing designed to capture price movement generated by an anticipated corporate event. The Event-driven category primarily includes: risk (or merger) arbitrage and distressed securities investing. It also includes Regulation D (Reg D) investing and high yield investing.

Event-driven represents 19 percent of all assets under management.

Risk Arbitrage   Risk arbitrage specialists invest simultaneously in long and short positions in both companies involved in a merger or acquisition. Risk arbitrageurs are typically long the stock of the company being acquired and short the stock of the acquiring company. The risk to the arbitrageur is that the deal fails. Risk arbitrageurs seek to capture the price differential between the stock of the target and the stock of the acquirer. Profits result as the price of the target stock converges with the stock price of the acquirer. Risk arbitrage positions are considered to be uncorrelated to overall market direction, with the principal risk being "deal risk"—that is, that the deal fails to go through.

Distressed Securities Distressed securities funds invest in the debt, equity, or trade claims of companies that are in financial distress, typically in bankruptcy. In this context, distressed means companies in need of legal action or restructuring to revive them, not companies in need of some approved medication. These securities generally trade at substantial discounts to par value. Hedge fund managers can invest in a range of instruments from secured debt (at the low end of the risk scale) to common stock (at the high end of the risk scale). The strategy exploits the fact that many investors are unable to hold below investment grade securities. Further, few analysts cover the distressed market, ensuring that many unresearched and inexpensive opportunities can exist for knowledgeable hedge fund managers prepared to do their homework.

Distressed managers can follow either an active or passive approach. Active managers get onto the creditor committees and assist the recovery or reorganization process. Passive managers buy the distressed securities and either hold them until they appreciate to the desired level or trade them. Distressed managers can benefit substantially from the creativity of financial engineers. The growing complexity of debt instruments can provide extensive opportunities for the credit analyst and distressed manager. Distressed debt investing often results in a manager holding "cheap" equity in a newly reorganized company.

(*Note: This is one of the few areas where long-only is included in the Tremont/TASS universe of hedge funds.*)

Regulation D This strategy, usually called Reg D, involves investing in micro- and small-capitalization public companies that are raising money in the private capital markets. The manager can invest via the stock, convertibles, or other derivatives. Investments usually take the form of receiving a convertible bond or convertible preferred issue in return for an injection of capital.

What is unique about these securities is that, unlike standard convertible bonds or preferreds, the exercise price either floats or is subject to a look-back provision. This has the effect of insulating the investor from a decline in the price of the underlying stock. Typically, the investor will be long the convertible, short a percentage of common stock and will also hold warrants. On the effective dates of the transaction, managers can exercise, if they choose to, and convert into common stock at a better market price.

High Yield Investing High yield investing, the politically correct phrase for "junk bonds," involves applying a buy/hold or a trading strategy to high yield securities. Managers may buy the high yield debt of a company that they think will get a credit upgrade or that might be in a position to redeem the outstanding high-coupon issue.

Other areas of opportunity include buying the discounted bonds of companies that are potential takeover targets. Some managers combine these strategies with levered pools of bank debt. Portfolio securities are generally sold when they reach upside or downside price targets or if the issuer of the securities or industry fundamentals change materially.

Until recently, high yield was primarily a U.S.-focused strategy. However, today it can be global. Some managers include emerging market bonds; others limit themselves to investment-grade countries only.

(*Note: This is one of the few areas where long-only is included in the Tremont/TASS universe of hedge funds.*)

Equity Market Neutral

This investment strategy is designed to exploit equity market inefficiencies and usually involves being simultaneously long and short in matched equity portfolios of the same size within a country. Market-neutral portfolios are designed to be either beta- or currency-neutral (equal currency, long and short) or both. Well-designed portfolios typically control for industry, sector, market capitalization, and other exposures. Leverage is often used to enhance returns.

Statistical arbitrage is theoretically designed to be an equity market-neutral strategy. To date, liquidity concerns have limited the activity primarily to the United States, Japanese, and United Kingdom equity markets.

Equity market neutral represents 6 percent of all assets under management.

Global Macro

Global macro managers carry long and short positions in any of the world's major capital or derivative markets. These positions reflect their view on overall market direction as influenced by major economic trends and/or events.

The portfolios of these funds can include stocks, bonds, currencies, and/or commodities in cash or derivative formats. The funds may use highly opportunistic investment strategies, investing on both the long and short side of the markets. The portfolios can be highly leveraged. Most of these macro hedge funds invest globally in both developed and emerging markets.

There are two schools of global macro managers: those who come from a long/short equity background and those who come from a derivative trading background. Macro funds run by companies such as Tiger Investment Management and Soros Fund Management were originally invested primarily in U.S. equities. The success of these managers at stock picking resulted in substantial increases in assets under management over time. As the funds increased in size, it became increasingly difficult to take meaningful positions in smaller-capitalization stocks (the stocks often preferred by equity hedge fund managers because they are generally under-researched by the brokerage community). Consequently, the funds started gravitating towards more liquid securities and markets in which bigger bets could be placed.

Funds run by Moore Capital, Caxton, and Tudor Investment Corporation developed from a futures trading discipline, which, by its very nature, was both global and macro-economic in scope. The freeing up of the global currency markets and the development of non-U.S. financial futures markets in the 1980s provided an increasing number of investment and trading opportunities not previously available to investment managers.

Global macro represents 8.5 percent of all assets under management.

Fixed-Income Arbitrage

The fixed-income arbitrageur attempts to profit from price anomalies between related interest rate instruments. The majority of managers trade globally, although a few focus only on the U.S. market. To generate returns sufficient to exceed the transaction costs, leverage may range from 10 times up to 150 times the net asset value employed. Genuine fixed-income arbitrageurs typically aim to deliver steady returns with low volatility, due to the fact that the directional risk is mitigated by hedging against interest rate movements or by the use of spread trades. Fixed-income arbitrage can include interest rate swap arbitrage, U.S. and non-U.S. government bond arbitrage, forward yield curve arbitrage, and mortgage-backed securities arbitrage.

Fixed-income arbitrage represents 5.6 percent of all assets under management.

Mortgage-Backed Securities Arbitrage   The mortgage-backed securities strategy specializes in arbitraging mortgage-backed securities and their derivatives. This strategy takes place primarily in the United States. The market is over the counter and extremely complex. The two greatest risks are prepayment and valuation; all securities are marked to market, but the pricing and valuation models used by the different participants may vary, and overall market liquidity has a huge impact.

Dedicated Short Bias

As recently as three years ago, there was a robust category of hedge funds known as "dedicated short sellers." However, the ravages of the 1990s' bull run have reduced their ranks to all but a handful of funds. Recently, a category of funds has emerged that is committed to maintaining net short as opposed to pure short exposure.

The short-biased managers invest mostly in short positions in equities and equity-derivative products. To be classified as a short-biased manager, the short bias of the manager's portfolio must be greater than zero constantly. To effect the short sale, the manager borrows the stock from a counter-party (often its prime broker) and sells it in the market. The broker keeps proceeds from the sale as collateral. An additional margin of typically 5 percent to 50 percent must be deposited in the form of liquid securities. The margin is adjusted daily. Leverage is created because the margin is below 100 percent.

Short-selling can be time-consuming and expensive. The manager needs very efficient stock borrowing and lending facilities. Because of this, short positions are sometimes implemented by selling forward—selling stock index futures or buying put options and put warrants on single stocks or stock indices.

It is generally accepted that the short side of the market can be much less efficient than the long side of the market. Restrictions on short-selling vary from jurisdiction to jurisdiction. For example, the United States has its "uptick" rule—namely, you cannot initiate a new short sell position when the price of the stock is going down. Europe does not have an uptick rule; in many emerging markets, short-selling is simply not possible. Derivatives can be used to get around some of these issues, particularly in the United States.

Dedicated short bias represents 0.4 percent of all assets under management.

Emerging Markets

This strategy involves equity or fixed-income investing, focusing on emerging markets around the world. Certain commentators regard emerging market hedge funds as a contradiction in terms. Many of the emerging markets do not allow short-selling, nor do they offer viable futures or other derivative products with which to hedge.

Emerging markets represents 3 percent of all assets under management.

(*Note: This is one of the few areas where long-only is included in the Tremont/TASS universe of hedge funds.*)

Managed Futures

The managed futures trading managers, otherwise called commodity trading advisers (CTAs), trade in the listed financial and commodity futures markets around the world. They may also trade in the global currency markets. Most traders apply their individual disciplines to the markets using a systematic approach although a small percentage use a discretionary approach. The systematic approach tends to use price and market-specific information in determining investment decisions. The discretionary approach tends to use price and market information as well as broader economic and political fundamentals in determining the investment decisions.

Most CTAs trade a diversified range of markets and contracts and seek to identify trends in each market/contract. Differences include time horizons, asset allocation, contract selection, contract weighting, the treatment of short-term market "noise," and the use of leverage. Most CTAs are regulated by the Commodity Futures Trading Commission instead of the SEC in the United States.

Managed futures represents 3 percent of all assets under management.

Funds of Funds

The funds of funds category is the hedge fund industry's closest equivalent to a mutual fund. The majority of funds of funds invest in multiple hedge funds (five to 100) with different investment styles. The objective is to smooth out the potential inconsistency of the returns from having all of the assets invested in a single hedge fund. Funds of funds can offer an effective way for an investor to gain exposure to a range of hedge funds and strategies without having to commit substantial assets or resources to the specific asset allocation, portfolio construction, and individual hedge fund selection.

A growing number of style or category-specific funds of funds have been launched during the last few years—for example, funds of funds that invest only in event-driven managers or funds of funds that invest only in equity market-neutral-style managers.

WHY HEDGE FUNDS MAKE MONEY

Previous studies have focused on the statistical robustness of returns that hedge funds offer investors. Although the preponderance of evidence suggests hedge funds over time offer equity-like returns with lower risk profiles, few studies consider the sources of the returns.

The Outsourcing of Proprietary Trading

To understand the inherent robustness of the hedge fund structure, one must grasp the significance of the changes hedge funds have wrought among traditional financial institutions. Although the hedge fund structure is relatively new, the investment activities conducted within them are not. These investment activities typically center on market-making and proprietary trading.

Historically, large financial institutions were the only organizations with the capital, infrastructure, and access to conduct the trading and investment activity now common to hedge funds. Senior positions on proprietary trading desks represented the top of the career ladder for professional traders. With the advent of hedge funds, another rung was added to this ladder. Traders who could establish a history of profitability and proven expertise could now ply their craft with investor assets, potentially earning both higher incomes and the opportunity to control their professional destinies.

Over the last decade, two trends have developed. The hedge fund structure is drawing top-flight talent off the trading desks at an accelerating pace. Further, in this era of shareholder value, financial institutions' appetite for risk and their willingness to accept the sometimes uneven return stream of proprietary trading have diminished, causing cutbacks and decreased trading lines. In broad terms, the risk capital funding the market-making and speculative activities of the largest proprietary traders is increasingly coming from private sources in the form of hedge funds.

The Inherent Return in Proprietary Trading

For decades financial institutions have been granted "unfair" trading advantages (or "edges," in industry parlance) in return for providing liquidity to the vast array of international capital and derivative markets and for taking speculative risk positions when hedgers needed to contract with a speculator to manage risk and cash flow and lock in future prices. These trading advantages include superior information (first call on breaking news), reduced transaction costs (either in the form of lower commissions or tighter quotes from the market-makers), and superior market access, as well as other structural and statutory benefits. These edges exist or were granted because the markets need these liquidity and speculative functions to be performed to ensure their smooth operation. They represent the first component of the inherent return in hedge funds.

A second level of inherent return is created by virtue of the fact that most of the specialized activities conducted within hedge funds require a substantial research infrastructure. It is not economic, in most cases, for traditional mutual funds to build the appropriate research capability, given the substantially lower fees they charge relative to hedge funds. Risk arbitrage, for example, requires specialized expertise from analysts and lawyers. Given the fact that there are a limited number of deals at any point in time and limited liquidity, it does not make economic sense for a fund charging 60 basis points to hire the individuals necessary to conduct the activity.

Virtually all hedge funds take advantage of some type of investment edge. Many enjoy multiple advantages. To take a basic example, a specialist on the floor of a stock exchange is granted market privileges that average investors do not receive. Most notably, they are allowed to see the buildup of orders above and below the current price of the stocks they are assigned. Further, they are allowed to take the opposite side of customer transactions in their own trading accounts as well as receive other statutory advantages from the exchanges. Finally, they execute their trades with the lowest possible transaction costs. Those factors are trading advantages, and the combination of those trading advantages means that even a specialist with a modest level of skill can ply his craft profitably.

But not all specialists are equally profitable. Even specialists who cover companies with tremendous similarity can vary greatly in profitability. That difference is considered to be a function of the trader's skill, or alpha.

Although alpha usually determines the degree to which any given hedge fund prospers, virtually all successful hedge funds exploit some type of trading advantage. These advantages include superior information, lower transaction costs, better market access, size advantages, and structural inequities in the markets in which they operate.

One of the most common advantages is superior information, which often manifests itself in situations where the hedge fund manager is dealing in a limited universe of securities and financial instruments. Typically, these managers will surface in an area where only a relatively small group of experts follows the instruments closely, though a larger group may follow the sector generally. In these situations, a mismatch of both expertise and objectives can be exploited to the benefit of the hedge fund manager.

For example, managers specializing in distressed securities develop tremendous expertise pertaining to a relatively small universe of companies. A given manager has the opportunity to learn more about a particular company than all but a handful of individuals. Further, activity in the securities of distressed companies (typically companies in Chapter 11) usually precludes involvement from large public investment funds. The fact that these large funds may invest in the securities at a later date once the company returns to health adds potential return to the hedge fund's holdings.

Relative size, either large or small, can be an edge. For instance, short-term or day-trading equity firms typically benefit from the fact that their small size (relative to large mutual funds) allows them to capture smaller market movements. Size advantages can generate other advantages. For example, managers dealing in below-investment grade debt in a particular emerging market country or region can find themselves among the largest investors in that narrow universe of securities. As some of the largest players, they are viewed by the market as buyers or sellers of last resort. As a result, these managers tend to get the first call on breaking news, leading to an advantage in superior information.

That same size advantage compounds into superior market access as market-makers will typically make deeper and tighter quotes to the active investor compared to the occasional participant. Large size usually translates into lower transaction costs. For example, most statistical arbitrage programs generate large volumes of equity trading, as every long position is matched against a short position. Furthermore, positions are usually turned over quickly. This makes them very desirable clients to their prime brokers, who offer them low commission rates in addition to the benefits of superior market access and first call on information.

Other types of managers will benefit from structural inequities in the marketplace. Derivative markets, for example, exist for the purpose of transferring risk. They typically facilitate transactions in which one party, saddled with an unwanted market risk, contracts with another to lock in a future price—a discipline known as hedging. In that transaction, the speculator usually assumes the risk position at some discount or premium to fair-market value. In essence, the hedger is paying what amounts to an insurance premium to the speculator who assumes the risk. Hedgers usually operate in derivative markets for non-economic reasons. Their motive is to operate their underlying businesses profitably rather that look to profit from their derivative market dealings.

Another advantage lies in the broad investment mandates that are typical of most hedge funds. Managers are not restricted to the long side only or to listed securities only. Hedge funds typically can employ a wider range of strategies to capture an investment idea than most traditional managers. Put simply, hedge funds function as vehicles to capture manager skill, or alpha. Virtually any financial activity can be packaged within the structure.

The additional profitability of a trading enterprise directly related to these trading advantages is the inherent return of hedge funds. Put another way, hedge funds collect the money that is left on the table, either by design or neglect, to encourage certain market participants to trade when others can't, choose not to, or must be on the other side of the transaction. As investment banks and other financial institutions retreat from the business of providing liquidity and speculative capital, that inherent return is being offered to investors in the form of hedge funds and other alternative investment vehicles.

Positive Selection of Alpha

The inherent returns of the activities are amplified by a key attribute of the hedge fund structure: incentive-based compensation. Performance-based compensation creates positive manager selection. Only managers with established industry pedigrees have the credibility to raise initial assets. Only managers who continue to deliver compelling net returns to investors keep and grow their assets.

The hedge fund structure is attractive to top-tier talent as it affords greater financial rewards to managers who can deliver net performance on large pools of investor capital. Further, it allows successful managers to build their companies in their own image, working where and when they want.

The incentive-based compensation structure amplifies the positive selection process. Unlike mutual funds, most hedge funds have limited capacity to invest assets. As a result, they depend on incentive fees and must generate profits consistently to maintain their financial viability. This typically influences the mindset of hedge fund managers away from the complacency that can occur among traditional managers who dwell in a benchmarked universe. A manager who must pay the bills every quarter draws little satisfaction from being down less than the S&P 500 Index if it means a dramatic loss of income to the company.

This mindset is further augmented by the fact that most managers invest their personal capital in the funds they manage. Many managers will require key employees to invest as well, ensuring that everyone's interests are aligned. The firm and its employees do only as well as the investors. Among the best managers, the internal investment can grow to such proportions that the company's investment income exceeds its fee income. It is not uncommon for successful hedge funds to close to new investments or even return capital to investors. This occurs because large hedge funds often earn more from incentive fees than from management fees. These factors coalesce to create an attitude where annual profitability is paramount.

Summing Up Returns

The inherent return in hedge funds is a function of the trading advantages that exist, either by design or neglect, to encourage investors to trade when others can't, won't, or need to be on the other side. These advantages can include cheaper costs, better market access, and superior information, as well as other structural and statutory benefits.

These advantages are not new. In fact, they have existed for decades, but prior to the emergence of hedge funds, they were in the exclusive domain of large financial institutions that traditionally supplied liquidity and speculative capital to the marketplace. The provision of these services is essential to the smooth operation of the world's capital and derivative markets.

Starting with the inherent return as a foundation, the potential benefits of this return are amplified through the positive selection of alpha. This positive selection occurs because of the performance-based compensation intrinsic to all hedge funds. Incentive-based compensation creates a Darwinian model in which only the most talented managers can far exceed the earning potential available within the financial institutions from which they emerged.

WHAT THE NUMBERS DEMONSTRATE

Hedge funds can deliver superior risk-adjusted returns. Table 2.1 shows the performance of a typical U.S. pension fund index (calculated by Tremont

	PFI	5%	10%	15%	20%
Average Annual Return (%)	9.1	9.6	10.1	10.5	11.0
Drawdown (%)	13.4	12.7	12.1	11.6	11.0
Standard Deviation (Annualized)	11.8	11.2	10.6	10.1	9.6
Semi Deviation (Annualized)	10.8	10.0	9.3	8.9	8.1
Sharpe Ratio (Annualized)	0.34	0.41	0.47	0.54	0.62

PFI – Typical Pension Fund Index
5% – Pension Fund Index plus 5% hedge funds
10% – Pension Fund Index plus 10% hedge funds
15% – Pension Fund Index plus 15% hedge funds
20% – Pension Fund Index plus 20% hedge funds

Source: Tremont Partners, Inc.; all data that has been used in this analysis is available from TASS.

TABLE 2.1 Fund performance including hedge funds at various levels.

Partners Inc.) compared with the same index that includes hedge funds, based on the TASS fund universe average, added at different levels—5 percent, 10 percent, 15 percent, and 20 percent. The hedge funds have been added uniformly, and no discretion has been used to either overweight or underweight the allocation.

What is interesting to note is that, as hedge funds are added, the index return increases and the volatility is reduced (see Figure 2.4 through Figure 2.9).

Fees

The fees in the hedge fund industry are much higher than those charged in the traditional fund management industry. Although a typical long-only manager may charge 10 to 85 basis points of assets under management, the hedge

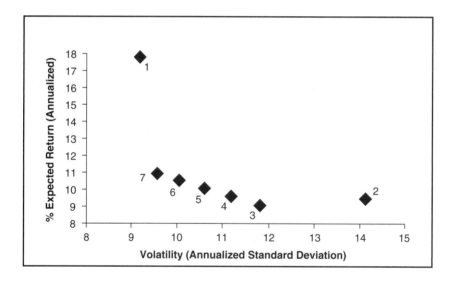

1. Long/Short Global Equity Group
2. MSCI $ Global Return Index
3. Pension Fund Index
4. Pension Fund Plus 5% Hedge Funds
5. Pension Fund Plus 10% Hedge Funds
6. Pension Fund Plus 15% Hedge Funds
7. Pension Fund Plus 20% Hedge Funds

FIGURE 2.4 PFI and long/short global equity group (January 1990 to March 1999).

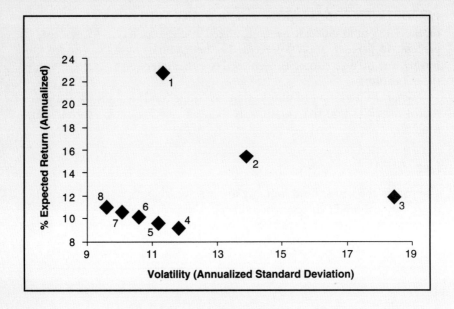

1. Long/Short U.S. Equity Group
2. S&P 500 Return Index
3. Russell 2000 Return Index
4. Pension Fund Index
5. Pension Fund plus 5% hedge funds
6. Pension Fund plus 10% hedge funds
7. Pension Fund plus 15% hedge funds
8. Pension Fund plus 20% hedge funds

FIGURE 2.5 PFI and long/short U.S. equity group (January 1990 to March 1999).

fund manager usually charges a management fee of 1 percent to 3 percent plus 20 percent of the profits. Hedge funds are able to command above-average fees because they have historically provided superior risk-adjusted returns and they have very limited capacity. This is simply a case of supply and demand; the relatively small number of superior hedge fund managers are in such demand that they are under no business-related pressure to acquiesce to the institutional investors by dropping their fees.

The high fees charged by hedge funds have created cultural difficulties for investors accustomed to fees measured in low basis points. The mitigating factor, however, is the fact that the hedge fund industry is a "net to the investor"

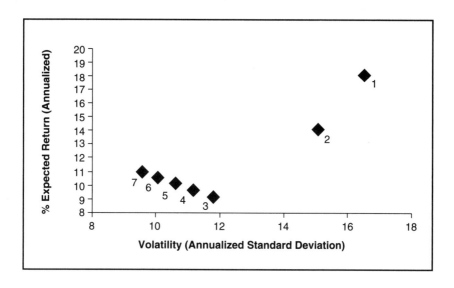

1. Long/Short European Equity Group
2. MSCI Europe Return Index
3. Pension Fund Index
4. Pension Fund Plus 5% Hedge Funds
5. Pension Fund Plus 10% Hedge Funds
6. Pension Fund Plus 15% Hedge Funds
7. Pension Fund Plus 20% Hedge Funds

FIGURE 2.6 PFI and long/short Europe equity group (January 1990 to March 1999).

business. Few institutional investors, if questioned, would choose to invest with managers offering lower fees at the expense of reduced performance.

Many of these hedge funds will give an institutional size discount, but their fees are still a multiple of standard institutional fees. Virtually all hedge fund managers recognize that their strategies work best when employed with a limited amount of capital. In contrast, most institutional funds are effectively open-ended, with the managers believing that no asset cap is necessary. The management of a hedge fund normally has a very large personal stake in the fund and will not jeopardize the potential return on its own assets by taking in more client assets than it believes are optimal.

The cost of operating a hedge fund varies with the size of assets and the scope of the investment approach. Extreme examples are a single practitioner

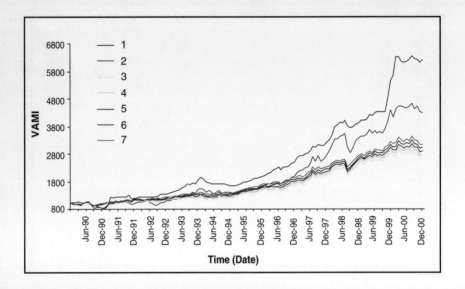

1. Long/Short European Equity Group
2. MSCI Europe Return Index
3. Pension Fund Index
4. Pension Fund plus 5% hedge funds
5. Pension Fund plus 10% hedge funds
6. Pension Fund plus 15% hedge funds
7. Pension Fund plus 20% hedge funds

FIGURE 2.7 MSCI Europe Index versus Long/Short European Equity Group and PFI (January 1990 to March 1999).

picking stocks, long and short, from a home office compared to a macro trading firm with 200 people based globally and executing complex, multi-instrument cross-border investment strategies. The management fees charged by hedge funds usually range from 1 percent to 3 percent of assets per annum. Generally speaking, managers expect to be able to cover the fixed costs of running their business with this fee revenue.

Expenses incurred when investing the fund's assets are paid out of the fund directly. Some managers take advantage of "soft-dollar" brokerage facilities, which allow them to direct brokerage business to vendors to pay for many of the necessary information and research services, as well as investment expenses. As with institutional fund managers, these management fees are due regardless of the performance of the underlying fund.

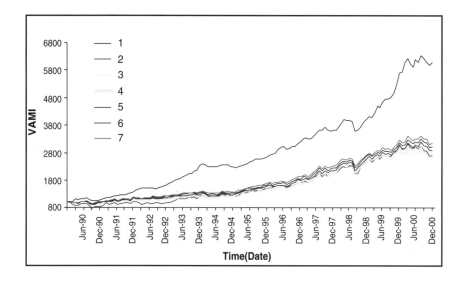

1. Long/Short Global Equity Group
2. MSCI $ World Return Index
3. Pension Fund Index
4. Pension Fund plus 5% hedge funds
5. Pension Fund plus 10% hedge funds
6. Pension Fund plus 15% hedge funds
7. Pension Fund plus 20% hedge funds

FIGURE 2.8 MSCI $ World Index versus Long/Short Global Equity Group and PFI (January 1990 to March 1999).

The distinguishing fee factor between hedge funds and institutional funds is the hedge funds' inclusion of performance or incentive fees. These fees are in addition to management fees and usually take the form of 5 percent to 50 percent of the profits charged on a schedule ranging from monthly to annual. No fee is earned if the fund has a negative return as the vast majority of funds only pay incentive fees to the manager on new profits to the investor. This is referred to as a "high-water mark." Some hedge funds use a "hurdle rate"—a minimum performance target that must be achieved before the incentive fee is charged.

This performance fee is key to understanding the motivations of a hedge fund manager. The arrangement provides the incentive to the manager to focus on generating absolute returns on a manageable asset base. Conversely, the

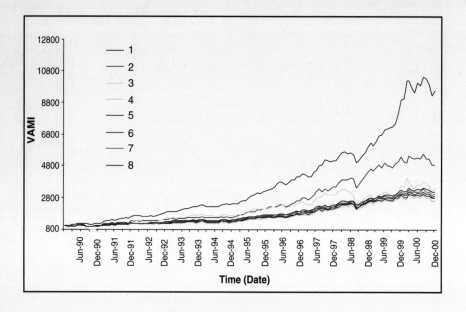

1. Long/Short U.S. Equity Group
2. S&P 500 Return Index
3. Russell 2000 Return Index
4. Pension Fund Index
5. Pension Fund plus 5% hedge funds
6. Pension Fund plus 10% hedge funds
7. Pension Fund plus 15% hedge funds
8. Pension Fund plus 20% hedge funds

FIGURE 2.9 S&P 500 Index and Russell 2000 Index versus Long/Short U.S. Equity Group and PFI (January 1990 to March 1999).

institutional manager is concerned primarily with tracking an index and gathering as much capital as possible. If successful in generating absolute returns, the hedge fund manager can earn as much as or more than a traditional manager running five or 10 times more capital. The structure of institutional funds rewards asset-gathering and does not penalize mediocre performance; the hedge fund fee structure focuses the manager on positive absolute returns and not degrading these returns by taking on too much capital.

The hedge fund fee structure benefits the fund by enabling it to attract the high-end talent necessary to run a successful fund. The chance to share in potential performance fees is a powerful recruiting tool and mirrors the type of compensation schemes used in investment banks and other sophisticated entities. Hedge fund managers can keep their overheads low by offering senior candidates a relatively modest salary with a healthy share of the performance fee.

One of the key questions for hedge fund investors is determining which individual funds actually deserve these premium fees. The proliferation of pools of capital managed with a hedge fund fee structure has made it extremely important to perform proper due diligence on the universe of managers to answer this.

This due diligence allows an investor to concentrate on the types of hedge funds that will add value, on a net of fees basis, to the overall investment strategy. An institutional investor with substantial long equity exposure may be very willing to pay a premium fee to a manager who has a record of generating returns that are not correlated to the equity market. The same investor would probably be unwilling to pay hedge fund fees to a leveraged long equity-focused fund.

A fund that provides the investor with superior investment talent is structured to enable this talent to implement rationally a disciplined investment approach, reward absolute performance, and produce robust risk-adjusted returns, all of which is worth the higher fees to an institutional buyer. The only caveat is that institutional buyers are unlikely to be able to invest as much of their portfolios into hedge funds as they would like because of the industry's inherent capacity constraints.

CAPACITY

Capacity is a structural issue that is influenced by many variables. When industry professionals talk about "capacity," they refer primarily to the maximum assets that a hedge fund can manage before performance starts to deteriorate. On a secondary basis, they may also be referring to the maximum number of people that a hedge fund may want to employ and the size of the infrastructure that they want to manage. Not all boutique hedge fund managers want their businesses to grow into substantial asset management companies with the operational, political, and bureaucratic characteristics typical in such companies.

It is well known that a limited number of managers demonstrate the ability to outperform over time. For many managers, performance often degrades once assets grow beyond a certain level. The reason for this is simple: slippage (sometimes called friction). Slippage is defined as the degree to which market prices are moved through the process of entering or exiting a position. The larger the position, the greater the effect of slippage.

Concern regarding assets under management varies from investment strategy to investment strategy. Funds focusing on investing in the currency markets should be able to manage much more money than funds focusing on exotic fixed-income arbitrage opportunities. Funds focusing on large-capitalization stocks should be able to manage more than those specializing in the micro- or small-capitalization arena. The overall health of the global economy, the liquidity in the markets, the types of market participants, and the regulatory environment all contribute to the "capacity factor."

TRANSPARENCY

Much noise has been made about the need for greater transparency since the bailout of Long Term Capital Management in the third quarter of 1998. Greater transparency is commonly associated with providing greater investor protection from both a performance and a fiduciary perspective. This is not always the case. Transparency is a double-edged sword with the potential to be misunderstood and misused.

Certain levels of transparency are essential for effective due diligence. Investors and asset allocators must have some ability to look through to the underlying portfolio to understand whether the manager is adhering to stated investment parameters and whether the investment methodology is consistent with stated objectives. This is particularly true for managers investing in unlisted securities and derivative instruments.

There is a curious dichotomy in the mindset of investors in alternative investments. Investors in private equity funds view lack of transparency and liquidity as par for the course and, often, as a benefit. However, lack of transparency and liquidity in a hedge fund can be regarded as a disadvantage.

Much of the recent clamor for transparency has focused on managers supplying full portfolio information to investors on a real-time basis. In this instance, transparency can have the ability to do more harm than good. The reasons are very straightforward:

- If the portfolio information is leaked to the marketplace, it can be used by other market participants against the manager and thereby against the best interests of the investors.
- It can cause the management of companies, in whose stocks a manager may be short, to cut off the flow of information. Again, this works against the best interests of investors.

Furthermore, we have seen no empirical evidence to show that the use of the ubiquitous value-at-risk (VAR) models (which are based on the mathematical formulae developed by some of the professionals who performed so badly in 1998) protects investors from major market setbacks. The reasons are threefold: (1) correlations are increasingly dynamic; (2) in a crisis, all correlations go to one; and (3) the Reverend Thomas Bayes[1] notwithstanding, modeling the unpredictability of human behavior is not yet a perfect science.

Real-time transparency is only valuable in two circumstances: (1) if you have real-time liquidity—that is, you can get in or out of the fund whenever you choose—or (2) if you can proactively manage the risk profile of the investment, such as overlay trading to act as a hedge. Few investors have either of these advantages. Hedge fund liquidity is usually monthly or quarterly, and few investors are in a position to second-guess the managers' investment decisions.

By definition, more transparency means more information. Fifteen years ago there were discreet advantages to having information ahead of the crowd because you could act on the information before its impact was generally understood. Today, by the time you get the information, it is old and everyone else has it, too. Therefore, you have no time to react before the herd.

The inherent return of hedge funds comes from providing investors with the premia that the markets make available to investment professionals who can take positions in securities when others can't, won't, or need to be on the opposite side. Full portfolio transparency may reduce the manager's ability to pick the premia off the table and thereby reduce the inherent return.

SUMMARY

There is a general perception that hedge funds are dangerous, high-risk vehicles designed only for the elite. The majority of statistical and intellectual evidence suggests otherwise.

As has been demonstrated, an inherent return in hedge funds exists partly because excess profit can be earned from consistently dealing in the world's capital and derivative markets on superior terms. However, by adding the positive selection of alpha, intrinsic in the structure of all hedge funds, the inherent return is enhanced. Hedge funds are paid—and have the incentive—to trade and invest when others cannot, will not, or need to be on the other side.

NOTES

[1]See essay towards solving a problem in the doctrine of chances, Philosophical Transactions of the Royal Society of London, 1764.

CHAPTER 3

Managed Futures

By Thomas Schneeweis

As was apparent in the last major market downturn at the end of 2000, managed futures are negatively correlated with the S&P 500 Index in its poorest months but are positively correlated in its best months. This academic research looks at the role of managed futures in maximizing the risk/return ratio within a diversified portfolio.

This chapter, updated with data through December 2000, is taken from "The Benefits of Managed Futures," a research paper originally commissioned by the Alternative Investment Management Association (AIMA) in 1996 and updated frequently since then. Reproduction or use of all or any part of the research is prohibited without the express written permission of both the author and the AIMA. The author and the AIMA retain all future publication rights to the original research paper and this chapter. © Schneeweis/AIMA (1996–2002)

OVERVIEW

The term managed futures represents an industry comprised of professional money managers known as commodity trading advisors (CTAs) who manage client assets on a discretionary basis, using global futures and options markets as an investment medium. However, for managed futures to grow as an investment alternative, individuals need to increase their knowledge of and comfort level with the use of managed futures in their investment portfolios.

Exactly what are the benefits of managed futures as part of an investor's overall asset portfolio? Basically, managed futures provide direct exposure to international financial and non-financial asset sectors while offering (through their ability to take both long and short investment positions easily) a means to gain exposure to risk and return patterns not easily accessible with investments in traditional stock and bond portfolios. Investors must come to appreciate that the investment benefits in managed futures are well-founded in financial theory and empirical evidence. Although it is impossible to convey all the details of the benefits of managed futures in a short synopsis, this chapter supports managed futures as a means to

- Reduce portfolio volatility risk
- Enhance portfolio returns in economic environments in which traditional stock and bond investment media offer limited opportunities
- Participate in a wide variety of new financial products and markets not available in traditional investment products

GROWTH AND BENEFITS OF MANAGED FUTURES

Futures and options have been used for centuries as both a risk management tool and a return enhancement vehicle. Yet, managed futures, as an investment alternative, have been available only since the late 1960s. Today, institutional investors, such as corporate and public pension funds, endowments and trusts, and bank trust departments as well as high net-worth individuals, include managed futures as one segment of a well-diversified portfolio.

As Figure 3.1 illustrates, the dollars under management for CTAs in the managed futures sector grew from less than $15 billion under management in 1995 to approximately $30 billion in 2000. Moreover, this number does not include the billions of dollars under management or in proprietary trading programs of major financial institutions, which trade similar strategies, but which do not report to traditional data sources. Assets under management in publicly traded funds or private pools remained in the range of $8 billion to $10 billion dollars over the period from 1995 to 2000.

This growth in investor demand for managed futures products indicates investor appreciation of the potential benefits of managed futures—for example, reduced portfolio risk, potential for enhanced portfolio returns, ability to profit in different economic environments, and the ease of global diversification. Futures/options traders receive other special benefits compared to trading traditional asset classes—for example, lower transaction costs, lower market impact costs, use of leverage, and trading in liquid markets. In addition, the market integrity and safety of trading on organized exchanges for futures/options contracts provide further assurances of transparency and regulation.

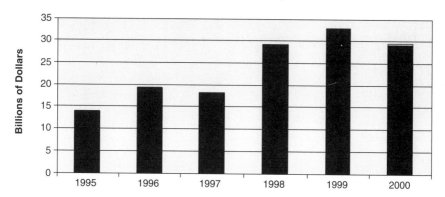

FIGURE 3.1 Commodity trading advisors: assets under management.

MANAGED FUTURES: RISK AND RETURN PERFORMANCE

Although funds placed with CTAs have often been regarded as high-risk investments, over the period from 1990 to 2000, the average annualized standard deviations of individual CTAs and the average annualized standard deviations of the 30 individual stocks in the Dow Jones Industrial Average were similar—that is, approximately 25 percent.[1] More important, investment theory has shown that assets should be compared on the potential benefit of their improving a portfolio's Sharpe ratio—such as, (mean return − risk free return)/standard deviation. Results (see Table 3.1) show that, over the 11 years from 1990 through 2000, investment in a portfolio of CTAs (Zurich CTA$ in this study) provides both stand-alone risk and return benefits generally similar to existing U.S. and world stock and bond investments as well as increased Sharpe ratios (return-to-risk ratios) when considered as an addition to widely diversified asset portfolios.[2]

For stocks, bonds, and CTA$, the individual Sharpe ratios are

Zurich CTA$ (0.60)
S&P 500 Index (0.71)
Lehman Brothers Government/Credit bond index (0.58)
Lehman Brothers World Government bond index (0.30)
MSCI world stock index (0.27)

At the portfolio level, the Sharpe ratio of the portfolios (Portfolio III of U.S. markets and VI of world markets) that include an investment in

TABLE 3.1 Performance Results (January 1990 to December 2000)

	Zurich CTA$	Zurich Fund of Funds Hedge Fund Universe	S&P 500	Lehman Gov./Corp. Bond	MSCI	Lehman Global Bond
Annualized Return	11.8%	10.8%	15.4%	8.0%	9.4%	7.3%
Annualized Stdev	10.4%	4.7%	13.9%	4.2%	14.1%	5.9%
Sharpe Ratio	0.60	1.12	0.71	0.58	0.27	0.30
Minimum Monthly Return	−6.0%	−6.4%	−14.5%	−2.5%	−13.3%	−3.7%
Correlation with Zurich CTA$		0.20	−0.06	0.24	−0.09	0.20

	Portfolio I	Portfolio II	Portfolio III	Portfolio IV	Portfolio V	Portfolio VI
	S&P 500 & Lehman Bond	S&P 500, Lehman Bond, and Zurich HF Fund of Funds	S&P 500, Lehman Bond Zurich HF Fund of Funds and CTA$	MSCI and Lehman Global Bond	MSCI, Lehman Global Bond, and Zurich HF Fund of Funds	MSCI, Lehman Global Bond Zurich HF Fund of Funds and CTA$
Annualized Return	11.90%	11.73%	11.81%	8.62%	9.11%	9.46%
Annualized Stdev	7.98%	6.91%	6.33%	8.54%	7.26%	6.62%
Sharpe Ratio	0.79	0.89	0.99	0.36	0.49	0.59
Minimum Monthly Return	−6.25%	−6.28%	−5.12%	−5.37%	−5.57%	−4.48%
Correlation with Zurich CTA$	0.01	0.02		0.00	0.01	

Portfolio I = 50% S&P 500 and 50% Lehman Brothers Gov./Corp. Bond
Portfolio II = 40% S&P 500, 40% Lehman Brothers Gov./Corp. Bond, and 20% Zurich HF Fund of Funds
Portfolio III = 90% Portfolio III and 10% Zurich CTA$
Portfolio IV = 50% MSCI and 50% Lehman Brothers Global Bond
Portfolio V = 40% MSCI, 40% Lehman Brothers Global Bond, and 20% Zurich HF Fund of Funds
Portfolio VI = 90% Portfolio V and 10% Zurich CTA$

managed futures, as well as investment in stocks, bonds, and hedge funds, dominate those portfolios that invest solely in traditional stock and bond investments (Portfolio I of U.S. markets and Portfolio III of world markets) or portfolios that invest solely in stock, bond, and hedge funds (Portfolio II of U.S. markets and Portfolio V of world markets). Although not reported, a portfolio of 45 percent S&P 500 Index (MSCI), 45 percent Lehman Bond (Lehman Global), and 10 percent CTA$ also outperforms, in terms of relative Sharpe ratios, equally weighted stock and bond portfolios.

For the U.S. markets, the Sharpe ratios for the portfolios are

Portfolio I (0.79)
Portfolio II (0.89)
Portfolio III (0.99)

For the world markets, the Sharpe ratios for the portfolios are

Portfolio IV (0.36)
Portfolio V (0.49)
Portfolio VI (0.59)

The benefits of managed futures in diversified portfolios is further illustrated in Figure 3.2. When the Zurich CTA$ is added to an S&P 500 Index-Lehman Brothers Bond index, as well as an equal-weighted S&P 500 Index and Lehman Brothers bond portfolio, increased risk-adjusted investment opportunities exist.

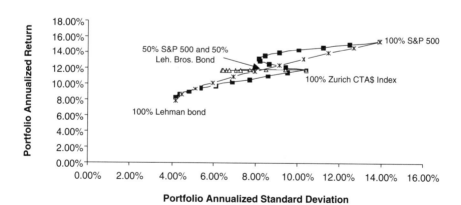

FIGURE 3.2 Risk and return of stock, bond, and Zurich CTA$ (January 1990 to December 2000).

ALTERNATIVE RISK/RETURN OPPORTUNITIES

Table 3.2 for the period 1990–2000 displays the performance of the Zurich CTA$ and various Zurich CTA strategy-based subsets as well as their correlation with other CTA-based investment strategies. In general, the correlation of CTA strategies with other CTA strategies depends on the degree to which the strategies are based on trend-following or discretionary approaches. Because most CTAs follow trend-following strategies, the overall dollar-weighted and equal-weighted indices are also highly correlated with other CTA strategies dominated by trend-following indices.

Table 3.3 displays the return and risk performance of the Zurich CTA strategies as well as their correlation with traditional stock and bond indices. On average, the correlations of the Zurich CTA$ and various Zurich CTA strategy-based subsets with traditional stock and bond indices are often close to zero. However, as shown in Table 3.4, CTAs may offer unique risk diversification benefits, especially in periods in which equity markets perform poorly. For instance, as Table 3.4 shows for the period from 1990 through 2000, the Zurich CTA$ is negatively correlated (−0.30) with the S&P 500 Index when the S&P 500 Index posted its 44 worst months, yet it is positively correlated (0.17) when the S&P 500 Index reported its best 44 months.

In contrast, as Table 3.4 and Figure 3.3 illustrate, other alternative investment strategies, such as equity-sensitive hedge funds (event-driven or global established), often have higher positive correlation with equity markets when the equity markets are falling than when the equity markets are rising. Thus, they may not provide the diversification benefits with equities offered by CTAs.[3]

The benefits of CTA investment in periods of extreme S&P 500 Index return movement is further illustrated in Figure 3.4, which indicates that, when S&P 500 Index returns were ranked from low to high and divided into four 33-month sub-periods, managed futures offered the opportunity to obtain positive returns in months in which the S&P 500 Index provided negative returns as well as in months in which the S&P 500 Index reported positive returns. In contrast, certain alternative investments, such as equity-based global established hedge funds, had negative returns in just those months in which the S&P 500 Index also performed poorly.

TABLE 3.2 Correlation

	Zurich CTA$	Zurich CTAEQ	Zurich Currency	Zurich Discretionary	Zurich Diversified	Zurich Financial	Zurich Trend-Following
Zurich CTA$	1.00						
Zurich CTAEQ	0.94	1.00					
Zurich Currency	0.70	0.68	1.00				
Zurich Discretionary	0.62	0.52	0.43	1.00			
Zurich Diversified	0.93	0.92	0.56	0.58	1.00		
Zurich Financial	0.92	0.87	0.63	0.45	0.83	1.00	
Zurich Trend-Following	0.96	0.95	0.72	0.50	0.92	0.93	1.00

TABLE 3.3 Performance: Zurich CTA Universe Strategies and Traditional Assets (January 1990 to December 2000)

	Return	Stdev	Sharpe Ratio	Minimum Monthly	Correlation S&P 500	Correlation Lehman Bond
Zurich CTA$	11.8%	10.4%	0.60	−6.0%	−0.06	0.24
Zurich CTAEQ	9.7%	9.8%	0.43	−5.4%	−0.09	0.20
Zurich Currency	10.8%	13.2%	0.40	−8.2%	0.00	0.16
Zurich Discretionary	12.9%	7.2%	1.01	−4.6%	−0.05	0.18
Zurich Diversified	10.1%	12.1%	0.37	−7.5%	−0.09	0.23
Zurich Financial	12.0%	13.6%	0.48	−8.6%	−0.02	0.32
Zurich Trend-Following	10.9%	16.5%	0.32	−10.4%	−0.07	0.24
S&P 500	15.4%	13.9%	0.71	−14.5%	1.00	0.37
Leh. Bros. Gov./Corp	8.0%	4.2%	0.58	−2.5%	0.37	1.00

TABLE 3.4 Correlations in Best and Worst 44 S&P 500 Ranked Months (1990 to 2000)

	All S&P Months	Worst S&P 500 44 Months	Best S&P 500 44 Months
Managed Futures			
Zurich CTA$	−0.06	−0.30	0.17
Zurich CTAEQ	−0.09	−0.37	0.22
Zurich Currency	0.00	0.14	0.26
Zurich Discretionary	−0.05	−0.08	0.03
Zurich Diversified	−0.09	−0.43	0.16
Zurich Financial	−0.02	−0.31	0.22
Zurich Trend-Following	−0.07	−0.35	0.23
Hedge Funds			
Zurich Event Driven Universe	0.47	0.64	−0.16
Zurich Fund of Funds Universe	0.52	0.61	0.09
Zurich Global Established Universe	0.78	0.71	0.34
Zurich Market Neutral Universe	0.31	0.55	0.15
Traditional Assets			
Lehman Gov./Corp. Bond	0.37	0.03	0.03

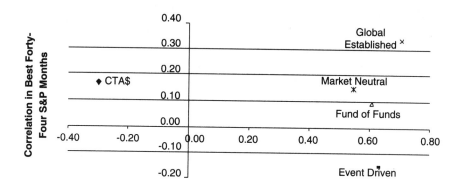

FIGURE 3.3   Correlations in best and worst 44 S&P 500 ranked months (1990 to 2000).

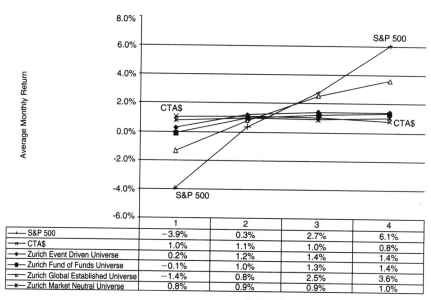

	1	2	3	4
S&P 500	−3.9%	0.3%	2.7%	6.1%
CTA$	1.0%	1.1%	1.0%	0.8%
Zurich Event Driven Universe	0.2%	1.2%	1.4%	1.4%
Zurich Fund of Funds Universe	−0.1%	1.0%	1.3%	1.4%
Zurich Global Established Universe	−1.4%	0.8%	2.5%	3.6%
Zurich Market Neutral Universe	0.8%	0.9%	0.9%	1.0%

Portfolio Groupings

FIGURE 3.4   Ranking by S&P 500 (January 1990 to December 2000).

RECENT PERFORMANCE

Table 3.5 shows that over the five-year period from 1996 through 2000, managed futures have continued to provide benefits as additions to existing stock and stock/bond portfolios. It must be pointed out that during that period, the S&P 500 Index generally outperformed managed futures as well as many other investment strategies. Investors must also realize the uniqueness of the time period. Average annual returns to the S&P 500 Index in the 1996–2000 period (17.2 percent) were greater than that achieved in the period from 1990 through 1995 (13.1 percent) while managed futures had higher returns in the first half of the 1990s (14.4 percent) than in the 1996–2000 period (8.0 percent).

DIFFERENTIAL SOURCE OF RETURNS TO MANAGED FUTURES, HEDGE FUNDS, AND TRADITIONAL ASSETS

The real benefit of managed futures is the provision of sources of returns that are uniquely different from traditional stock or bonds or even hedge funds. For instance, hedge funds have been marketed as offering unique risk and return properties that are not easily available through traditional investment securities or investment products. These return opportunities stem from the expanded universe of securities available to trade and to the broader range of trading strategies.

One reason for the supposedly low correlation and potential diversification benefit is that hedge funds often describe themselves as employing skill-based investment strategies that do not explicitly attempt to track a particular index. Because their goal is to maximize long-term returns independently of a proscribed traditional stock and bond index, they emphasize *absolute returns* and not returns relative to a predetermined index. It is important to realize, however, that although hedge funds do not emphasize benchmark tracking, this does not mean that their entire return is based solely on manager skill or is independent of the movement of underlying stock, bond, or currency markets.

Hedge fund managers often track a particular investment strategy or investment opportunity. When appropriately grouped, these hedge fund strategies have been shown to be driven by the same common market factors, such as changes in stock and bond returns or stock market volatility, that drive the traditional stock and bond markets. For instance, Table 3.6 reports the performance of various hedge fund strategies relative to stock and bond markets as well as other factors that have been shown in prior

TABLE 3.5 Performance Results (January 1996 to December 2000)

	Zurich CTA$	Zurich Fund of Funds Hedge Fund Universe	S&P 500	Lehman Gov./Corp. Bond	MSCI	Lehman Global Bond
Annualized Return	8.0%	10.9%	17.2%	6.0%	11.9%	3.3%
Annualized Stdev	8.5%	5.6%	16.1%	3.9%	14.3%	5.7%
Sharpe Ratio	0.93	1.95	1.07	1.55	0.83	0.59
Minimum Monthly Return	−4.8%	−6.4%	−14.5%	−2.4%	−13.3%	−3.4%
Correlation with Zurich CTA$		0.07	0.03	0.46	0.02	0.16

	Portfolio I S&P 500 & Lehman Bond	Portfolio II S&P 500, Lehman Bond, and Zurich HF Fund of Funds	Portfolio III S&P 500, Lehman Bond Zurich HF Fund of Funds and CTA$	Portfolio IV MSCI and Lehman Global Bond	Portfolio V MSCI, Lehman Global Bond, and Zurich HF Fund of Funds	Portfolio VI MSCI, Lehman Global Bond Zurich HF Fund of Funds and CTA$
Annualized Return	11.8%	11.7%	11.4%	7.8%	8.5%	8.5%
Annualized Stdev	8.6%	7.6%	7.0%	8.0%	7.0%	6.4%
Sharpe Ratio	1.37	1.53	1.62	0.98	1.21	1.32
Minimum Monthly Return	−6.3%	−6.3%	−5.1%	−5.4%	−5.6%	−4.5%
Correlation with Zurich CTA$	0.13	0.13		0.07	0.08	

Portfolio I = 50% S&P 500 and 50% Lehman Brothers Gov./Corp. Bond
Portfolio II = 40% S&P 500, 40% Lehman Brothers Gov./Corp. Bond, and 20% Zurich HF Fund of Funds
Portfolio III = 90% Portfolio III and 10% Zurich CTA$
Portfolio IV = 50% MSCI and 50% Lehman Brothers Global Bond
Portfolio V = 40% MSCI, 40% Lehman Brothers Global Bond, and 20% Zurich HF Fund of Funds
Portfolio VI = 90% Portfolio V and 10% Zurich CTA$

TABLE 3.6 Factor Correlations (1990 to 2000)

	S&P 500	Leh. Bros. Bond	Change in Credit Spread Moody's (Baa-Aaa)	Change in VIX
Managed Futures				
Zurich CTA$	−0.06	0.24	−0.06	0.15
Zurich CTAEQ	−0.09	0.20	−0.03	0.17
Zurich Currency	0.00	0.16	−0.05	0.06
Zurich Discretionary	−0.05	0.18	−0.07	0.09
Zurich Diversified	−0.09	0.23	−0.05	0.21
Zurich Financial	−0.02	0.32	−0.08	0.13
Zurich Trend-Following	−0.07	0.25	−0.07	0.18
Hedge Funds				
Zurich Event Driven Univ.	0.47	0.11	−0.33	−0.45
Zurich HF FOF Univ.	0.52	0.20	−0.16	−0.35
Zurich Global Est. Univ.	0.78	0.20	−0.29	−0.48
Zurich Mkt. Neutral Univ.	0.31	0.11	−0.21	−0.15
Traditional Assets				
S&P 500	1.00	0.37	−0.09	−0.63
Leh. Bros. Bond	0.37	1.00	−0.02	−0.15

Change in Credit Spread is the change in the spread between Baa and Aaa yield indices. A positive (negative) value indicates an increase (decrease) in the returns of the strategy as the spread increases.
Change in VIX is the change in the VIX index (that is, implied volatility of the S&P 100). A positive (negative) value indicates an increase (decrease) in returns when the VIX (implied volatility) increases.

studies to explain returns such as increase in risk, reflected by change in the VIX index (S&P 100 Index implied volatility).

As expected, results show that equity-biased hedge fund strategies have a high correlation with the same factors as long equity strategies (for example, the S&P 500 Index). In contrast, managed futures universe returns are not correlated with the stock and bond markets or changes in equity market volatility, but track indices that reflect trend-following return patterns. As Table 3.7 shows, certain managed futures strategies, which are systematic and trend-following in nature, are highly correlated with simple passive trend-following indices. In contrast, managed futures programs that are not trend-following in structure are not correlated with these trend-following indices such that investments across trend-following and non-trend-following strategies may offer diversification.[4]

TABLE 3.7 Factor Correlations: Zurich Managed Futures (1996 to 2000)

	S&P 500	Leh. Bros. Bond	Change in Credit Spread Moody's (Baa-Aaa)	Change in VIX	Trend-Following Interest Rate	Trend-Following Currency	Trend-Following Stock
Zurich CTA$	0.03	0.46	-0.09	0.06	0.61	0.53	0.35
Zurich CTAEQ	0.01	0.42	-0.05	0.09	0.64	0.58	0.37
Zurich Currency	0.07	0.20	-0.01	-0.09	0.09	0.79	-0.03
Zurich Discretionary	0.18	0.24	-0.27	-0.07	0.37	0.21	0.26
Zurich Diversified	-0.04	0.44	-0.08	0.16	0.62	0.39	0.48
Zurich Systematic	-0.01	0.41	-0.03	0.05	0.58	0.53	0.33
Zurich Financial	-0.01	0.47	0.00	0.09	0.67	0.50	0.29
Zurich Trend-Following	-0.02	0.46	-0.04	0.13	0.63	0.51	0.39
S&P 500	1.00	0.20	0.07	-0.66	0.04	-0.01	-0.06
Leh. Bros. Bond	0.20	1.00	0.20	-0.02	0.45	0.15	0.28

*CTA returns are Zurich Universe Medians

**Trendfollowing Interest Rate, Currency, and Stock are Passive Systematic CTA Indices (See www.CISDM.org)

SUMMARY

The results of this chapter provide important information to the investment community about the benefits of managed futures.

1. Managed futures trade in markets that offer investors the same market integrity and safety as stock and bond markets. Managed futures investment, as is the case for stocks and bonds, provide investors with the assurance that their investment managers work with a high degree of government oversight and self-regulation and trade primarily in closely regulated markets.

2. Managed futures are not more risky than traditional equity investment. Investment in a single CTA is shown to have risks and returns that are similar to investment in a single equity investment. Moreover, a portfolio of CTAs is also shown to have risks and returns that are similar to traditional equity portfolio investments.

3. Most traditional money managers (and many hedge fund managers) are restricted by regulation or convention to holding primarily long investment positions and from using actively traded futures and option contracts (which offer lower transaction costs and lower market impact costs than direct stock or bond investment). Thus, in contrast to most stock and bond investment vehicles, managed futures offer unique return opportunities, which exist through trading a wide variety of global stock and bond futures and options markets and through holding either long or short investment positions in different economic environments (for example, arbitrage opportunities, rising and falling stock and bond markets, and changing market volatility).

As a result of these differing investment styles and investment opportunities, managed futures traders have the potential for a positive return, even though futures and options markets in total provide a zero net gain among all market participants. Thus, managed futures are shown on average to have a low return correlation with traditional stock and bond markets as well as many hedge fund strategies and to offer investors the potential for reduced portfolio risk and enhanced investment return. As important, for properly constructed portfolios, managed futures are also shown to offer unique downside risk control along with upside return potential.

Simply put, the logical extension of using investment managers with specialized knowledge of traditional markets to obtain maximum return/risk tradeoffs is to add specialized managers who can obtain the unique returns in market conditions and types of securities not generally available to traditional asset managers—that is, managed futures.

REFERENCES

Schneeweis, Thomas. "Dealing With Myths of Managed Futures," *The Journal of Alternative Investments*, (Summer 1998): 9–18.

Schneeweis, Thomas. *The Benefits of Managed Futures*. AIMA, 1996.

Schneeweis, Thomas, and Joe Pescatore, editors. *The Handbook of Alternative Investment Strategies: An Investor's Guide*. Institutional Investor, 1999.

NOTES

[1]The annual and monthly returns presented in their nominal form. Annualized standard deviations are derived by multiplying the monthly data by the square root of 12.

[2]Zurich Commodity Trading Advisor Universe and Managed Futures Pools and Fund Universe returns replace the Managed Accounts Reports (MAR) data used in previous studies. Zurich recently purchased the MAR CTA and hedge fund databases.

[3]In the exhibits in this study, Zurich CTA and hedge fund universe returns are used. CTA$ is the dollar-weighted CTA universe. CTAEQ is the equal-weighted CTA universe. The additional CTA indices are segmented by CTA reporting strategy (for example, currency, financial, diversified) or style (discretionary, trend-following). For hedge funds, event-driven indicates the median of the reporting hedge funds grouped as distressed and risk arbitrage. The Zurich Fund of Funds is the median of reporting fund of funds where capital is allocated among a number of hedge funds. The Zurich Global Established is the median of the reporting hedge fund managers who are primarily hedge equity managers with a long bias who pay attention to economic changes, but are more bottom-up oriented in that they tend to be stock-pickers. The Zurich Market Neutral is the median reporting long/short stocks, convertible arbitrage, stock index arbitrage, and fixed-income arbitrage managers. It is important to note that the Zurich CTA and hedge fund universe returns used in this study are not the same as the Zurich hedge fund indices that are designed specifically to track particular strategies that meet predefined criteria and are, by design, more style pure.

[4]See **www.cisdm.org** for data and description of trend-following indices.

CHAPTER **4**

Distressed Securities

By Tremont Advisers

For much of the 1990s, distressed investing posted some of the best risk-adjusted returns among all strategies. However, growing default rates, a growing supply of distressed securities, and dwindling hedge fund and bank demand reduced its attractiveness. It may still have a place in the investment spectrum for the person who has a superior ability to value a firm's assets and thoroughly understands all investment risks. (For another look at this category, see Chapter 11 on high yield investments.)

PERFORMANCE AND MARKET PROFILE

Risk-adjusted performance for distressed securities investors appeared rather strong throughout most of the 1990s while equity market correlation held remarkably low. Notwithstanding some very serious issues regarding mark-to-market pricing of these inherently illiquid securities, the asset class has been a successful complement to many fund-of-fund strategies when viewed over the long term, based on its counter-cyclical nature. (Mark-to-market pricing, or the lack of it, has undoubtedly smoothed the monthly volatility, an issue I will discuss in depth later).

Since the inception of the Tremont/CSFB Index Universe in 1994, the mid- to high-teen annualized percentage returns experienced by the distressed market were accompanied by volatility in the 3.5 to 5 percent range, yielding Sharpe ratios in excess of 2.0 (greater than 4 in some instances). Prior to that, in the 1980s and early 1990s, distressed managers soared, annualizing 25 to 40 percent with few statistical outliers. Volatility, although certainly higher during these boom years, was not overly so, yielding Sharpe ratios in excess of 2.0.

The investment opportunities in the early 1990s (considered the glory days of distressed investing) typically consisted of sound businesses with over-leveraged balanced sheets, facing operational cash-flow difficulties stemming from cyclical downturns, failed or expensive acquisitions (including leveraged buyouts), or expensive takeover defenses. The fall of Drexel Burnham Lambert and the high yield market overall made the opportunity especially attractive for value investors with a long-term perspective.

Investors liquidated these positions en masse, due to the negative stigma associated with these defaulted or soon-to-default securities or by obligation due to their investment charter. Savvy distressed investors bought them back below intrinsic value, held (or advised) them throughout the reorganization/restructuring process, in control and noncontrol positions, ultimately profiting from the sale of such securities, asset liquidations, or buyouts.

A good example of the typical 1990s distressed play was U.S. Gypsum Corporation (USG), which attempted to repeal a takeover attempt through a leveraged recapitalization. USG's investment adviser for the leveraged recapitalization worked on the assumptions of a sound business plan, strong new housing starts, and steady commodity (gypsum) prices. The economic slowdown and gypsum pricing pressure in the early 1990s sapped USG's cash flow, causing the company to miss interest payments on its debt obligations. This created valuable investment opportunities for distressed investors, who scooped up cheaply priced debt and turned a nice profit upon USG's emergence from bankruptcy. (As a side note, USG has once again filed for Chapter 11 bankruptcy protection as a result of the mounting threat of asbestos litigations).

Poor asset quality, low default rates, and a strong equity bull market made distressed investing both uninteresting and highly directional towards the middle and latter half of the 1990s. Passive approaches to the asset class were particularly dismal, as poor management, misguided business models, and operational difficulties made many businesses not worth saving. High yield credit quality deteriorated significantly, and much of what was outstanding had little to speak of in terms of asset quality and recurring cash flow. Although default rates remained low, record levels of high yield debt outstanding produced record default volume. The distressed market grew by default, while the high yield market, which often serves as an incubator to distressed securities, still traded at a historically low spread to Treasuries, despite the deteriorating new issuance credit quality. What would normally have traded at a greater than 1000 basis point spread to comparable Treasuries priced much richer, discounting the risk of default.

High yield investors continued to demand new product, and corporations, seeing an excellent financing opportunity, rushed to issue high yield securities. Investment banks jumped at the opportunity to generate fee income off the sale of such securities to the market and did not do a proper job in weeding out flawed businesses from the high yield market. Although large high yield new issuance resulted in a larger supply of distressed securities (albeit with low default rates), it did so only on an absolute-dollar basis. Some distressed investors and commercial and investment banks continued to allocate capital to the distressed sector, albeit across an inferior investment opportunity set.

Supply and Demand Factors

These factors all contributed to growing default rates, and a rapidly increasing supply of distressed securities. In addition, the demand for distressed securities dwindled as hedge funds and commercial and investment banks quickly reduced leverage or exited the business following the credit and liquidity crisis in the Fall of 1998. The estimated $18+ billion in hedge funds and segregated accounts (not including proprietary bank capital) chasing distressed securities was cut dramatically. According to a second quarter 2000 TASS Investment Research report on hedge fund asset flows, total event-driven asset flows declined by approximately $1 billion in both the fourth quarter of 1998 (7.1 percent) and the first quarter of 1999 (6.5 percent) of total event-driven assets. The second quarter of 2000 witnessed an additional $500 million in net outflows, or 3 percent of total event-driven assets.

The Event-Driven Index includes both distressed and risk arbitrage managers, implying a much more severe quarterly outflow for the distressed sector (see Figure 4.1). Once the negative outflows from proprietary sources are factored in, the total withdrawal of capital became monumental. Hence, with rising default rates, poor quality merchandise, and record high yield new issuance, distressed supply quickly outstripped demand.

A Primer on the Bankruptcy and Restructuring Process

Investing in distressed situations involves purchasing the claims of companies that have already either filed for Chapter 11 or Chapter 7 bankruptcy protection, are trying to avoid Chapter 11 through an out-of-court debt restructuring with their creditors, or are in immediate danger of doing so. Companies in danger of filing will typically trade at a wide spread to Treasuries, reflecting this risk. This includes originally issued high yield securities, or "fallen angels," which were originally deemed investment grade.

There are basically two general investment philosophies to distressed securities investing:

1. The "private equity" approach.
2. The much shorter-term, passive, "relative value" approach, which is principally the domain of most hedge fund investors.

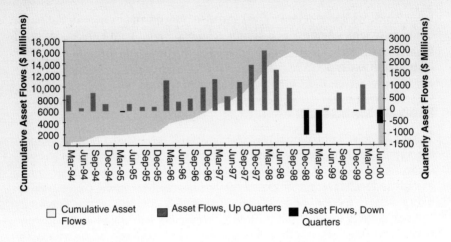

*Asset flows refer to money flowing into/out of the industry. Asset growth/contraction as a result of performance is not included.
Source: TASS Investment Research Limited Asset Flows Report, Third Quarter 2000

FIGURE 4.1   Event-driven asset flows* (quarter-end, March 1994, through quarter-end, June 2000, million U.S. dollars).

    The first model is called "private equity" due to the capital-call nature of investing, the occasional activist approaches taken, and the required three- to seven-year lock-up periods often associated with those investment vehicles. Within the passive "relative value" model, investors can purchase deeply discounted securities, issue new debt, or attempt to arbitrage one capital structure versus another. In the "private equity" model, investors purchase these claims during or before Chapter 11 so they may exert influence on the terms of the reorganization, or they wait until the debt is converted into an equity stake that can be used similarly afterwards. Relative value investors will choose a more passive approach and, to some extent, ride the coattails of the activist investors who seek to add value in the reorganization process.

    Distressed investments vary widely in terms of the type of security available: Investment debt, bank loans, trade claims, private placements, real estate mortgages, and lease contracts are examples of the most common types. Distressed investments can also take the form of direct investments and debtor-in-possession (DIP) financings. The supply of available distressed debt is highly cyclical in nature, based on a variety of economic, capital market, company specific, corporate structure, and technical factors.

Distressed investors generally attempt to profit on pricing inefficiencies associated with such securities, the negative stigma associated with such claims, or simply an inability on behalf of the original investors to value such claims accurately or direct their legal interests during restructuring proceedings. When considering a potential investment, distressed investors consider a variety of factors. Industry practitioners Barnhill, Maxwell, and Shenkman summarize the most important considerations as follows:

Why is the company in distress?
- Excessive leverage?
- Industry weakness?
- Poor management?
- Lawsuits?

Corporate and relevant industry characteristics
- Industry structure.
- Industry trends.
- Competitive forces.

Restructuring options available
- Prepackaged bankruptcy.
- Out-of-court restructuring.
- Chapter 11 or 7.

Capital structure positioning
- Senior secured to junior subordinated.
- Control or noncontrol.

Other creditors and their interests
- Banks.
- Debt holders.
- Stockholders. Liability claimants.
- Others.

Bankruptcy judge and the legal jurisdiction
- What is the judge's record?
- How involved will the judge be in the reorganization?

Investment timing
- Creditor disputes.
- Operating results.
- Working capital.

Potential exit strategies
- Outright sale of security (debt or converted equity).
- Acquisition.
- Initial public offering (IPO).

Investments in distressed securities can occur throughout many separate and distinct stages of a bankruptcy life cycle. Distressed investors generally categorize the life cycle in any or all of the following four stages:

1. *Pre-filing (prior to bankruptcy filing; duration is variable)*
   - Companies in the pre-bankruptcy stage acknowledge their distressed situation.
   - Bondholders committees may be formed, and informal discussions are held to consider restructuring options.
   - During this stage, distressed claims are entering investor "radar screens," and the investigation process begins.
2. *Early-stage bankruptcy (can last six months to one year after filing)*
   - The corporation at this point commences bankruptcy filing; legal advisers, creditor groups, and consultants are all very active here.
3. *Middle-stage bankruptcy (can last from six months to two years after filing)*
   - In-depth due diligence commences among legal advisers, financial advisers, and creditor groups.
   - Cash-flow difficulties should begin to stabilize, and the picture becomes somewhat more clarified.
4. *Late-stage bankruptcy (can last from one to several years after filing)*
   - Creditor disputes are resolved, enterprise value is established, and the new security baskets are distributed to claimholders.

The various stages will differ in the length of the associated investment period, the price level of the security purchased, the level of fundamental due diligence required, issues being addressed, and the potential impact of a passive or active investment approach. Depending upon in which stage an investor is investing, the investment firm may get involved in any of the following restructuring stages:

- *Chapter 7 filing.* Companies filing for Chapter 7 bankruptcy protection are preparing for liquidation of the firm's assets and are seeking court-aided supervision during the liquidation process.
- *Chapter 11 filing.* Companies filing for Chapter 11 bankruptcy protection are seeking a court-supervised reorganization of the firm while affording relief from interest payments due to existing creditors. Firms generally opt for Chapter 11 when the value of a firm as an ongoing concern exceeds the firm's saleable liquidation value. Chapter 11 filings can be voluntary or involuntary in nature. A company's senior management and board of directors have the authority to opt for voluntary Chapter 11 filings. Involuntary Chapter 11 filings can

be enacted by a minimum of three creditors with aggregate claims exceeding $100,000.

■ *Out-of-court restructurings.* In an out-of-court restructuring, creditors and debtors agree on a private exchange offer. A firm's existing financial claims are exchanged for a new basket of claims. The firm's objective is to reduce total debt in the firm's capital structure. An out-of-court restructuring may be in the best interests of both parties to avoid associated deadweight costs such as legal and administrative expenses and the lengthy time constraints often associated with bankruptcy proceedings.

Active and Passive Approaches

As I have already alluded, there are three general approaches to distressed investing. The first two relate to a proactive investment approach. The investor may attempt to increase the present value of the firm by deploying the firm's assets more efficiently. The investor may also attempt to increase his/her percentage ownership of the outstanding firm value at the expense of other investors. The third investment approach, which is the domain of a passive investor, is a simple buy-and-hold strategy, purchasing undervalued securities trading at distressed levels that are suffering from general investor disinterest.

Hedge fund investors typically become involved in this stage, as the more activist approaches require a long-term investment horizon. The potential for partnership asset/liability mismatches require that, for the most part, the two partnership structures operate distinct strategies, although some hedge funds have involved themselves in some combination of the two. Although we believe the private equity model of distressed investing is generally superior to the relative value model due to the longer-term nature of distressed investing, multi-strategy approaches in distressed hedge funds many times make sense.

The appropriateness of the three investment approaches will depend on the strength of the investor as an active or passive investment entity, the successful execution of his or her investment strategy, and the time involved, relative to resources dedicated to such an approach.

Proactive investment strategies involve active investor participation in the reorganization process. The following three proactive strategies aim for a *control* position, with the purpose of directing how the firm's assets are employed (to improve profitability) through its investment and operating policies:

1. The investor may choose to submit his or her own reorganization plan to claimholders, specifying what each claimholder will receive, as well

as an amended business plan for the firm upon emergence from bankruptcy.

2. The investor may purchase outstanding debt claims with the intent of
   transferring these claims into voting common stock upon reorganization.
3. The investor may also purchase new voting stock that is to be issued
   subsequent to the reorganization.

Another proactive investment strategy involves the investor's attempt to
increase percentage ownership of the outstanding firm value (at the expense
of other investors) by acquiring a sufficiently large percentage of an outstanding debt issue so as to block a firm's reorganization plan. Debt issues
are categorized according to a number of separate claim (bond) "classes:"

- Senior secured
- Senior unsecured
- Senior subordinated
- Subordinated
- Junior subordinated

Each of these debt classes votes separately on whether or not to approve
a reorganization plan. A plan will be accepted by the debt class as long as
two-thirds in value and greater than one-half of the number of claimholders in that class vote in favor of the plan. If an investor controls greater than
one-third of the value of an outstanding debt class, he or she can effectively
block a reorganization plan (this practice is known as "bondmail"). By
effecting bondmail, the investor can hold up the reorganization until he/she
is given a higher recovery. This investor, however, cannot force the debt class
to approve its own reorganization plan.

The dissenting debt class, by holding up the reorganization process, may
coerce the other class holders to acquiesce them by increasing its recovery
rate. An investor's ability to put into effect his/her investment strategy via
bondmail is limited by the effect of what is called *debt cramdown*. A bankruptcy judge will refute an investor's blocking position, effectively cramming
down that debt class interest, if the firm's assets are too little to satisfy any
additional payments to that (junior) class.

Barnhill, Maxwell, and Shenkman categorize three key qualities essential to successful distressed investing:

1. *A superior ability to value a firm's assets.* This is a very labor-intensive
   process, requiring a skilled and fundamentally oriented investment
   infrastructure (investment personnel), a comprehensive and wide-
   ranging network of information resources, and an operationally sound

procedure for collecting and synthesizing information. A thorough understanding of the company as well as some extent of top-down industry and even macro considerations is vital as well. Getting a handle on asset valuation will help the investor understand the downside risk, which is essential to any absolute return strategy.

2. *Superior interpretation, negotiation, and bargaining skill.* This depends very much on the accuracy in evaluating firm assets and in understanding the firm's entire capital structure, who the other claimholders are, and interpretation of bankruptcy law. For passive approaches, interpretation and successful investment execution based on that is critical.

3. *A thorough understanding of all investment risks,* including how these risks correlate and how to mitigate these risks. Experience here is critical as well. Understanding the options embedded in this strategy can offer added insight as to what those risks are and how they may play out.

Distressed investors may also leverage competitive advantages such as superior deal flow, investment flexibility due to size and scope, and partnership investment horizon/liquidity terms.

The Investment Process

Again, a distressed investor needs to consider a variety of factors before initiating a distressed security investment. These factors include the cause of distress, the industry and company operating results, the available restructuring options, what level in the capital structure to invest in, the composition of the creditor's committee, the bankruptcy judge's record, and the timing of the investment and exit strategy. As asset valuation is of paramount importance in distressed investing, a thorough analysis will require inquiry into the following:

- *Individual assets.* The analyst will review comparable equity-market valuations and recent business sales to come up with probabilistic values for a firm's discrete units.
- *Enterprise value.* This determines the value that creditors will divide upon the reorganization of the firm. The two methods used are discounted cash-flow analysis and industry comparables. Discounted cash-flow analysis, as used in traditional valuation models, prices the present value of the stream of current and future cash flows as well as the firm's terminal value, divided by the firm's weighted average cost of capital (WACC). Comparable analysis involves:

1. Attaching a market value to a firm's assets, based upon the assumption of similar multiples priced for other firms operating in the same space. The multiples usually used include price/sales, price/EBITDA, and price/EBIT, or a combination of the three.
2. Valuation of a firm's securities, based on the rankings of specific claims. Again, the priority list ranks as follows: Secured claims; debtor-in-possession claims; priority claims such as legal/professional fees, wages, employee benefit claims, consumer deposits, alimony, tax claims; unsecured claims; and, finally, equity holders. These creditor claims must be ranked in terms of priority. The dollar amount sought by each claimant will be confirmed or rejected by the bankruptcy judge. Under the absolute priority rule, no claimants will receive anything until higher-priority holders are "made whole."

■ *Plan value.* The corporation plan value relates to the entire package of cash, bonds, and equity distributed for the newly reorganized entity.
■ *Tranche.* The value of the corporation's post-reorganization equity securities, usually held by the more junior tranche holders.

Sources of Risk

Numerous risks are involved with distressed securities investing. Most of these risks are firm- and situation-specific. This is what practitioners refer to as *event risk*. Due to the event-driven nature of distressed securities investing, the majority of the responsibility for the final outcome depends on the skill and expertise of the distressed investor. Market-related risks such as the economy, interest rates, and the state of the equity markets would have a minimal impact on long-term distressed investments (due to their event-driven nature) except in times of severe overall market stress, when correlations tend to increase significantly. To the extent that the above affects market liquidity, market-related risks will have a significant impact on the distressed investment strategies.

Liquidity (Market) Risk   During an investment period, mark-to-market losses can occur due to non event-oriented factors. Market liquidity is perhaps of most importance. Although market liquidity in distressed securities has improved significantly in recent years, this area is still significantly less liquid than other securities markets. Market liquidity can also be very cyclical in nature, dictated by supply and demand for such securities.

Liquidity risk is potentially very troublesome for investment partnerships whose liabilities (investor claims in and ownership in the limited partnership) are mismatched with regards to the position's investment horizon. For distressed funds with quarterly liquidity provisions to investors, trading out of distressed claims can be prohibitively expensive unless there are interested buyers for them. (If the investment fund holds control positions, it is actually prohibited from immediately exiting the investment, due to its ownership interests). In addition, these redemption requests will seldom coincide with the investment fund's exit strategy. A distressed investment's exit strategy may generally be executed simply by trading out of the position; swapping its interests for that of an acquiring entity (in the event of a merger); or via an IPO upon an equity stake's going public. "Private equity" approaches are obviously much less susceptible to this risk.

Firm-Specific Risk   The following event risks are much more firm specific. The majority of these risks can be mitigated via thorough due diligence, a solid knowledge of bankruptcy law, and the experience to understand exactly how these risks correlate.

- *J Factor Risk.* What Barnhill, Maxwell, and Shenkman define as the *J Factor* risk is a very important input to be considered before making an investment. The judge's track record is vital in making probabilistic assumptions and sensitivity analysis on the outcome of bankruptcy proceedings. How actively involved might the judge get in the proceedings? How much of his/her time is dedicated to the specific case? What about his/her track record? Does the judge usually rule in favor of stockholders or management? Does the active investor run the risk of having the bankruptcy judge disqualify his/her voting rights?
- *Mechanic Risk.* Refers to the vagaries and operational steps involved in the transferring of creditor claims. Have (security) title transfers been accurately reported and disclosed in a timely fashion? Have creditors with disputed or contingent claims filed a "proof of claim?" Has the investor submitted a claim transfer in time to have his/her voting rights included?
- *Claim Liability Risk.* Refers to the risk of purchasing claims with liabilities that the new purchaser of such security had no role in creating, yet becomes subject to after their purchase. These liability transfer risks are known as fraudulent conveyance, avoidable preferences, equitable subordination, or environmental liability risk.
- *Disputed/Contingent Claims.* Represent another risk to purchasers of distressed securities. Where exactly in the capital structure and what the exact size of each claim purchased will be might not be determined until the disputed claims are actually resolved. The prices paid for such

securities have an obvious effect on the investor's yield upon the closing of the proceedings and are based on certain assumptions regarding the dispute outcomes.

- **Holding Period Risk.** Relates to the effect of time on annualized returns. The passage of time also coincides with increased legal and administrative expenditures, which directly affect recovery values. In addition, holding period risk can cause serious pain to distressed investors who value their portfolio on a mark-to-market basis and have to raise capital to satisfy investor redemptions.

There are a host of other risks associated with distressed investing, such as *lack of information* about other purchases and purchasers, Chapter 7 (liquidation) risk, insider trading issues, and tax issues.

The Economy and Its Impact

Moody's believes (in a third quarter 2000 report) that the relationship between the economy and default rates is not linear, in that default rates cannot necessarily be derived by looking at measures of aggregate economic activity such as gross domestic product (GDP), industrial production, or corporate profits as a percent of GDP. In fact, U.S. industrial production and default rates are weakly correlated. During the 1920 to 1999 sample time period, the correlation between the U.S. Industrial Production Index and the Moody's All Corporate trailing 12-month default rate was −0.14. Prior to 1965, increases in the default rate lagged after weakness in the economy, not during it. After 1965, however, increases in the default rate occur in advance of a weakening in the economy.

Moody's believes that the proportional relationships between these economic indicators and default rates also depend on the level at which an economy is functioning. It believes that default rates over time vary due to other factors that are independent of the macro-economy (at least, indirectly) for a certain range of fluctuations in the growth of that economy. Only above a certain threshold does economic growth impact default rates. Helwage and Kleiman (1995 and 1996) model this threshold level at 1.5 percent GDP growth.

Other factors that exhibit stronger explanatory power for default rates, such as credit quality and aging bias, could be correlated with macroeconomic activity and affect default rates through those channels. So the belief here is that, unless the economy slides into a full-fledged recession, macroeconomic conditions will be almost irrelevant. The true issue related to economic strength is the possibility of a widespread credit crunch throughout the economy. For us to be in a true credit crunch, however, interest rates must not be a "market-cleared price" but rather be determined by credit rationing among borrowers in the presence of high yields and spreads.

Distressed Securities Valuation Methodology

The distressed investment sector will always represent a concern due to a lack of an efficient pricing mechanism for such securities. Depending on their investment focus, managers may hold an entire portfolio of illiquid and rarely traded debt instruments, leaving the onus on the manager (or their dealers, who may be biased) to self-mark their portfolio. As long as these securities are not traded regularly on an organized, widely agreed upon pricing source, auditors will defer judgment on pricing to the manager. Auditors will require that the report conforms to generally agreed accounting principles and that the manager is consistent in his valuation methodology.

The manager may use a variety of pricing sources, all of which may or may not be in agreement with each other, particularly if the security is defaulted (and not recently traded). Sources used include independent brokers (of which there may be many, as much as six); independent pricing services (for example, Bridge, ADI, IDC, Muller, Merrill, FIPS); and, of course, the manager's own discretion. Under audit rules, the manager's pricing must be justified by any of the above or the manager's own information, which may or may not be reflected in the quoted prices. In addition, prices quoted by the brokerage community and pricing services may be outdated, simply inaccurate, or "nonfirm" prices. The nonfirm prices are quotes that may be limited in size or volume and otherwise "not real" bids.

Depending on the manager's investment focus, nondefaulted securities may constitute a large portion of the aggregate portfolio, in which case there will tend to be a more accurate and widely agreed upon price quote.

REFERENCES

Theodore Barnhill, William Maxwell, and Mark Shenkman. *High Yield Bonds*. New York: McGraw Hill Companies Inc., 1999.

CHAPTER 5

Convertible Securities

By Tremont Advisers

Convertible bonds offer corporations a third way to raise new capital, giving investors a moderate current income in exchange for the opportunity to participate in a potential rising stock value by converting the bond instrument into company shares using essentially an embedded call option.

CONVERTIBLE BONDS AND THE OUTRIGHT MARKET

Corporations needing new capital may choose from an extraordinarily wide variety of instruments that have been built and marketed by investment banks. But, at a very basic level, they face two choices:

1. Issue more *equity*, which further dilutes earnings per share but has low current financing costs.
2. Issue more straight *debt*, which, whereas not dilutive, may have high current financing costs, depending upon interest rates and the company's credit rating.

However, there is a third choice that is a hybrid of the above two: Issue *convertible bonds*.

Convertibles typically offer the instrument purchaser (bondholder) a moderate current income with lower current financing costs (coupons) than the company could typically offer for its straight debt. The buyer receives lower current income (versus straight debt) in exchange for the potential of participating in the equity upside of the company by converting the instrument into some agreed-upon number of the company's common equity shares at some agreed-upon future price.

This potential for equity participation comes essentially in the form of an embedded call option within the convertible instrument. The buyer pays option "premium" in the form of accepting the lower coupons and/or paying an outright bond premium in excess of the investment value of substitutable straight debt. In the event that the company's future share price rises, the convertible instrument might also rise, going "in the money," sometimes resulting in the buyer converting the bond into shares of the underlying company—in other words, "exercising the conversion option." The conversion event would then, of course, be dilutive to the company's earnings. On the other hand, in the event that the share price does not rise, the company will not suffer a dilutive event, and it may even get the chance to "call in" or redeem the issue and refinance the bond more cheaply if interest rates decline in the future.

Like the regular equity and fixed-income markets, convertible instruments have supply- and demand-driven equilibrium growth rates and size constraints at any moment in time. Changing economic conditions may induce or dissuade corporations to issue new convertible instruments versus equity or straight debt, and corporate issuers of convertible instruments may find it economically prudent to retire certain instruments from time to time. Additionally, the general fortunes of the fixed-income and equity markets will affect the convertible market capitalization by causing prices of convertible bonds already issued to rise and fall. Very often, convertible issuance is driven by merger activity in that the capital raised from the issuance allows companies to pursue their acquisition strategies. Together, these effects imply that the market capitalization of the convertible bond sector will ebb and flow rather than rise indefinitely.

Both outright buyers and arbitrageurs must take these shifting capital flows into account. Importantly, the composition characteristics of the issuance will vary over time by credit quality (for example, investment grade, high-yield, junk), concentration in sectors (for example, telecommunications, biotechnology, financial), and so on.

The degree to which the market's composition can change and the speed at which it can change was illustrated in the U.S market in the first half of 2000. By May, new issuance had proceeded at a record clip of more than $30 billion for the year to date, but technology/media/telecom (TMT) companies had issued 68 percent of this amount, and biotech (Bio) companies had issued 17 percent! The new issuance had come on top of existing issuance that was already heavily skewed in these sectors, bringing the total TMT/Bio percentage from about 56 percent of the market to about 66 percent from January through May 2000—well above its average of around 20 percent during the 1990s.

As companies within both of these sectors tend to have high cash requirements, raising capital via convertibles made sense. However, due to their rapid use of cash (or "burn rates"), their credit quality tends to be lower than for other sectors and, in many cases, these companies are practically startups with little operating history and no credit rating whatsoever. So only about 30 percent of the secondary convertible market in the United States in the third quarter was investment grade, significantly lower than in past years! For comparison, in Europe at the same time an estimated 85 percent of the convertible market was investment grade, including nonrated bonds, though Europe's TMT/Bio portion also rose substantially in 2000. Similarly in Japan, more than 85 percent of existing issuance was investment grade, though important differences in accounting methodologies might tend to overestimate their average credit quality by U.S. standards.

Also, as the TMT/Bio stocks tend to be more volatile than other sectors, their convertible premiums tend to expand (reflecting the higher value placed upon the embedded option), making these bonds more expensive. The combination of highly concentrated sectors with high Internet stock valuations and low credit quality plus expensive bond premiums presents a new set of risks and opportunities unlike those seen in the market two, four, or six years ago. For example, during the Internet shakeup in the second quarter of 2000, these speculative grade TMT/Bio convertibles were affected to a much greater degree, falling more than 8 percent in value on average, though hedged managers were able to make profits on the short stock positions. The best convertible arbitrageurs will evaluate these changing macro-driven factors and respond through diversification, careful analysis, and hedging away of unwanted risks.

For example, as average credit quality has fallen, some arbitrageurs are paying more attention to an issuer's cash flows, debt servicing and debt levels, financial performance and overall capitalization, experience of the management team, and accuracy of earnings reports, and so on. This information can be built into their pricing models, thereby requiring more "cheapness" in price than usual before they would consider a lower credit bond to be "mispriced." Hedge funds may enter into "asset swaps" when practical and when possible to remove or reduce credit risk to an issuer.

CONVERTIBLE BONDS: MAKE-UP AND NEW ISSUANCE

Convertible securities come in many varieties. In the United States, for example, regular coupon-paying convertible bonds made up about 47 percent of the market in 2000. The rest is made up of convertible preferred stock at 21 percent, mandatory convertibles (wherein convertibles must be converted at the issuer's option) at 17 percent, and zero-coupon convertibles at about 15 percent. Though the composition of these types of securities changes over time, the ratios in the United States have not differed greatly since 1994.

Figure 5.1 illustrates the make-up of the convertible market as of October 1999. Figure 5.2 shows new issuance as of the second quarter in

Region	Billions USD	Share
Japan	160	38%
U.S.	130	31%
Europe	101	24%
Emg Mkts	29	7%
Total	**421**	**100%**
Approximately, as of October 1999		
Source: http://www.gabelli.com/		

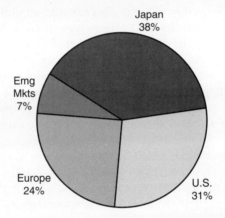

FIGURE 5.1   Global convertible market share (October 1999).

2000. Figure 5.3 shows the size of the U.S. market in mid-2000 at approximately $170 billion, down somewhat from a peak of about $190 billion earlier in the second quarter. Notable is the record surge in the United States in both new issuance and global share over the previous two years. Also notable is the relative trickle from Japan of new issues from 1996 to 2000. There were net retirements in Europe in the first half of 2000 as redemptions during that period actually exceeded issuance. Of note also in Europe is the concentration of new issuance in the TMT sectors.

In Japan, several issues surround the "callability risk" inherent in many convertible bonds. Although there has historically been an assumed immunity from callability, issuers facing financial troubles might be required to call in expensive debt that they have traditionally allowed to survive beyond

New Issuance, Billions USD			
	U.S.	**Europe**	**Japan**
1995	15	n/a	10
1996	28	n/a	34
1997	27	15	5
1998	31	27	2
1999	40	33	8
2000 YTD	43	15	1
Approximately, as of 2nd Qtr 2000			
Source: Goldman Sachs Investment Research			
Convertible Arbitrage Monitor—March 30, 2000			
Source: Merrill Lynch			
Global Convertibles—July 2000			
Source: http://www.convertbond.com/			

FIGURE 5.2 Global convertible issuance (new issuance in billion U.S. dollars).

U.S. Total Market Cap	
Year ending	**Billions USD**
1994	99
1995	102
1996	106
1997	125
1998	132
1999	166
2000 2nd Qtr	167
Source: Merrill Lynch	
Global Convertibles—July 2000	
Source: Saloman Smith Barney	
Convertible Special Report—May 2000	

FIGURE 5.3 U.S. convertible market capitalization.

call covenants. Due to the poor amount of new issuance in Japan since 1996, investors have bid up prices on the existing inventory of securities, in some cases to higher prices than might be expected based upon the de facto call risk. A systemic risk, prompted by an unexpected shock to the Japanese economy, for example, might cause many issuers to call in such bonds simultaneously, thereby causing a sudden premium contraction. Though such a risk should not be ignored, profitable opportunities still exist, and arbitrageurs who have strong relationships with market-makers and issuers may enjoy limited, yet unequal, protection or advantage in the event of call-ins.

FEATURES AND CATEGORIES OF CONVERTIBLE SECURITIES

Convertible bonds and securities, such as convertible preferred stock, can take many different forms.

Convertible bonds pay a coupon until maturity and then repay the face amount (unless conversion occurs first). They are debt securities so they legally rank senior to equity securities in a default scenario, but they may have other more senior debt above them. As bonds, their value depends on, among other things, prevailing interest rates and the credit quality of the issuer. A convertible bond has an embedded long call option feature giving the bondholder the right, but not the obligation, to convert the face (par) amount of the bond into shares of the company's common stock at a predetermined rate or "conversion ratio" (alternatively, convertibles may be viewed as a bond plus call option or a stock plus put option, depending upon where the bond lies in the spectrum).

A five-to-one (5:1) conversion ratio gives the bondholder the right to exchange $100 (par) of a company's convertible bonds into its common stock shares at $20 per share. Typically somewhat protected against dilution from stock splits or dividends, the conversion ratio is thus fixed and is essential in determining the strike price (or level at which an option goes "in the money") of the embedded option. As the stock price rises or falls, the number of shares that would be owned upon conversion of the bond into common stock is variable; thus, arbitrageurs frequently reset their hedges.

Convertible bonds have "call in" and "put back" features that must be taken into account when evaluating them. A bond issuer may elect to call in its debt if prevailing economic conditions make this a prudent choice, thereby causing the embedded option within the bond to expire early. Because this "optionality" was purchased at a premium and because the investor would suddenly lose that premium due to the early expiry, bond purchasers must carefully take into account the callable provisions within the bond's covenants. Investors often pay a higher premium for bonds that have significant "make whole" or "provisional" call protection in their covenants. Some bonds may also allow the buyer to "put" all or part of the bonds back to the issuer at some predetermined price or level, thereby protecting some of the unredeemed coupons or the premium paid to purchase the bond against adverse risks (for example, premium contraction, stock dilution, or early "call in").

In the event of the issuer's calling the convertible bond for redemption at its first opportunity, bondholders face three possibilities: They can allow it to be redeemed, sell it in the market, or convert it and sell the stock. Their decision will be based primarily upon whether the common stock price is then above the "breakeven" price, in which case they would convert; if lower, then they would redeem for cash and/or stock.

Arbitrageurs prefer to hold a convertible bond position while it is protected from call-ins because the bond's price and risk are easier to evaluate. They typically buy the convertible bond and sell the common stock of the same company. In effect, they are isolating the embedded long call option within the bond and, thus, making an option "bet" on the underlying equity. Like all option buyers, they must pay a premium (conversion premium, investment premium, and time premium) to own the option, and that premium is at risk due to time decay, credit exposure to the company, and so on. However, unlike conventional option buyers, they earn a current income due to the bond's coupon interest payments. Thus, an important implication of a carefully established hedged convertible bond position is that it can be near to self-financing for an extended period of time, whether the underlying stock price rises, falls, or does not fluctuate much.

Current income taken together with varying economic conditions, with the "callable" and "put-able" covenant provisions and with the varying (with stock price) number of shares of common stock owned upon conversion combine to offer the arbitrageur a nonconventional long American-style call option that has a floating strike and a floating expiry.

Convertible preferreds (prefs) are convertible into common stock shares, similarly to a convertible bond, but they represent equity rather than debt in the company. Importantly, convertible preferred stock is subordinated to debt of the issuing company. There are other differences between convertible bonds and prefs from the issuer's and buyer's perspectives. Prefs typically pay dividend income rather than coupon payments. Dividend payments may be treated differently from interest by taxation authorities, so issuers and purchasers have differing tax-related incentives for desiring prefs. Like convertible bonds, their convertibility allows arbitrageurs to set up a hedge using common stock that isolates the embedded option within the pref.

Mandatory convertibles must be converted at the issuer's option. These securities include automatically convertible equity securities (ACES), provisionally redeemable income debt exchangeable for stock (PRIDES), debt exchangeable for common stock (DECS), stock appreciation income-linked securities (SAILS), preferred equity redemption cumulative stock (PERCS), and yield-enhanced equity-linked debt securities (YEELDS). The list of product acronyms goes on, evolving as economic conditions, tax laws, and issuer and investor preferences change. These products also have varying impact on the issuer's balance sheet.

Mandatory convertibles may be structured as debt, curbing the upside (DECS-type), or structured as preferred stock, capping it (PERCS-type). Investors typically receive higher current income in exchange for somewhat lower participation in common stock appreciation. Although holders of conventional convertible bonds may elect never to convert and, thus, enjoy the fixed-income instrument should the stock perform worse than expected, this downside protection is absent in a mandatory because conversion to stock is a foregone conclusion from the start. These instruments typically are a small fraction of an arbitrageur's portfolio due to their limited upside and unlimited downside.

BASIC COMPONENTS OF CONVERTIBLE SECURITIES

The portion of a convertible bond's value that is equivalent to a conventional bond is called its investment value. A convertible bond's conversion value, however, is equivalent to its value if converted into stock at current price levels. Figure 5.4 shows how these values shift with changes in the underlying equity price. Because the conversion value is a fixed ratio set at issuance, it has a linear relationship to the underlying equity price. The investment value is also mostly linear with respect to the underlying equity price because a bond is a predictable fixed-income investment, except that it falls rather sharply at very low values of the underlying equity price. This reflects the increased risk of issuer default accompanying a very large drop in the stock's price. Figure 5.5 expands upon Figure 5.4 and shows the convertible bond's fair value as a dashed line. The dashed line is always greater than both the investment value and conversion value. The excess over the

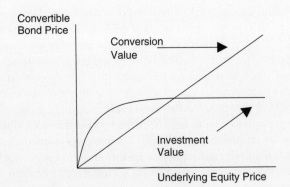

FIGURE 5.4   Convertible bond value components.

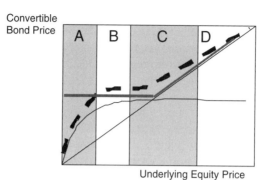

FIGURE 5.5   Convertible premiums.

conversion value is the conversion premium; the excess over the investment value is the investment premium.

Note how the general shape of the dashed line is quite similar to the familiar profit/loss graph of a long American-Style call option position (illustrated by the bold angled line) up until the bond enters into Region A, where the bond's investment value begins to drop off precipitously. Also, note that in regions A and B (the speculative, low-grade to busted parts of the spectrum), the bond has a relatively high conversion premium; conversely, in investment-grade regions C and D, the conversion premium is relatively lower. Meanwhile, the investment premium in regions A and B is much less than in regions C and D. Notably in region D, the slope of the fair value line tends to approach the slope of the conversion value line, and the bond behaves much like the equity (delta = 100). In A and B, the convertible bond acts more like the substitutable straight fixed-income instrument.

Region A typically includes distressed companies; convertible bonds whose prices fall within this region, though cheap, are considered credit bets. The optionality in the convertible bond in Regions A and B is considered "out-of-the-money," in region C, "at-the-money," and in region D, "in-the-money."

EMBEDDED OPTIONS WITHIN CONVERTIBLE BONDS

As previously discussed, the "optionality" embedded within convertible bonds may be viewed alternatively as a bond plus a call or as a stock plus a put.

Arbitrageurs may establish a hedged convertible bond position with any of several goals in mind. They may construct either a volatility trade (see the following "Typical Convertible Arbitrage Strategy" for a more detailed example), a cheap (low premium) put or a cheap call (a credit play). Some arbitrageurs focus on one of those three types of trades; others use a blended approach. In all cases, they have the opportunity to earn varying amounts of standstill income from coupon interest and rebates and to employ leverage.

First, referring again to Figure 5.5, Region C is the typical province of volatility trading, where neutral hedged positions are established and the arbitrageur earns standstill income while waiting and hoping for either significant upward or downward moves in the stock price. Neutral hedges are established after determining the bond's delta. "Delta" refers to the change in the convertible bond's price for a very small change in the underlying stock price and ranges from 0 to 100. Due to the long gamma, or "change in delta," inherent in the hedged bond position, arbitrageurs will make profits whether market prices rise or fall. So it is essentially a market-neutral position, and any volatility should result in a profit.

As the stock price fluctuates toward Region D, the arbitrageur adjusts the hedge by selling more stock short, in accordance with the higher delta. As the stock price fluctuates toward Region B, the arbitrageur realigns the hedge by buying back some of the short stock, in accordance with the lower delta. Arbitrageurs trading volatility strategies typically do not have a definite time frame for exiting the trade (other than before call protection expires) nor do they use a "stop-loss" level because they are market-neutral. Instead, the hedged convertible bond position is maintained in anticipation of an eventual move in the underlying stock.

Second, the trader may construct a cheap put in Region D, wherein the deep-in-the-money-call option can be alternatively viewed as a cheap, out-of-the-money put if it is highly hedged. In this case again, standstill income is earned and the low premium/high delta position will have the same upside potential as the stock itself. But, if the stock were to fall significantly, the arbitrageur would make quite a gain on the downside, as bond losses should be greatly exceeded by short stock gains.

Finally, in Region A, the inexpensive, out-of-the-money call option embedded in the convertible bond offers the opportunity to profit from a significant improvement in the credit quality of the underlying issuer or from a large rise in the issuer's stock. Though the bonds in this region trade at a low delta and act more like straight fixed income, they still have some correlation to the already depressed stock price. Any improvement to the stock price therefore is likely to represent an improvement in the credit scenario for the bond as well.

However, arbitrageurs may also take directional bets by hedging either much heavier or much lighter on the shorting of stock. They may take event-oriented positions on "distressed" convertible securities by developing their understanding of a particular company through deep credit analysis. Some managers may also enter into private placement convertible opportunities, though these typically have a longer investment time horizon.

In evaluating the price of a convertible bond, therefore, an investor needs to analyze its straight fixed-income value plus the value of the various options embedded in the security. Quantitative options pricing models, similar to Black-Scholes, are used to determine fair value. In addition to the long, American-style call embedded in the bond, there are some other implicit, yet important, options that bear mentioning.

Noted previously in regard to the discussion about call protection is the issuer's right to call in the bond. From the investor's point of view, this is similar to a short American-style call position, though longer-dated than the investor's long American-style call on equity conversion.

Also, the issuing company always has the option to default on its obligations, so the investor is essentially short a deep out-of-the-money put on the company's equity, wherein they may be given the company's assets in the event of default.

So bankruptcy management experience is important for arbitrageurs dealing in the busted or distressed parts of the spectrum where that short put is not so out-of-the-money anymore. In this regard, the investor is long an even deeper out-of-the-money put on the issuer's equity, which means that there should at least be some "recovery" value above zero (from the bricks and mortar, for example) if the company does default since bondholders get paid out before equity holders.

In addition to default risk, convertible investors face other risks. One of the most immediate risks is premium erosion. If an arbitrageur overpaid for a convertible security due to mis-analysis, it could be due to errors in the models the arbitrageur is using (model risk) or due to poor volatility or credit assumptions. The longer a hedged position is held, in theory, the more opportunity there is for such mistakes to surface, so holding period risk is important. Also, the average duration of the arbitrageur's entire portfolio is subject to interest rate risk should the entire yield curve shift suddenly, causing an adverse dislocation in the bond floor (for all investment values at once).

Issuing companies also introduce specific risks to a portfolio, such as event risk from acquisition, which might suddenly cause the stock's "borrow" (supply available for short selling) to drop to very low levels. In this case many, but not necessarily all, arbitrageurs would have to exit their positions when their broker calls their short stock away from them. The simultaneous exiting of many arbitrageurs might cause the long convertible bond position's premium to erode suddenly.

Arbitrageurs will typically seek to hedge some of these market risks and issuer-specific risks through various swap deals. For example, they will attempt to hedge away any currency risks they may face if they trade a global portfolio. Often, this exposure is limited to monthly or quarterly profits and losses, because the arbitrageur is typically long and short linked instruments denominated in the same currency. Hedging currency risk for convertible arbitrage therefore is typically not too expensive.

However, funds have various approaches to hedge away other risks, such as interest rate risks and credit risks, and these hedges can be very costly, both in terms of "insurance premiums" paid to establish them and in terms of losses if not properly executed. For example, if interest rates were to rise, this should hurt an arbitrageur's returns because he is long convertible bonds whose price should fall as all "bond floors" (investment values) fall at once. If the arbitrageur had placed a short U.S. T-Bond position as a hedge against interest rate hikes, then the profit from hedging should help offset the loss on the convertible bonds. However, due to their special nature as a "safe investment," in the event of global market turmoil, such as a liquidity/credit crisis, investors tend to flock en masse into U.S. T-bonds in a "flight to quality" versus other assets. So, maintaining a short U.S. T-bond position as an interest rate hedge at just the wrong time can be a "double whammy." The arbitrageur can lose on the quality flight out of (long) convertibles and into (short) T-bonds.

Therefore, many hedge fund managers use a mixture of different duration and credit securities and derivatives (short-term paper, Eurodollars, corporate bonds, and high-yield junk) to hedge interest rate risk. Such hedges, often in the form of a swap plus an out-of-the-money put, are usually imperfect and cost capital up front plus foregone returns.

Asset swaps (or credit swaps) may be used to reduce the credit exposure of a portfolio to one specific issuer; however, these are typically expensive hedges to create in markets with lower average credit quality, such as the United States. However, in markets with higher credit quality, such as Europe, if an issuer has straight fixed-income debt as well as convertible debt, it is straightforward to hedge out the credit exposure in the (already high quality) convertible bond, further isolating and extracting its embedded "optionality." In a lower credit market, however, hedgers must typically pay away a larger spread to induce the counter-party in the swap to assume their credit exposure. This swap itself is an over-the-counter (OTC) deal and, as such, entails additional counter-party risk and is usually subject to legal indemnity from situations involving *force majeure*. In a credit crisis, such as the Russian debt default in 1998, just when hedgers might most need the terms of their expensive OTC credit swaps to protect them, they could face possible counter-party risks and claims of *force majeure*.

TYPICAL CONVERTIBLE ARBITRAGE STRATEGY

Typically, here are the features you will find in the structure of a convertible arbitrage deal:

- Intended to be a market-neutral source of return.
- Intended to produce current "standstill" income.
- Intended to exploit pricing inefficiencies between two related equity or equity-linked securities, such as a company's stock and its convertible bond.
- Intended to capture profits proportionately from volatility, regardless of whether the company's stock price rises or falls. Volatility trading is the core strategy for many convertible arbitrageurs, focusing on the "at-the-money" part of the convertible spectrum.
- Sometimes, intended to introduce a slight directional bias to the market-neutral investment to capture profits disproportionately, depending if the stock price rises or falls.
- Sometimes, intended as a "cheap" call or put option on the issuer's stock. These strategies focus on the deep "out-of-the-money" or "in-the-money" parts of the convertible spectrum.
- Leverage is employed to enhance returns.
- Overall portfolio is constrained and affected by credit quality and supply of issuance.

Typical Deal Structure: A Hedged Convertible Bond

Buy a company's convertible bond and simultaneously sell short a delta-equivalent amount of its underlying stock. Typically, this investment will be neutrally hedged on an ongoing basis, in other words, the number of shares of short underlying stock will be adjusted periodically (zero delta hedged) to keep the combined position (hypothetically) immune to adverse overall market fluctuations and price fluctuations in the underlying stock or bond.

The investment produces standstill income:

- The convertible bond investment generates interest income from the bond's coupon, less stock dividends.
- The short sale of stock generates rebate income from the broker, typically the risk-free rate of interest less certain costs charged by the broker for borrowing the stock and/or for using leverage.

Broker costs may vary according to the size and nature of the particular securities in a deal and the client relationship between the prime broker and hedge fund manager. A typical U.S. convertible arbitrage fund might borrow money (use leverage) from the broker at the Fed Funds rate plus 75 basis points (bp) and loan money (earn short rebate) at the Fed Funds rate plus 50 bp. Actual leverage costs will vary, based upon the particular onshore Joint Back Office (JBO) or offshore agreement terms between the hedge fund (acting as a broker-dealer) and its prime broker-dealer, but it can be assumed for simplification that capital requirements will be 10 to 15 percent of the unhedged long market value of the convertible bonds plus the bond's premium over equity conversion value. This implies a maximum leverage of about 6 to 10 times, but many managers use less leverage than this.

The investment has some downside protection:

- The convertible bonds should only fall in value as low as (that is, converge with) their "investment value"—that is, the value of the same company's straight (nonconvertible) debt. This "bond floor" exists as such because a drop in a company's equity value, if unaccompanied by a deterioration of their fundamental credit quality, should not largely affect the value of the company's debt.
- If the stock's price drops, loss in the equity value of the hedged convertible bond investment is offset to an extent by the short stock position.

The investment may generate *delta* trading profits due to stock price moves in either direction:

- Delta refers to the change in the convertible bond's price for a very small change in the underlying stock price and ranges from 0 to 100. Practically, delta is always changing, and a movement in delta between two levels is defined as the rate of change in the bond's price versus the product of the change in stock's price and the conversion ratio. (The conversion ratio is a constant, fixed when the bond was first issued.) The rate of change of the delta is called the "gamma" and is convex (nonlinear) due to the convertible's convergence to the "bond floor."
- The arbitrageur maintains a "delta-neutral" position, seeking to capture profits due to volatility in the underlying stock. Such increased volatility would be expected to raise the value of the embedded option owned within the convertible, thereby raising the price (premium) of the bond. As such, the typical arbitrageur is said to be long volatility or long gamma.

- After profits are realized due to price movements in the underlying stock, the arbitrageur typically reestablishes the "proper" delta-neutral hedge ratio (number of short underlying stock shares), thus enabling the possibility of further delta trading profits.
- As much an art as a science, the reestablishment of the "proper" hedge ratio is based upon both quantitative models as well as the arbitrageurs' trading skill, fundamental credit analysis, and particular assumptions about market sentiment. It may also be influenced by their differing transaction costs and the composition characteristics of their overall portfolios. As such, perhaps no two managers would reset their hedges on a particular bond at exactly the same point, even though their quantitative models would likely be in very close agreement. As a simplification, however, assume that managers reset their hedges (adjust the amount of stock sold short) for at-the-money convertible bonds after a three-percentage-point move in delta (such as, from 75 to 72).

The long convertible bond investment faces three possibilities common to investments: prices may go up, down, or stay the same. However, as a market-neutral investment that is earning standstill income, the hedged position is intended to make money in any of the three outcomes, barring adverse risks discussed elsewhere in this chapter. However, due to the convexity of the long gamma in the hedged position, the return profile for the three outcomes differs substantially. Consider a highly simplified illustration (see "Sample Trade") of the return components in a typical convertible arbitrage trade:

- Assume the manager will buy and hold the position for a year and, after initially establishing the delta hedge ratio, will not need to adjust it regularly. Rather, assume that the entire move in stock price (Cases 2 and 3) occurs upon maturity in one year. In a realistic case, the hedge ratio would be adjusted frequently.
- Assume the bond is significantly mispriced, in that it is purchased for no conversion premium.
- The profitability in all three cases includes standstill income. Notice that the strategy also makes money regardless of whether the stock rises or falls (Cases 2 and 3).

Sample Deal Structure Assumptions
- Company XYZ convertible bond, 5 percent coupon.
- Maturing in one year at par of $1,000.
- Exchangeable into 100 shares of (nondividend-paying) XYZ common stock.

- Greatly mispriced bond purchased for no premium at $1,000 conversion value (100 shares × $10 per share).
- XYZ common stock currently valued at $10 per share.
- Investment value (based on XYZ straight debt) of XYZ convertible bond is $920.
- Arbitrage strategy (hedge against the convertible bond) is established via a short position with 50 shares of underlying XYZ common stock at price of $10.
- Short rebate interest of 5 percent. No leverage used.

Sample Deal Analysis

- All three cases return a profit, which includes standstill returns.
- Case 1 returns only standstill returns.
- Case 2 has a greater gain on the long bond than the loss on the short stock.
- Case 3 has a smaller loss on the long bond than the gain on the short stock.
- The arbitrage strategy succeeds in Cases 2 and 3 due to the long gamma (or long volatility) inherent in the position. Volatility in either direction (25 percent up or down) for the stock price resulted in profitability for the arbitrageur (see Figure 5.6).

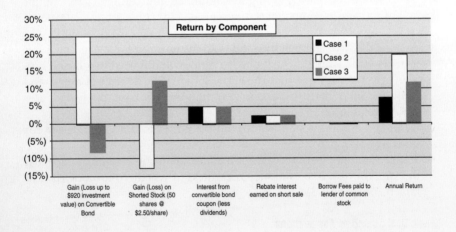

{Delta Trading Profit (Loss)} + {Current Yield + Short Rebate − Dividends}
x {Leverage} − {Financing} = {Total Return}

FIGURE 5.6   Return by component.

Sample Trade

Case 1: Assume no change in stock price (standstill income).

Coupon payments on $1,000 convertible bond (5 percent)	$50
Rebate interest earned on $500 short sale (5 percent)	$25
Fees paid to lender of common stock (0.25 percent per year)	($1.50)
Net cash flow	$73.50
Annual return (standstill income only)	7.35%

Case 2: Assume 25 percent gain in stock price.

Gain on convertible bond	$250
Loss on shorted stock (50 shares at $2.50/share)	($125)
Interest from convertible bond coupon	$50
Rebate interest earned on short sale	$25
Borrow fees paid to lender of common stock	($1.50)
Net trading gains and cash flow	$198.50
Annual return	19.85%

Case 3: Assume 25 percent drop in stock price.

Loss on convertible bond (up to $920 investment value)	($80)
Gain on sorted stock (50 shares at $2.50/share)	$125
Interest from convertible bond coupon	$50
Rebate interest earned on short sale	$25
Borrow fees paid to lender of common stock	($1.50)
Net cash flow	$118.50
Annual return	11.85%

CONVERTIBLE ARBITRAGE PERFORMANCE AND GROWTH: 1994–2000 Q2

The convertible arbitrage sector of the CSFB/Tremont hedge fund manager universe has produced relatively steady long-term returns since 1995 with three notable exceptions—namely, the poor performance in 1994, the sizable drop in the third quarter of 1998, and the sizable (volatility-induced) pickup in rate of return beginning in the first quarter of 2000 (see Figure 5.7). The 1994 losses were related to the broader fixed-income crisis that began with the Valentine's Day Massacre (for a closer look, see the next section, "Sources of Risk"). The large drop in the third quarter of 1998, though related to the Long Term Capital Management (LTCM) debacle, Russian debt default, and the ensuing credit/liquidity crisis, was nonetheless less drastic for convertible arbitrageurs than for some other hedge fund managers. For example, from July 31, 1998, to October 31, 1998, the overall CSFB/Tremont Hedge Fund Index fell about −14 percent whereas the

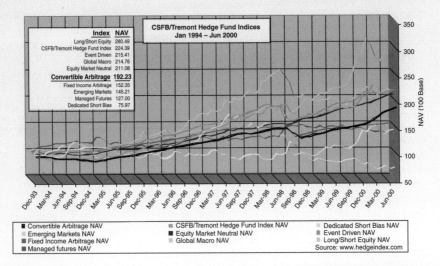

FIGURE 5.7 CSFB/Tremont Hedge Fund Index and Sub-Indices (Quarterly NAV, January 1994 to June 2000).

Convertible Arbitrage Sub-Index fell only −12 percent; some other Sub-Indices (for example, Emerging Markets, Global Macro) fell more than that −20 percent over the same period.

The estimated number of hedge funds principally focused on convertible arbitrage grew from less than 50 in 1995 to more than 120 by mid-2000. Figure 5.8 illustrates the flow of assets into convertible arbitrage strategies versus all hedge funds from January 1994 through June 2000, as tracked by TASS (whose methodology adjusts for the change in hedge funds' assets that is attributable to profits, losses, and net new investment). The total manager universe includes about 2,200 hedge funds with assets (as of June 2000) of $205 billion, of which $10 billion (or 4.9 percent) is invested in convertible arbitrage funds. Over the period illustrated, an estimated $57.5 billion in new investments flowed into all hedge funds, of which $5.25 billion (or 9 percent) flowed into convertible arbitrage strategies.

With a global (United States, Europe, and Japan) market capitalization for convertible bonds of $434 billion as of June 30, 2000, and assuming that the $10 billion in convertible arbitrage strategies is leveraged at about 4× to 8×, then outright buyers would own approximately 80 to 90 percent of the outstanding convertible issues while those hedge funds in the TASS database would own approximately 10 to 20 percent—up significantly since 1994. This increased participation of hedge funds in the convertible mar-

Hedge Fund Asset Flows, Millions USD				
	Convertible Arbitrage		All Hedge Funds	
Year ending	Annual	Cumul.	Annual	Cumulative
1994	14	14	7,636	7,636
1995	240	254	3,537	11,173
1996	1,189	1,443	10,788	21,961
1997	1,953	3,396	22,213	44,174
1998	1,268	4,664	8,819	52,993
1999	307	4,971	3,443	56,436
2000 2nd Qtr	281	5,252	1,091	57,527

Note: Dec. 31, 1993 = Zero Baseline

Source: Tass+ Asset Flows Report—as of June 30, 2000

Universe includes 2,200 hedge funds with assets under management of $205 billion. Estimated total hedge fund

FIGURE 5.8 Hedge fund asset flows: convertible arbitrage as an asset class (January 1994 to June 2000, in million U.S. dollars).

ketplace is not trivial, and several large hedge funds are not included. Thus, the actual portion owned by hedge funds is significantly higher. Some practitioners estimate that hedge funds may now control more than 60 percent of the marketplace.

On the one hand, hedge funds provide increased demand and liquidity for both new issues and for the secondary market. However, because these arbitrageurs typically sell short the common stock of the issuer, there is always the concern that a particular convertible bond might undergo intense selling pressure if the ability to borrow the issuer's common stock suddenly became hampered (that is, due to a corporate merger event). If stock "borrow" became difficult on a systemic basis (that is, due to a credit or liquidity crisis), a sharp drop in convertible bond values might be expected, as many hedge funds would simultaneously unwind their leveraged positions as they did in the third quarter of 1998.

Of note in Figure 5.8 is the sharp reduction in the rate of new asset flows that occurred after 1998 in the convertible arbitrage sector, as well as within hedge funds in general. Leading up to the LTCM debacle and subsequent events of the third quarter that year, asset flows into convertible arbitrage were proceeding on a near-record pace. Interestingly, though falling convertible bond premiums (associated with the global credit/liquidity crisis) hurt many investors within the strategy, there were no meaningful outflows of assets from within the convertible arbitrage sector during that time. This contrasts dramatically with the overall outflow of more than $8.2 billion from other hedge funds in the universe between the fourth quarter of 1998 and the first quarter of 1999.

Investors who remained faithful to the asset class after the LTCM/Russia crash, perhaps perceiving the sector to be too "cheap," were rewarded for their patience and loyalty. From October 31, 1998, to July 31, 2000, the Convertible Arbitrage Sub-Index returned more than +42 percent. Only the Long/Short Equity Sub-Index at +64 percent and Emerging Markets Sub-Index at +47 percent did better, whereas the overall Hedge Fund Index returned just +31 percent over the same period.

Interestingly, on a risk-adjusted basis, the convertible arbitrage sector's Sharpe Ratio of 1.04 ranks as the third best, behind only Equity Market Neutral and Event-Driven (see Figure 5.9). By comparison, the Sharpe Ratio of the S&P 500 Index with dividends reinvested (DRI) was 1.18. And, as Figure 5.10 shows, convertible arbitrage was the best sector of the CSFB/Tremont Hedge Fund manager universe for the first half of 2000, producing a net return of +19.8 percent. Equity Market Neutral and Event-Driven were next best. By comparison, the S&P 500 DRI lost −0.4 percent, the NASDAQ Composite Index lost −2.5 percent, the Merrill Lynch Corporate Master Index (investment-grade bonds) made +2.2 percent, and the Merrill Lynch High Yield Index lost −1.2 percent. Both the convertible arbitrage and equity market neutral sectors fared especially well in the first half of 2000 due to high equity market volatility. During this period, con-

	Jan 1, 1994–Jun 30, 2000				
Index	Return	Draw Down	Std Deviation	Semi Deviation	Sharpe Ratio
CSFB/Tremont Hedge Fund Index	13.06	−13.81	10.10	6.53	0.79
Sub-indices					
Long / Short Equity	16.96	−14.21	12.68	8.25	0.94
Event Driven	12.36	−16.05	6.77	6.55	1.08
Global Macro	12.31	−26.79	14.63	11.21	0.49
Equity Market Neutral	12.02	−3.54	3.50	2.42	1.98
Convertible Arbitrage	10.44	−12.03	5.17	5.03	1.04
Fixed Income Arbitrage	6.60	−12.48	4.50	5.95	0.34
Emerging Markets	5.83	−45.14	20.79	20.55	0.04
Managed Futures	3.70	−17.74	11.11	9.29	−0.12
Dedicated Short Bias	−4.09	−41.93	18.16	16.67	−0.50
S&P 500 DRI Index	21.47	−15.37	13.96	10.92	1.18

Source: CSFB/Tremont Hedge Fund Index

FIGURE 5.9 Performances of the CSFB/Tremont Hedge Fund Index and Sub-Indices (1994 to June 30, 2000).

Index	YTD (Jun 30, 2000)
CSFB/Tremont Hedge Fund Index	1.9%
Sub-indices	
Convertible Arbitrage	19.8%
Equity Market Neutral	10.9%
Event Driven	5.2%
Fixed Income Arbitrage	3.4%
Long / Short Equity	1.1%
Emerging Markets	1.0%
Global Macro	−0.7%
Dedicated Short Bias	−6.8%
Managed Futures	−8.0%
S&P 500 DRI Index	−0.4%
Source: CSFB/Tremont Hedge Fund Index	

FIGURE 5.10 Compound performances of the CSFB/Tremont Hedge Fund Index and Sub-Indices for the first half of 2000.

vertible arbitrage truly lived up to its promise to serve as a "put option" on the equity market.

SOURCES OF RISK

Here is a further review of selected economic crises mentioned previously and their effects on convertible bonds.

St. Valentine's Day Massacre—1994

The U.S. Federal Reserve began to raise interest rates for the first time in five years on Feb. 4, 1994 (see Figure 5.11), sparking hedge funds to dump huge quantities of government bond futures, driving prices of the underlying bonds down sharply. The shockwave spread rapidly to the rest of the world's bond markets, and global interest rates rose sharply, cutting investor expectations for productivity growth.

In the following two months (see Figure 5.12), the S&P 500 Index fell 9 percent and the MSCI World Index 6 percent, and the U.S. dollar began its historic slide from 110 to less than 100 Japanese yen. Unfortunately, the trouble in the stock, bond, and currency markets persisted long after

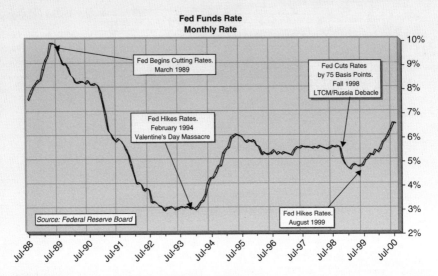

FIGURE 5.11 Fed rate moves, 1988 to 2000.

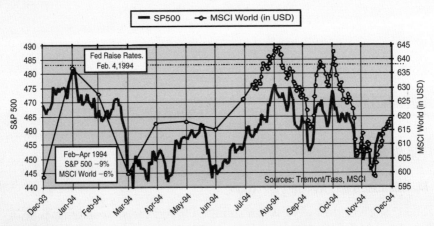

FIGURE 5.12 Stock market moves, U.S. and world, 1994.

February, stifling Wall Street, European, Japanese, and Emerging Markets through at least the rest of the year.

Among the biggest losers from the global turmoil were legendary hedge fund managers George Soros and Michael Steinhardt. Steinhardt, who by early April had reportedly lost about $1 billion since the beginning of the year (or roughly 25 percent of the funds under his management), finished 1994 with significant drawdowns. Soros was also caught up in the interest rate-driven mayhem, which insiders at Quantum Fund dubbed the "St. Valentine's Day Massacre." Soros reportedly lost more than $500 million in a single day on Feb. 14 by incorrectly assuming that the U.S. dollar would rally against the yen (see Figure 5.13).

More broadly, all hedge fund managers (as represented by the CSFB/Tremont Hedge Fund Index) did very poorly in the initial period after the rate hike. From February through April 1994, the index was down more than 9 percent, though the managers struggled back to end the year down only about 5.4 percent from the January peak versus −4.3 percent for the S&P 500 Index and −3 percent for the MSCI World Index (in U.S. dollar terms).

The hedge fund managers in the CSFB/Tremont Convertible Arbitrage Sub-Index fared even worse in 1994 than did those managers in the broader index. Though initially down only 3.3 percent from February through April, the subindex ended the year down 8.5 percent from its January peak (see Figure 5.14).

To understand why the convertible arbitrageurs did so poorly, one must consider the combined effects of leverage and the declining bond floor. As Figure 5.15 makes clear, long-term and short-term government bonds as well as high-yield bonds had a poor year starting from February, with the long bonds being hurt the most. Note also that the UBS Warburg Global Convertible Index (UBSWGCI—a market capitalization-weighted,

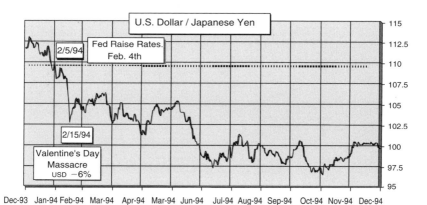

FIGURE 5.13 U.S. dollar versus Japanese yen, 1994.

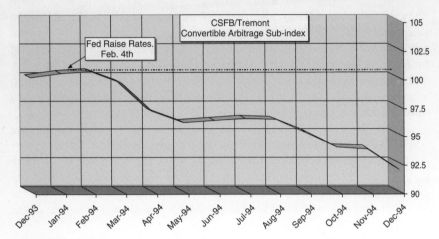

FIGURE 5.14 CSFB/Tremont Convertible Arbitrage Sub-Index, 1994.

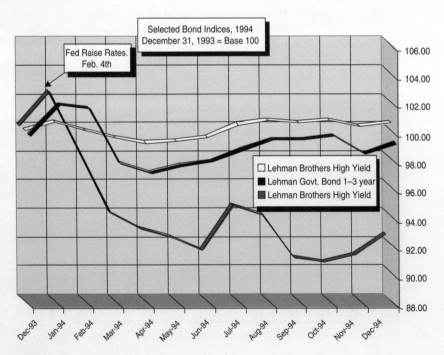

FIGURE 5.15 Selected bond indices, 1994.

liquidity-based, tax-exempt, total return index of global convertible bonds, calculated in U.S. dollars and maintained independently by Mace Advisers) fell initially by more than 4 percent and, near the end of the year, was down 6.7 percent (see Figure 5.16). The rate hikes had brought Fed Funds rates from around 3 percent in February to around 5.25 percent by December. When the bond floor fell at once for so many fixed-income securities, managers holding long bond positions began dumping them, and the selling pressure was added to their losses, causing the worst year for the CSFB/Tremont Convertible Arbitrage Sub-Index on record.

Asian Contagion—1997 Q2 to Q3

The Asian currency and financial crisis in 1997 led to a severe drop in the region's demand and output that quickly spread from the crisis countries (Thailand, Indonesia, Korea, Malaysia) to peripheral countries (Hong Kong, Philippines, Singapore, and Taiwan). The cause was initially a credit/debt crisis and ultimately an emerging market crisis, brought about by unsustainable borrowing levels for foreign direct investment into too many nonperforming corporate loans. High national and corporate debt-to-equity ratios in these countries, plus high inflation and interest rates, led first to large conglomeration defaults and then to loss of faith in the countries' ability to service their debt. That led to investors and speculators running out

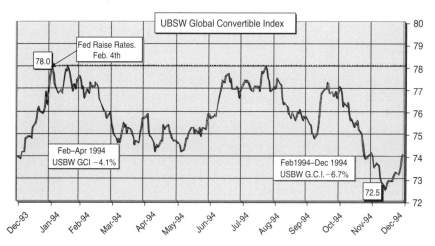

FIGURE 5.16 UBSW Global Convertible Bond Index (UBSWGCI), 1994.

of the currencies and eventually devaluation, accompanied by enormous losses on the Asian stock markets.

As the figures at the end of this chapter illustrate, convertible arbitrage did well in 1997 (+14.5 percent) and was not too greatly affected by the crisis. The effect on emerging market managers, for example, was much worse. The predominant convertible issuance at the time, like today, was from the United States, Europe, and Japan; thus, the global convertible market was not adversely influenced. However, since May 1997, Japan had been in a policy-induced recession, trying to correct an enormous budget deficit via lower government expenditures and higher taxes. In light of this, Japanese imports from its Asian neighbors fell sharply, exacerbating the contagion problem. Although Japan remained in an economic slump for many quarters, its convertible new issuance, which had been decent in 1996, took a sharp downturn to a mere trickle (refer to Figure 5.2), from which it has struggled to recover.

Long Term Capital Management (LTCM)/Russian Debt Default—1998 Q3

The third quarter of 1998 saw enormous upheaval in equity and financial markets. The Convertible Arbitrage Sub-Index was down, peak-to-trough and month-on-month, about 12 percent versus the overall CSFB/Tremont Hedge Funds Index at −13.8 percent. The crisis was initiated by loss of liquidity and the sudden massive widening of credit spreads, which reached their widest point in a decade.

The trouble began when Russia defaulted on its debt on August 17, 1998, causing the collapse of the Russian ruble and a halt to its free exchange. Investors and speculators, already nervous from the previous year's Asian crisis, fled into high-quality instruments, such as the most liquid U.S. government bonds and sovereign bonds of G-7 countries in general. They simultaneously poured out of lesser-quality securities, especially noninvestment grade corporate debt. To make matters worse, many hedge funds had geared up their leverage to try and boost returns from trading, as many spreads were thought to be converging.

LTCM was notoriously caught up in the trouble, as mark-to-market losses, compounded by high leverage, brought the firm to the brink of ruin, necessitating an eleventh hour consortium of banks to provide capital for margin calls and orderly liquidation. As Figure 5.17 depicts, the Convertible Arbitrage Sub-Index was highly correlated to other bond indices from 1994 to 2000 and especially tracked the High-Yield Index during the 1998 debacle. The combination of flight to quality and sudden reduction of leverage caused many convertible arbitrageurs to find themselves holding bonds with rapidly contracting premiums in very difficult stock borrow conditions.

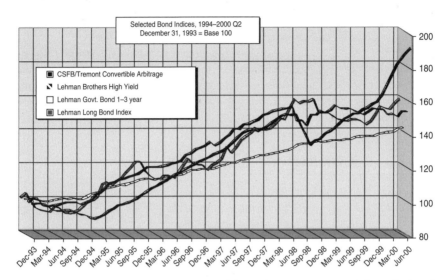

FIGURE 5.17 CSFB/Tremont Convertible Arbitrage versus Selected Bond Indices, 1994 to 2000 Q2 (December 31, 1993 = 100).

Unable to hold "unhedged" bonds that were dropping fast, many managers were forced to liquidate at the literal bottom of the market.

A few managers that had started the period with better stock borrow terms and lower leverage and higher credit quality issues in their portfolios managed to fare better during the "mark-to-market" period from October to December 1998. Liquidity steadily improved after the crisis period, but credit did not bounce back strongly. However, so many issues were so "cheap" that the sector had one of the best recoveries, +42 percent, between the trough and July 31, 2000. If a similar credit/liquidity event occurs, it seems certain that managers with better quality issues and lower leverage will again fare better than those highly leveraged.

Internet Stock Washout—April 2000

During the Internet stock washout from March 14 to April 14, 2000, the NASDAQ Index fell from about 5,000 to about 3,265 or −35 percent. Over the same period, the S&P 500 Index fell only about 5 percent. But convertible arbitrageurs and hedge fund managers in general who were surveyed at the time reported no noticeable "drying up" of the stock "borrow"— instead, they said liquidity was very good.

Though the Fed had begun tightening in August 1999, the stock market kept riding the end-of-year tech stock rally. When the market finally had enough, the sell-off was quick, but credit spreads did not widen tremendously nor was there any wide-scale "flight-to-quality" panic. Arbitrageurs, in fact, had one of their best quarters on record as the massive equity volatility made money in almost any delta-trading scenario, and higher short-term interest rates meant higher standstill income.

GENERAL OBSERVATIONS AND CONCLUSIONS

Because of the St. Valentine's Day Massacre, 1994 remains the worst year on record for the CSFB/Tremont Convertible Arbitrage Sub-Index (see Figure 5.18). Another fixed-income market shock of a nature similar to the St. Valentine's Day Massacre of 1994 could be expected to have like consequences.

Year	1994	1995	1996	1997	1998	1999	2000 YTD July
Return %	−8.07	16.57	17.87	14.48	−4.41	16.04	19.85

FIGURE 5.18 CSFB/Tremont Convertible Arbitrage Sub-Index, 1994 to 2000 Q2.

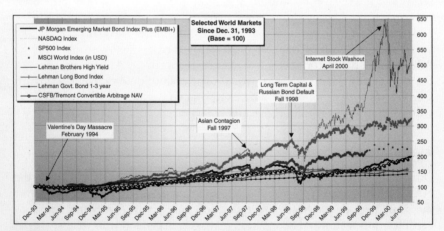

FIGURE 5.19 Selected world markets, 1994 to 2000 Q2 (December 31, 1993 = 100).

Figure 5.19 shows how various markets fared through the crises mentioned previously. It seems clear that a falling bond floor as in 1994 or a credit/liquidity crisis as in 1998 would adversely affect the convertible market. The 1994 events took much longer to recover from than those of 1998, not only for convertible arbitrage but also for most other hedge fund strategies as well. It is interesting to note that the credit/liquidity crisis of 1998 might be viewed by a cynical investor as merely a brief "mark-to-market" issue: The rebound in returns was very strong, and a hedge fund that managed to avoid selling off inventory at the very bottom (through good borrow terms, lower leverage, higher credit quality, and/or liquidity names, etc.) was rewarded by a strong comeback. However, for managers that were forced to liquidate at just the wrong time, the losses were locked in without the chance to participate in the market rebound.

Meanwhile, the best conditions for a convertible arbitrageur are clearly high equity volatility without any substantial credit or liquidity problems, as in April 2000. Perhaps most of the "easy money" has been made since the LTCM/Russian debt debacle, and arbitrageurs may face new interest rate or credit challenges to come.

CHAPTER 6

Real Estate

By Mark G. Roberts

Institutions have had to rethink how to deploy real estate in multiasset portfolios over the last 20 years because of macroeconomic events. As their investment in real estate evolved, they learned a few lessons, particularly concerning risk management and diversification.

Institutional investing in real estate has experienced significant evolutionary changes over the last 20 years. In the early years of institutional investing in the late 1970s and early 1980s, investors readily embraced the diversification benefits and inflation-hedging characteristics of real estate. However, by the late 1980s, they were sorely disappointed with the performance brought about by volatile changes in national tax policies, deregulation in the savings-and-loan industry, and the onset of risk-based capital regulations. Ultimately, these events took their toll on the industry, resulting in the real estate crash of the late 1980s and early 1990s.

With it, industry participants began to address some fundamental issues that previously may have been disregarded to some degree. Issues, such as investor control and discretion, liquidity, sales discipline, and alignment of interests, soon became the preeminent topics of discussion at most industry conferences. In turn, institutional investors adopted new or different operating models that more fully defined the discretionary authority of the manager.

Today, the issues are more focused on exceeding the "benchmark" and addressing questions such as

- How did the manager add value?
- Was value added through "sector rotation" or "asset selection?"

Although these phrases may seem uncommon to some real estate industry participants, they are tools that drive performance evaluation in the equity market.

However, in light of certain embedded characteristics in real estate—investment size and time horizon, life cycle, and the nature of the appraisal process—can real estate investing really embody the benchmarking principles of the broader equity market? If it can, it has the potential to create a more efficient marketplace, which would inevitably increase the productivity of plan sponsor capital while also expanding the set of investment opportunities available for managers.

This chapter will reflect on some of the evolutionary shifts that have occurred in real estate investments in the 1990s and will address strategic issues to consider in developing and benchmarking the performance of a portfolio of real estate assets.

STRATEGIC ROLE OF REAL ESTATE

After determining the financial obligations that a plan sponsor has to its participants and beneficiaries, one of the first questions the sponsor must confront is how to diversify assets prudently. *Because real estate has a low or even negative correlation with both stocks and bonds, it has been demonstrated that a strategic allocation to this asset class can enhance the diversification of a multiasset portfolio.* Due to its competitive return and its lower relative risk, including private real estate in a multiasset portfolio improves the efficient frontier, thereby enhancing the risk-adjusted returns of the overall portfolio (see Figure 6.1).

A 10 to 15 percent allocation to the real estate asset class can either enhance return performance by roughly 44 basis points or alternatively lower risk by roughly 41 to 47 basis points (see Table 6.1). The diversifying benefits are achieved due to the low correlation that real estate exhibits to the other major asset classes (see Table 6.2).

Additionally, real estate exhibits a positive correlation to inflation, unlike either stocks or bonds, which have exhibited a negative correlation. Even though the inflationary environment may be favorable, real estate should offer an embedded hedge against unexpected inflation when supply and demand in the property market are in relative balance. In fact, high inflationary pressures during the 1970s produced negative real rates of return in the stock and bond markets whereas real estate produced positive real rates of return (see Table 6.3).

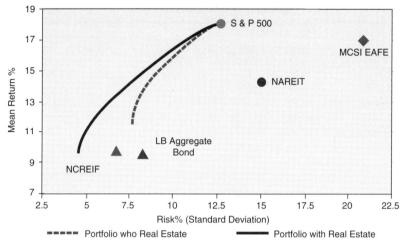

Source: Ibbotson and Associates, INVESCO Realty Advisors Research, NCREIF

FIGURE 6.1 Efficient frontier, 1978 to 1999.

TABLE 6.1 Historical Returns and Risk, 1978 to 1999

	10% Real Estate		15% Real Estate	
	Return	Risk	Return	Risk
60% Stocks/40% bonds	14.63%	9.40%		
60% Stocks/Bonds/NCREIF[1]	14.63%	8.93%	4.63%	8.74%
65% Stocks/Bonds/NCREIF[2]	15.07%	9.40%	15.07%	9.15%
(Risk Reduction)/Return Enhancing	0.44%	−0.47%	0.44%	−0.41%

[1]Real estate lowered the bond allocation to either 25 percent or 30 percent.
[2]Real estate lowered the bond allocation to either 20 percent or 25 percent.
Source: Ibbotson and Associates, INVESCO Realty Advisors Research, NCREIF

Real estate flourished for two primary reasons:

1. During the 1970s and into the early 1980s, the U.S. economy experienced tremendous demographic shifts as the baby boom generation entered the workforce and the economy began shifting from a manufacturing-based economy to a service-based economy. The shift to a service-based economy created tremendous demand for real estate. In turn, this demand

TABLE 6.2   Asset Correlations

	S&P 500	MSCI EAFE	LB Agg	Inflation	NAREIT	NCREIF
S&P 500	1.00					
MSCI EAFE	0.28	1.00				
Lehman Agg. Bond	0.38	0.07	1.00			
U.S. Inflation	(0.18)	(0.15)	(0.33)	1.00		
NAREIT—Equity	0.37	0.13	0.23	0.18	1.00	
NCREIF Property Index	0.12	0.19	(0.22)	0.52	0.02	1.00

TABLE 6.3   Annualized Compound Returns, 1971 to 1979

	Nominal	Real
Stocks	6.15	−1.4%
Bonds	5.0%	−2.4%
Real Estate	11.5%	3.6%

Note: Percentage result from cumulative rounding and compounding.
Sources: "Managing Real Estate Portfolios," INVESCO Realty Advisors Research, Ibbotson

created high levels of rental earnings growth, which allowed buildings to appreciate at rates in excess of inflation, thereby attracting many investors to the asset class.

2. In the early 1980s, the Economic Recovery Tax Act (ERTA) created a capital market shift and increased the after-tax benefits of owning real estate.

Prior to 1981, it was assumed that "normal" rates of returns could be achieved in the office market if the general level of occupancy rates remained in the range of 93 percent to 96 percent (see Figure 6.2). However, the fiscal and regulatory stimulus of the early 1980s shortened the depreciable life of an asset, thereby increasing the after-tax rate of return on real estate. These higher rates of return attracted tremendous amounts of investment capital into real estate, and this increased the level of construction. Eventually, an increasing amount of supply lowered the level of occupancy and rental income that a building needed to generate "normal" rates of return. This

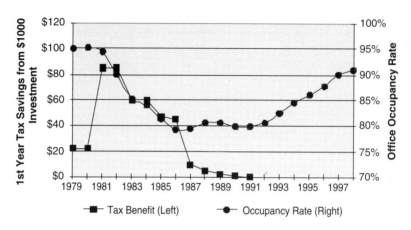

Source: Ernst & Young, Torto-Wheaton Research, INVESCO Realty Advisors Research

FIGURE 6.2 Tax impact on real estate.

was an example of how supply-side economics increased growth in the economy and simultaneously helped to lower inflation by decelerating the rate of rental growth in commercial real estate.

As such, this tax stimulus initially increased asset level returns. Eventually, however, as new product was delivered and rent growth declined to a normalized level, the market value of the asset declined. Had tax rates remained constant, it can be argued that real estate values would have stabilized. Instead, asset values declined further when the 1986 Tax Reform Act repealed many tax shelters and eroded the after-tax benefits of owning real estate. After several years of excess supply, the market finally stabilized by the mid-1990s and began generating more "normalized" performance.

From an institutional perspective, the question the industry addressed was whether investors could diversify macroeconomic risks, such as changes in tax policies, within the real estate portfolio. Systematic risks such as these cannot be diversified within the asset class itself. The only means truly available to diversify these risks to some degree is by altering the allocation among stocks, bonds, and real estate at the portfolio level.

To alter the allocation strategy at the portfolio level, investors believed they needed more control over liquidity in their real estate portfolio. Thus, as the market collapsed and liquidity evaporated, investors began thinking about real estate in a broader portfolio context and began to address plan sponsor control and liquidity.

RESTRUCTURING PHASE

Although investors still recognized the intrinsic portfolio benefits of real estate, they began to develop tailored portfolio guidelines that addressed their particular needs by utilizing a separate account structure. Toward the latter half of the 1980s, investors began to embrace more fully a separate account structure. In 1991, the preferred investment vehicle that institutional investors used to invest in real estate was a commingled fund. As Figure 6.3 indicates, plan sponsors invested 56.3 percent of their real estate investments in commingled funds versus 43.7 percent in separate accounts. By 1998, though, the percentage investing in real estate through separate accounts had increased to nearly 68 percent whereas the share directed toward commingled or coinvestment vehicles had declined to roughly 22 percent and the

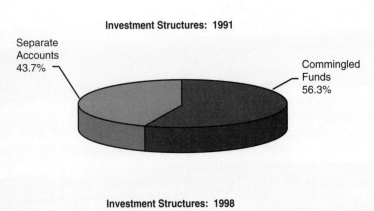

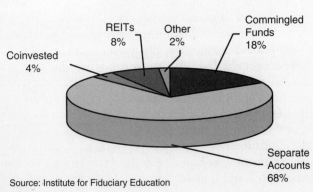

Source: Institute for Fiduciary Education

FIGURE 6.3   Investment structures.

share of real estate investment trusts (REITs) and others had increased to nearly 10 percent.

One of the first questions investors faced in this evolution was what level of discretion the investment manager should retain. There was a broad spectrum of issues to address that determined the level of discretion that a plan sponsor would delegate. Across this spectrum are degrees of discretion that have an economic cost to the plan that could not be overlooked.

On the one hand, nondiscretionary relationships offered the plan sponsor the highest degree of control. However, the management intensity of their activities also increased and caused the plan sponsor to assume greater levels of fiduciary responsibility. Also, the bid/ask spread oftentimes increased for nondiscretionary investors, which can lower the expected return. From a benchmarking perspective, the plan sponsor retained control over the sector rotation and asset selection decisions. In light of these issues, the plan sponsors examined the cost/benefits of such a structure.

To remedy the situation to some degree, plan sponsors and consultants began to soften the edges of their real estate guidelines in the mid-1990s and moved towards semidiscretionary or "discretion-in-a-box" relationships. These actions delegated more of the fiduciary responsibility to the investment manager and created guidelines by which the investment manager could be held more accountable to the plan for the performance of their allocation. These guidelines addressed matters, such as diversification by property type, investment size, and a minimum number of investments, along with the expected holding period of the investment.

For the most part, this alignment serves both the plan sponsor and the investment manager well. The guidelines used for discretion-in-a-box appear to balance the plan sponsor's goal of achieving control (hence, liquidity), risk management, and accountability with the manager's goal of enhancing investment access in an efficient and productive manner.

In light of the broad use of "discretion-in-a-box," it would seem that the industry has successfully adopted portfolio guidelines that have improved conditions in the market. However, benchmarking the performance of private real estate can still be a challenge. Some of the obvious practical impediments reflect the appraisal nature of the index. In other instances, program guidelines may emphasize that investment activity should be focused on balancing the diversification of the plan sponsor's overall real estate portfolio. In this case, some might argue that the plan sponsor has retained control over the allocation decision and delegates the asset selection decision to the manager. In the following section, we address these issues briefly and examine their implications.

DIVERSIFICATION

The initial "semidiscretionary" programs of the early 1990s focused on balancing diversification of the real estate portfolio at the plan sponsor level. In doing so, the first step was to evaluate the current exposure of the portfolio by geographic or economic region and by property type. New investment activity would then focus on those markets and property types where the portfolio had limited exposure.

In the early to mid-1980s, office, malls, and industrial assets dominated the investment exposure by sector in a plan sponsor's real estate portfolio as evidenced by the National Council for Real Estate Investment Fiduciaries (NCREIF) Index (see Figure 6.4). As a result, many separate account strategies in the early 1990s initially delegated the discretion to invest in smaller assets, such as multifamily, industrial, and neighborhood shopping centers, in an effort to construct a more diversified real estate portfolio. By focusing on these areas, investors were able to reduce risk in a couple of ways.

First, because apartments, warehouses, and neighborhood retail assets have a relatively lower correlation to office and large retail investments, investors were able to lower property-specific risk in their overall real estate portfolio. Second, due to the fundamental operating characteristics and return attributes of these sectors, they appear to be inherently less risky than the other property types.

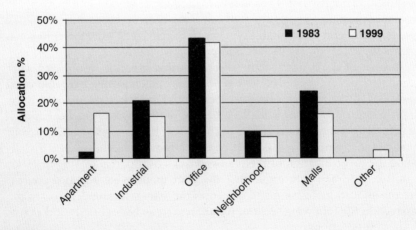

FIGURE 6.4   NCREIF allocation by sector.

As Table 6.4 and Figure 6.5 indicate, even though the historical return of these smaller assets is comparatively lower by 34 basis points on an annualized basis since 1978, the level of risk is also substantially lower by 277 basis points. Consequently, these smaller assets have offered favorable "risk-adjusted" returns that have served to lower risk in the plan sponsor's overall real estate portfolio.

From a strategic perspective, property types that have higher levels of embedded risk, such as large office assets, have generated lower risk-adjusted returns and are likely to have more pronounced market cycles. Conversely, those sectors that offer higher risk-adjusted returns, such as apartments, appear less volatile and offer more defensive characteristics. During market recoveries, the evidence appears to suggest the more volatile larger-cap property types are more likely to outperform the more defensive sectors.

TABLE 6.4 Real Estate Risk/Return

	Return	Risk	Return/Risk
Small Market Value Real Estate	9.34%	6.29%	1.49
NCREIF Property Index	9.65%	6.71%	1.44
Large Market Value Real Estate	9.68%	9.06%	1.07

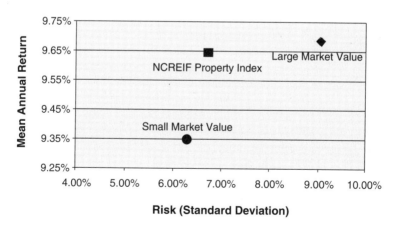

FIGURE 6.5 NCREIF Index, 1978 to 1999.

From a size perspective, an investor can also acquire more individual assets, which can lower property-specific risk (addressed in the next section). From a benchmarking perspective, then, it may be necessary to decompose the index to reflect the investment guidelines because they may vary substantially from the index. For this reason, the NCREIF Web site (**www.NCREIF.org**) provides a tool for investors to construct specific indices of one or a combination of geographic regions and property types to evaluate the relative performance of the assets they own to those within the index.

How Large Does the Allocation Need to Be to Minimize Risk Prudently?

Many real estate guidelines emphasize the need to invest in a minimum of 10 assets in an effort to diversify property-specific or nonsystematic risk in the portfolio. We find that investing in a minimum of 10 assets appears to reduce asset-specific risk by as much as 95 percent (see Figure 6.6). Once this level of exposure is achieved, 20 additional investments are required to reduce property-specific risk by the remaining 5 percent.

In light of this analysis, what becomes readily apparent in structuring a well-diversified portfolio is that the first 10 investments in the portfolio are likely to have the greatest impact on reducing overall risk in the real estate portfolio. Coincidentally, it will likely be difficult to alter the return profile of the portfolio over the near term once the "style tilt" of these initial investments is embedded in the portfolio due to the low turnover associated with real estate. Extending this analysis further, if we assume the allocation to real estate grows at roughly 5 percent per year and that average turnover in the portfolio is roughly 10 to 15 percent per year, then it may require as many as two to four years to alter the initial style and return profile.

As a side note, one means to enhance the return profile of a well-structured, low-risk core portfolio on a shorter-term or tactical basis is to broaden the set of investment choices at the margin. Plan sponsors are, in fact, augmenting the return profile of their portfolios by increasing their exposure to such investments modestly. A recent survey of tax-exempt real estate investors undertaken by Institutional Real Estate Inc. describes the historical and expected composition of the "average" plan sponsor's real estate portfolio. As Figure 6.7 illustrates, plan sponsors are broadening the set of investment choices by allocating capital to limited-life opportunity funds, REITs, "value-added" direct investing, and international real estate.

Within the private equity market, investors also use a number of tactical strategies to increment return. Although Figure 6.8 is by no means an exhaustive list of strategies, it broadly defines the attributes of risk at the

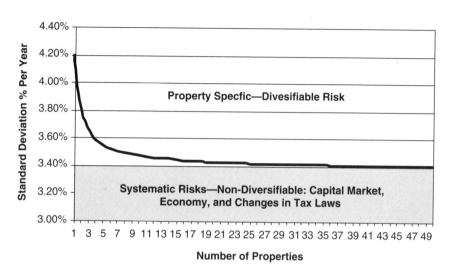

FIGURE 6.6 Risk reduction and portfolio size.

property level for a given strategy and the incremental increase in the unleveraged return that an investor is likely to expect under normal market conditions. These strategies range from the lower risk, lower return nature of core, unleveraged, stabilized assets to pure development, and entity investing at the high risk/high return end of the spectrum.

As measured by the NCREIF Index, core, unleveraged, stabilized assets at the low risk end of the spectrum historically have generated a total return of roughly 9 to 11 percent, depending on property type. This level of return is frequently used as the minimum return for pricing expected return along the risk spectrum. The return spread over unleveraged assets can typically range from 200 to 300 basis points for re-capitalization strategies to more than 600 to 800 basis points for entity level investments in real estate-related operating companies. Applying leverage to the transaction will increase these spreads, depending upon the level of debt applied to the strategy.

Although the nature of the risks are described in Table 6.4, the risk-adjusting pricing of each of these strategies depends upon the nature of leasing, construction, development, or partner risk an investor is willing to assume for an expected level of return. Suffice it to say, an investor will consider the nature of these risks for the return they are attempting to achieve

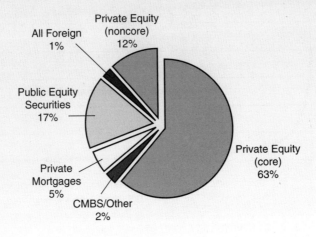

Investment Choices: 2001

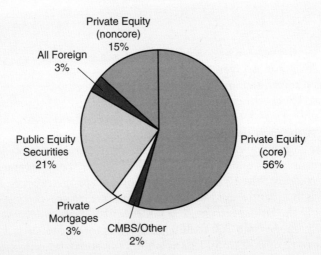

FIGURE 6.7   Investment choices.

and develop guidelines accordingly. As described with the investment vehicles previously, investors are allocating a portion of their real estate investment to a consistent and predictable base of core assets and incrementing return by tactically allocating a portion of capital to these higher risk/higher return strategies.

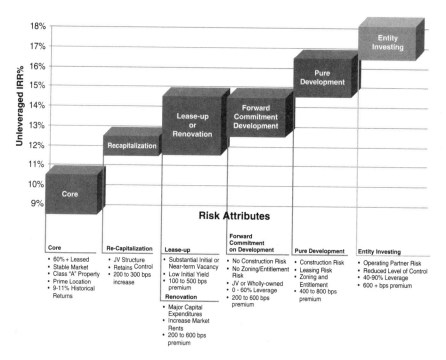

FIGURE 6.8   Tactical investment strategies in private real estate.

PORTFOLIO CONSTRUCTION

Returning to the question of plan size, the average asset size of investments in the NCREIF Index was roughly $20 to $30 million at the end of 1999, as Table 6.5 highlights. On the surface, it would appear that a plan sponsor would need to allocate a minimum of roughly $200 to $300 million to construct a diversified base of directly held unleveraged core assets to obtain the "purest" diversification benefits that real estate offers for a multiasset portfolio. Because the majority of plan sponsors investing in real estate allocate roughly 7 to 10 percent to the asset class, this suggests that overall size of the plan sponsor's portfolio would need to be a minimum of $2.0 billion or higher to construct a diversified separate account real estate portfolio.

Some plans, though, have allocated discretion to a narrower segment of the NCREIF universe to capture the diversification benefits of real estate. This segment of the market comprises those sectors marked with a single asterisk in Table 6.5. Together, they comprise roughly 63 percent of the NCREIF

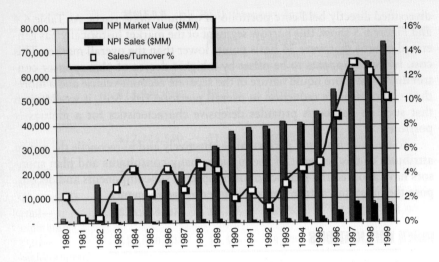

FIGURE 6.9 Sales turnover in NCREIF Index, 1980 to 1999.

impact on the performance of the overall index. However, as sales turnover has increased since 1994, the impact of the appraisal lag on the total return of the index appears to have increased.

Several implications need to be considered then when using the NCREIF Index for benchmarking. First, it appears fair to assume that we can expect higher turnover in the index, given the industry's emphasis on maintaining an active sales discipline in contrast to the 1980s. Should this occur as expected, then it is equally fair to assume that turnover in mature, stabilized portfolios will likely reflect turnover percentages in the index. As a result, it would seem that, despite the appraisal lag, the index would reflect activity in the marketplace and be a reasonable barometer to benchmark performance.

In less mature portfolios that are in the early stages of construction, the turnover percentage is likely to be lower than that of the index. In these instances, value is still accruing at the asset level and may not be fully recognized through the appraisal process due to the lag effect. As a result, the returns on less mature portfolios may lag the index to some degree over the short term because there will be fewer sales. Conversely, when these assets are sold and value is recognized, the evidence suggested from Figure 6.10 indicates a high likelihood that net sales proceeds would exceed the last reported value due to the appraisal lag. In these instances, comparing per-

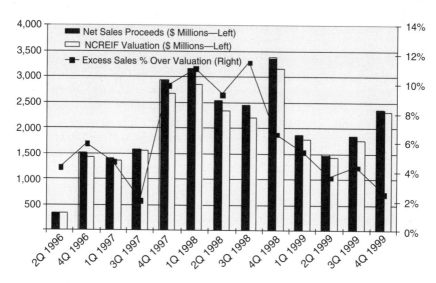

FIGURE 6.10   Market value versus sales proceeds: evidence of appraisal lag.

formance to NCREIF over the holding period or life cycle of the investment may be more appropriate than either a one- or three-year measurement that may reflect appraisal bias.

Admittedly, though, utilizing a holding period measurement to judge performance may run contrary to plan objectives if it diminishes or detracts from the importance of maintaining an active sales discipline on the part of the manager. To reconcile the potential conflict and diminish the impact of appraisal bias on benchmarking performance, many plan sponsors have elected to measure performance for directly held assets on either rolling five- or seven-year periods as opposed to merely focusing on one- or three-year performances.

INDUSTRY RESOURCES

Since 1983, the market capitalization of the institutional private real estate market, as reflected by the NCREIF Index, has grown from roughly $8.5 billion to almost $87.5 billion as of the second quarter of 2000. As such, the capitalization of the NCREIF Index has grown in excess of 14 percent annually.

As institutional ownership of real estate has grown, so too has the information available necessary to service growing investor demand to the asset class. With enhanced access to information through the Internet, industry efforts are underway to enhance the timely dissemination of information to investors and other industry participants. Conceptually, such informational efficiency is likely to bode well for investors by improving transparency into the asset class and raising the productivity of plan sponsor capital.

Although many Web-based sites have been developed for the real estate market, a few key sites provide timely content as well as links to other industry resources and databases:

- *www.NCREIF.org* National Council for Real Estate Investment Fiduciaries. NCREIF is an association of institutional real estate professionals. Its members contribute quarterly return data on investments owned by tax-exempt plan sponsors. In addition to producing quarterly return indices, NCREIF has worked diligently with other industry associations, such as the Pension Real Estate Association and the National Association of Real Estate Investment Managers, to develop the Real Estate Information Standards. This document recommends a series of standards appropriate for the industry.

- *www.PREA.org* Pension Real Estate Association. This Web site provides educational and research information to the pension real estate community. PREA promotes high standards of industry practice and professionalism and holds several meetings per year to promote interactive forums on leading issues impacting the asset class.

- *www.NAREIT.com* National Association of Real Estate Investment Trusts. This Web site is an information source on REITs and publicly traded real estate. NAREIT provides a wealth of information on companies as well as industry performance statistics. NAREIT also provides timely information on many key legislative issues affecting the asset class.

- *www.IREI.com* Institutional Real Estate Inc. is a media and consulting firm that offers links to many other industry Web sites and real estate-related data sources in addition to those highlighted above. Under the "Trade Association and Organization" link, for example, investors will find links to the Appraisal Institute, the Urban Land Institute, and the International Council of Shopping Centers in addition to many other important industry organizations and databases.

SUMMARY: STRATEGIC IMPLICATIONS

As has been identified, there are several strategic and tactical issues to consider in constructing a well-diversified portfolio of real estate assets within a multiasset institutional portfolio.

As real estate portfolio management has evolved over the last 20 years, institutional investors initially focused on allocating exposure to the asset class in light of high inflation. However, systematic shocks to the economy in the 1980s severely impacted the value of real estate. Because many were invested in commingled funds, investors were restricted in their ability to reallocate capital among the asset classes. As time passed, investors continued to recognize the intrinsic benefits of real estate but also emphasized the need to reallocate capital should the investment outlook change. This has resulted in the broad use of the separate account investment vehicle coupled with commingled or REITs vehicles that offer tactical strategies and an ability to increment return while managing risk and liquidity needs in the overall real estate portfolio.

From a benchmarking perspective, one of the major issues to consider when constructing a well-diversified portfolio is the size of the overall plan. Practically speaking, this question will establish how an investor can tactically allocate capital to the asset class. The next questions are: "What is the portfolio's current exposure to the asset class?" "What is the anticipated rollover?" From here, the investor can identify the appropriate sectors to target that will balance the diversification of the portfolio.

Finally, the plan sponsor needs to address its liquidity requirements. As noted, many plan sponsors are establishing a well-diversified base of directly held core assets with average holding periods in the range of seven to eight years and incrementing return by accessing more liquid, higher-yielding, or tactical investment structures and strategies. Such a strategy allows the institutional investor to maximize control over their real estate portfolio, increment return and facilitate rebalancing necessitated by potential macroeconomic shocks to the economy.

REFERENCES

Booltz, Charles C.L., *Cyclicality in Commercial Real Estate Market*, Brookfield, VT: Ashgate Publishing Co., 1996.

Brown, Gerald R., "Reducing the Dispersion of Returns in U.K. Real Estate Portfolios," *Journal of Real Estate Portfolio Management* no. 2 (1997): 129–140.

Eagle, Blake and S. Hudson-Wilson, *Real Estate Markets: A Historical Perspective, Managing Real Estate Portfolios*, New York: Irwin, 1994.

Young, Michael S., and R.A. Graff, "Measuring Random Appraisal Error in Commercial Real Estate," *Real Estate Review* no.4 (Winter 1999): 57–62.

NOTES

[1]"Small cap" refers to that segment of the NCREIF Index consisting of those sectors that generally have a smaller average asset size and less volatility in returns. "Large cap" refers to larger average asset sizes or sectors that have higher volatility in returns. The specific sectors of these style categories are discussed later in the chapter.

[2]See Brown reference at the end of this chapter for the derivations of the values in Figure 6.6.

[3]This variation between appraisal and transaction value appears consistent with the work of other industry research (please see references at the end of this chapter).

CHAPTER 7

Mortgage-Backed Securities

By Tremont Advisers

Market-neutral mortgage-backed hedge funds seek high yields and low volatility of returns, strategies that are particularly appropriate for periods when the spread differentials between mortgage yields and benchmark Treasuries or LIBOR are high.

INTRODUCTION

Outstanding mortgage-backed securities (MBS) in the United States are now valued in excess of $4 trillion and collectively represent the second largest fixed-income market in the world. The success of the MBS market in the United States is due to three primary factors:

1. Government and quasi-governmental issuers provide standardization and credit support for mortgage issuance.
2. The government encourages home ownership—the tax deductibility of mortgage interest represents the single largest opportunity for taxpayers to reduce their overall tax burden.
3. Greater availability of consumer credit information, the enhanced financial engineering capability of issuers, and the increased sophistication of MBS buyers have allowed for the creation of new MBS debt structures and classes of securities, increasing the size of the market appreciably.

Residential Mortgage-Backed Securities (RMBS)

The largest percentage of MBS is backed by first mortgage liens on primary residences. Government agencies including Ginnie Mae, Fannie Mae, and Freddie Mac (starting in 1970), as well as numerous private issuers (beginning in 1977), aggregate mortgages with similar coupons, maturities, and credit quality into pools that serve as collateral for pass-through mortgage securities. A pass-through security allows a bondholder to receive the interest and principal from a specific mortgage pool.

Since 1983, pass-through securities have been further structured as collateralized mortgage obligations (CMOs) to allow buyers to negate or assume certain risks specifically associated with MBS. In the 1980s, issuers created adjustable rate mortgages (ARMs) on which they received a fixed premium over an index, usually U.S. Treasury bonds, which reset according to a predetermined schedule. In the 1990s, issuers were able to securitize pass-throughs from homeowners who had limited or poor credit histories, smaller down payments than the traditional 20 percent, and more or less documentation as to their employment or financial status. These innovations in structure and credit analysis are the engines behind the burgeoning MBS marketplace.

Commercial Mortgage-Backed Securities (CMBS)

After the real estate crisis in the United States in the late 1980s, securitization of commercial real estate loans became more prevalent. By developing consistent underwriting standards, standardized loan documentation, and documented financial histories on real estate assets, Wall Street has become a primary source of capital for the commercial real estate industry.

In each commercial loan sector—multifamily, retail, office, and hotels—rating agencies, issuers, and buyers of CMBS analyze the assets as to their location, quality of borrower, quality of tenants and lease terms, property condition and management, and asset capitalization (equity, debt, and reserves). This information is used along with debt service coverage ratios and loan-to-value data to create credit tranches for the CMOs backed by the commercial asset(s). CMBS buyers can then select from a range of AAA-rated instruments to those securities structured to assume the first losses on a pool of commercial properties. Outstanding CMBS in the United States exceeds $500 billion.

Structured MBS

Between 1986 and 1993, the volume of mortgage securities issued increased noticeably as volatile interest rates touched 25-year lows. During this period, the issuance of structured MBS grew distinctly to accommodate buyer demands for specific types of instruments. These included "floaters," whose coupon varied based upon a spread over an index (like LIBOR), "PACs" or planned amortization classes, which mimic U.S. Treasuries by offering a defined set of principal payments if prepayments were in a certain range, and interest-only and principal-only bonds (IOs and POs).

Floaters allow commercial banks to offset index-based liabilities. PACs allow mutual fund managers to earn higher spreads with minimal increases in duration risk. IOs and POs serve as natural hedging instruments for mortgage portfolios. However, the increase in structured CMO issuance also created securities with few natural buyers. For example, inverse floaters and certain PAC support classes had few institutional buyers. Heavily structured MBS derivatives and such residual securities are often purchased by hedge funds and other alternative investment vehicles because of their greater return potential, if properly hedged.

AVAILABLE MBS INVESTING STRATEGIES

There are three general categories of MBS investing: long-only, market-neutral, and directional trading, each with its own risk/return profile.

Long-only mortgage investing is most common and is done predominantly by mutual funds and pension funds that use mortgage securities exclusively or as part of a mix of fixed-income portfolio securities. Many of these funds are prohibited by charter from using hedges or from taking short positions. Long-only strategies work best in falling interest rate environments, where certain higher coupon structured mortgage securities benefit in price.

Directional trading in MBS and MBS derivatives is comparatively rare and is undertaken by alternative and hedge fund managers who use these securities to take views on interest rates or prepayments. By purchasing derivatives and using certain hedging techniques, managers can profit from rising or falling interest rates while hedging a portion of their risks in the event that they are wrong. Such managers often use leverage to enhance their results. Directional traders performed especially poorly in 1994 to 95, brilliantly in 1996 to 97 and into the first half of 1998 before being hit very hard during the Russian debt crisis in the second half of the year.

Market-neutral MBS investing is most common among hedge funds. Unlike long-only or directional trading strategies, market-neutral managers attempt to capture the spread between a portfolio of MBS securities and an index such as Treasuries or LIBOR. Such a strategy has four components:

1. Assemble a portfolio of mortgage securities that have a substantial spread in excess of the target index. To create such a portfolio, managers can elect to purchase MBS or MBS derivatives and assemble a portfolio of positions, which in the aggregate, resembles a bond.
2. Hedge the portfolio to reduce its exposure to a variety of risks, including changes in interest rates, the shape of the yield curve, interest rate volatility, and convexity.

3. Establish a short position in either LIBOR or Treasuries or a combination of the two to serve as the spread capture mechanism.
4. Create a hedge, wherever possible, to deal with changes in the spread differential between mortgages and their LIBOR or Treasury hedge due to fundamental factors.

Mortgage-backed, market-neutral hedge funds capture spreads between mortgages and other indices. They also establish positions that counter the effects of changes in mortgage prepayment, interest rates, and other factors on their portfolios. They are one of the few "hedge funds" that are genuinely hedged against known risks.

MBS hedge fund portfolios have lasting value. Once a manager assembles and hedges a valuable MBS portfolio, the performance it generates can last for up to two years. Investors who buy into existing funds immediately obtain portfolios with wide spreads and long lives.

HOW MBS HEDGE FUNDS MANAGE RISK

The most sophisticated MBS hedge funds utilize hedging tools to reduce the risks of MBS ownership. Generally speaking, there are three risks that must be managed: interest rate risk, prepayment risk, and default risk. There are two crucial strategies in dealing with these risks:

1. The manager should subdivide these risks into more specific components and then hedge each dimension separately.
2. Because every potential type of adverse occurrence, or shock, can occur to different degrees, a manager should adjust the hedges frequently. The manager should also include instruments in the hedging strategy that are particularly sensitive to large shocks.

As an example of the first step, interest rate risk can be broken into four more specific risks: parallel shifts in the yield curve, steepening (or flattening) of the yield curve, increased (or decreased) curvature in the yield curve, and changes in the volatility of interest rates. Statistical studies show that, although there are an infinite number of imaginable changes in the yield curve, well over 90 percent of changes in the yield curve can be decomposed into combinations of these first three shifts.

Prepayment risk can be decomposed into turnover risk, homeowner cost changes, and homeowner alertness changes. Again, while there may be an infinite number of reasons for prepayments to change unexpectedly, the majority of past surprises can be explained by combinations of these three components.

Default risk, as well, can be decomposed into factors that affect perceptions about all markets (and thus can be hedged by shorting LIBOR), mortgage specific risks, and geographically related mortgage risks. The last two dimensions pertain to the general credit-worthiness of homeowners and consumers more generally and are influenced by changes in housing prices, total debt, and income.

Different mortgages are differentially affected by these various shocks. An inverse IO, for instance, is particularly buoyed by a steepening of the yield curve. This occurs because its coupon goes up when the short interest rate goes down, and its horizon extends when prepayments go down, as they will when long interest rates rise.

A successful hedge fund must be aware of all these risks, be able to quantify the sensitivity of each bond to each risk, and know how to hedge them all if it chooses to do so. No hedge fund will choose to hedge all risks completely as the cost would be prohibitive. Near the point of perfect hedging, for instance, the benefit from further hedging is practically zero and typically not worth the expense. An experienced hedge fund will protect itself against large losses from any of these shocks and expose itself to small shocks only when it has good reason to think a particular kind of shock is more likely to be positive than negative.

To illustrate the second strategy, consider a straight pass-through mortgage. As interest rates fall, the mortgage (like any fixed-income instrument) will tend to rise in value because its cash flows are discounted at lower rates. A hedge fund can cope with this by modifying its hedge dynamically, making changes as interest rates fall little by little. To protect itself against a sudden and large change in interest rates, however, the fund can also hedge with out-of-the-money swaptions or caps. Managers who use dynamic hedging and incorporate tools to mitigate large, unforeseen changes in interest rates or other variables may offer the best risk-adjusted returns.

Numerous risks of MBS ownership explain why they trade at a yield premium to U.S. Treasury securities. In the residential MBS, the greatest risk assumed by a buyer of a mortgage-backed security is prepayment risk. Homeowners can prepay a mortgage without penalty (in most cases) and will do so to varying degrees if available mortgage rates fall below the coupon on their mortgage. Conversely, if mortgage rates rise above their mortgage coupon, consumers will avoid refinancing their mortgages, doing so only if they elect to move, for example. This "one-way" option means that the duration of RMBS can vary widely, depending upon prevalent interest and mortgage rates.

Although interest rates explain a majority of consumer prepayment behavior, other factors are also of material importance. These include the state of the economy (people move more when incomes rise and, conversely, default more often when unemployment rises), the amount of information a consumer gets (more data increases the refinancing rate), and the costs associated with refinancing (lower costs make refinancing more affordable), to name just three of many additional factors. One final risk is that, whereas government agencies provide a guaranteed return of principal on the RMBS they issue, private issuers (called "nonagencies") do not provide such guarantees.

Different risks have impacted MBS hedge funds over time. In 1998, the high levels of leverage used by some hedge funds caused a near panic in the financial markets, which resulted in losses to those MBS hedge funds that were forced to sell their securities. In contrast, those MBS funds that did not have to sell suffered much smaller losses. In 1994, the Askin affair and the effective shutdown of Kidder Peabody by its parent, General Electric, roiled the MBS markets. Historical experience suggests that proper hedging and the use of moderate leverage are the keys to avoiding these risks.

Of course, there are circumstances one could envision that would even impact a low-leverage, broadly diversified MBS portfolio. A worldwide financial liquidity crisis would drive spreads of all fixed-income securities wider. A change in government policy, such as altering the tax deductibility of mortgage interest, would affect MBS values greatly. A major recession in the United States and a real estate price collapse would similarly devastate MBS values.

Although each of these scenarios is plausible, the fact is that the remaining top-tier MBS market-neutral managers are operating their funds with lower leverage and better risk controls than at any time in the past decade.

WHY MARKET-NEUTRAL, MORTGAGE-BACKED HEDGE FUNDS?

Market-neutral mortgage-backed hedge funds seek high yields and low volatility of returns. Such strategies are particularly appropriate for periods when the spread differentials between mortgage yields and benchmark Treasuries or LIBOR are high. During such periods, market-neutral strategies can capture an attractive "run rate" (the return from holding the hedged portfolio, assuming no change in spread) as well as incremental profits in the event that spreads between mortgages and the benchmarks return to historical norms. Market-neutral MBS investors can cite several other positive traits:

- Managers who are most effective in implementing these strategies need not assume any substantial credit risk to achieve their returns.
- Unlike other fixed-income hedge fund strategies, a properly hedged MBS portfolio can generate positive returns for up to two years.
- Excess leverage is unnecessary.

In a period where interest rates are more likely to rise than fall and when interest rate volatility is likely to remain high, market-neutral hedge fund strategies are an appropriate way for risk-averse investors to participate in the MBS marketplace. In comparison, long-only funds will suffer losses in a rising rate environment, and directional traders are often whipsawed in periods of unusual, sustained volatility.

MBS market-neutral hedge funds, operated by experienced management and research teams and armed with excellent analytical and risk management tools, can be extremely attractive for investors in a variety of circumstances.

SELECTING THE RIGHT MBS HEDGE FUND

To put money to work in this sector, we recommend the following:

- The hedge fund should use leverage of no more than three-to-one. This means that, for every dollar of invested capital, the firm owns no more than three dollars of MBS.
- The hedge fund should be broadly diversified in its portfolio, holding numerous MBS positions across a variety of mortgage sectors and MBS types.
- The hedge fund should utilize dynamic and out-of-the-money strategies to minimize the effect of changes in prepayments, interest rates, volatility, and convexity on the value of its MBS portfolios.
- The hedge fund should be managed by experienced MBS traders who conduct proprietary research to create their own models for managing prepayment and other risks.
- The hedge fund should use independent third-party valuations of their positions and allow investors to see their marks on their positions upon request.

HISTORICAL BACKGROUND

The mutual and hedge fund marketplace for MBS is in its adolescence, and, like most adolescents, it is prone to emotional outbursts. Three times in the 1990s, the mortgage-backed market and the funds that invest in MBS encountered sudden and dramatic volatility, followed by a sustained and material dislocation in the pricing of their MBS portfolios.

In the wake of that volatility, investors were presented with an opportunity to acquire AAA-rated MBS securities and derivatives that yielded double-digit returns with low volatility by investing with market-neutral MBS hedge funds. Managers of these specialized MBS hedge funds captured the spread differential between highly rated mortgage securities and U.S. Treasury bonds or LIBOR while managing risks that include rising interest rates and shifts in prepayment behaviors.

In the period from 1995 to 1996, which represents a more consistent interest rate environment, market-neutral MBS returns were high and risk was low, thus providing significant value to investors. With the advent of substantial volatility and uncertainty because of financial crises in Asia, Russia, and Long Term Capital Management, combined with the sudden loss of liquidity and high use of leverage during the subsequent two-year period, risk increased markedly and returns fell.

In the fall of 1999 after the most tumultuous year since 1994, MBS hedge fund managers could look at four remarkable changes, stemming from the crisis of the third quarter of 1998 to confirm a new investment opportunity for mortgage investing in general and for hedge funds specializing in mortgage-backed securities in particular.

First, spreads between the average outstanding mortgage and the average Treasury became wider than they had been in more than five years. The spread difference between the coupon mortgage and the Treasury of comparable average life (the seven-year treasury) was consistently wider than at any time in the previous decade. Thus, even plain vanilla mortgages (properly hedged) presented an opportunity to earn a handsome return. More important, the dramatic spreads were an indicator of dislocations that would take time to resolve. However, they had a great probability of returning to normal levels for both historical and fundamental reasons and offered significant standstill returns in the interim.

Second, there had been a consolidation of many of the most sophisticated and talented mortgage traders. Among investment banks, the legendary Salomon arbitrage group had closed down, the Goldman Sachs arbitrage group had reduced operations markedly, and Nomura had cut back proprietary trading due to capital losses. Among hedge funds, Long Term

Capital Management had nearly collapsed and lost many of those partners with the mathematical ability to assess mortgages, including its two Nobel Laureates. Many other hedge funds had either disappeared or greatly reduced their exposure to mortgage-backed securities. In addition, new regulations prohibited Home Loan Banks from increasing their mortgage positions.

This pullback is a typical occurrence at cyclical high points in spreads. Calmer markets and above-average returns should attract new players, instigating the narrowing of spreads. However, one suspects that the expertise to evaluate mortgage securities now rests in fewer places than before. The result will be that fewer players will share future opportunities.

Third, one of the greatest risks to holding mortgage-backed securities—prepayments—had been reduced significantly as interest rates had begun to move up again. The rate at which homeowners pay off their mortgages (known as the prepayment rate) affects the price of mortgage securities greatly. For example, in falling interest rate environments, prepayment rates are high, as many homeowners can refinance their homes (prepaying an old mortgage and obtaining a new one) to reduce interest costs. During such periods, mortgage-backed pass-through securities issued by FNMA and GNMA would see their durations shorten markedly, reducing their value.

After sustained periods of falling interest rates, most homeowners have taken advantage of these refinancing opportunities. Thus, when rates begin to rise again, homeowners are "locked-in," meaning that there is a substantial disadvantage associated with refinancing their mortgage. As rates rise and more homeowners become locked in, the prepayment risk of owning MBS is reduced accordingly.

Last, unlike high-yield bonds, emerging markets debt and certain other fixed-income security types, including asset-backed and convertible bonds, the preponderance of mortgage-backed securities issuance is AAA rated. This is either because the bonds are issued by government agencies or because nonagency issuers (those who specialize in larger mortgages above about $250,000) seek rating agencies to assess the credit-worthiness of their bonds. In fact, the vast majority of MBS derivatives, including interest-only and principal-only strips, do not present any credit risk to their owners.

The absence of credit risk in a period when prepayment uncertainty is low and spreads are wide made mortgage-backed portfolios an excellent vehicle for high risk-adjusted returns in that economic environment.

CHAPTER 8

Investing in Gold and Precious Metals

By Richard Scott-Ram

During the runup in the value of stocks and the weakening status of gold, investors may have forgotten that gold is a unique asset with a negative correlation to most other assets, especially equities. Its role as a diversifier can reduce portfolio risk in either quiet or inflationary periods.

Most investors have a fixed perception of gold and may not be aware of its ability to control portfolio risk. In fact, many investors are surprised to hear that gold can help portfolio managers solve some interesting problems and meet their fiduciary responsibilities when used as a risk management tool.

Some basic characteristics of gold make it a unique asset. First, it is primarily a monetary asset. As much as two-thirds of gold's total accumulated holdings relate to "store of value" considerations. Holdings in this category include central bank reserves, private investments, and high-caratage jewelry bought primarily in developing countries as a vehicle for savings.

Second, gold is partly a commodity although less than one-third of gold's total accumulated holdings can be considered a commodity. These holdings include jewelry bought in Western markets for adornment and gold used in industry.

The distinction between gold and commodities is important. Gold has maintained its value in after-inflation terms over the long run while commodities have declined.

Some analysts like to think of gold as a "currency without a country." It is an internationally recognized asset that is not dependent upon any government's promise to pay. This is an important feature when comparing gold to conventional diversifiers, such as T-bills or bonds that, unlike gold, do have counter-party risks.

PRICE FACTORS

Econometric studies indicate that the price of gold is determined by two sets of factors: supply and macro-economic factors.

Supply and the gold price are inversely related. In addition to supplies from new mining, the available supply of gold in the market is made up of three major "above-ground" sources:

1. Reclaimed scrap or gold reclaimed from jewelry and other industries such as electronics and dentistry
2. "Official," or central bank, sales
3. Gold loans made to the market from official gold reserves for borrowing and lending purposes

In recent years, the growth in gold supply has come from above-ground sources.

In the case of macro-economic factors, the U.S. dollar tends to be inversely related to gold while inflation and gold tend to move in tandem with each other. Also, high real interest rates are generally a negative factor for gold.

GOLD AS A DIVERSIFIER

What makes gold such a highly effective portfolio diversifier?

"Including gold within an existing portfolio could improve investment performance by either increasing returns without increasing risk or by reducing risk without adversely affecting returns," concludes Raymond E. Lombra, professor of economics at Pennsylvania State University.

This statement summarizes the usefulness of gold in terms of Modern Portfolio Theory, a strategy used by many investment managers today. Using this approach, gold can be used as a portfolio diversifier to improve investment performance.

Figure 8.1 demonstrates why gold is such a helpful diversifier when you compare the correlation between gold, on the one hand, and various asset classes on the other. Gold is negatively correlated with most other asset classes. For example, whenever long-term bonds decline, there is a tendency for gold prices to go up. Whenever equities decline, there is an even greater tendency for gold prices to go up.

Figure 8.2 shows that gold is more negatively correlated to U.S. stocks than any of the other asset classes that are typically used as portfolio diversifiers (such as bonds, emerging market equities, and real estate investment

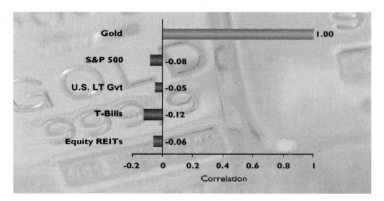

FIGURE 8.1   Gold is negatively correlated to other asset classes, (January 1991 to December 2000).

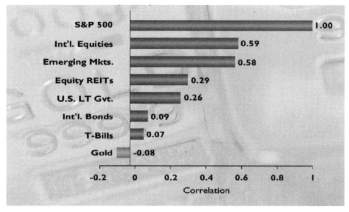

FIGURE 8.2   Gold is negatively correlated to U.S. equities, (January 1991 to December 2000).

trusts or REITS). This makes gold an especially effective diversifier for equity-oriented portfolios.

Let's examine the relationship between gold and equities a little further. Historically, the price of gold has generally moved in the direction opposite to the trend in equities. In particular, the price of both equities and gold tend to "revert to the mean" at certain points in history. During the years of strength in the stock market and weakness in the gold price in the last half of the 1990s, many portfolio managers had reason to question what role, if any, gold could play in a portfolio's performance.

Historically, however, they could look at the levels of each market and quickly conclude that the stock market was at an unusually high level and that the gold price, in contrast, was unusually low with an upside potential perceived to be greater than the downside potential. Figure 8.3 captures these two developments—high stock prices and low gold prices.

The key questions for portfolio managers as the 21st century began were: When will the stock market "revert to the mean"—that is, move downward —and when will gold prices revert to their mean—that is, move up? Regardless of whether they were a bull or a bear on the stock market, the mere threat of a market correction should have alerted them to the advantages of diversifying their portfolio into alternative assets such as gold.

Figure 8.4 displays the ratio of the Dow Jones Industrial Average to the gold price since 1885. The ratios of these investments have experienced marked peaks and valleys during major market cycles, peaking once in 1928, a second time in 1965, and a third time in July 1999 (at 45). Since 1999, the ratio has turned downward, prompting the question: Will the ratio continue to decline?

The valleys in the ratio came in 1896 at a time of financial turmoil and William Jennings Bryan's "Cross of Gold" speech, in 1932 at the bottom of the stock market cycle, and in 1980 at the end of an inflationary boom that resulted in the erosion of the value of financial assets.

When the stock market was trading at record high levels, gold was selling at the low end of its historical range. History suggested that this ratio

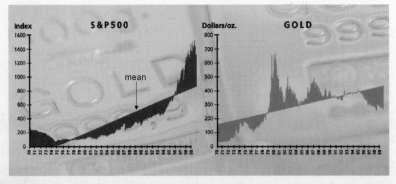

FIGURE 8.3   Reversion to the mean: Will equities move down to their mean? Will gold move up? (1970 to 2000).

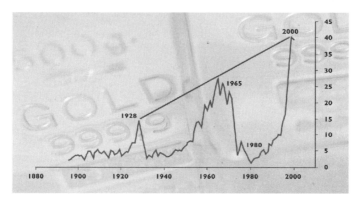

FIGURE 8.4 Ratio of Dow Jones Industrial Average to gold, (1895 to 2000).

would turn downwards—either the price of gold would rise and/or the value of the stock market would decline.

STRESS FACTOR

Traditional methods of portfolio diversification often fail when they are needed most—that is, during periods of financial stress or instability. On these occasions, the correlations and volatilities of return for most asset classes (including traditional diversifiers such as bonds and alternative assets) increase, thus reducing the intended cushioning effect of a diversified portfolio. Consequently, the portfolio does not perform as originally expected, leaving investors disappointed.

Figure 8.5 depicts an efficient frontier curve using a new optimization procedure that recognizes that periods of stress do, in fact, occur. The portfolios included on the efficient frontier contain the following asset classes: large-cap equities, international equities, Treasury bills, long-term Treasury bonds, small-cap equities, and gold. The assumption made in developing this efficient frontier is that there is an equal likelihood of either a stress or non-stress period occurring. Notably, gold appears in many portfolios along the efficient frontier, ranging from very conservative, low-risk portfolios (mainly bonds and T-bills) to aggressive, high-risk portfolios (mainly equities).

Next, Monte Carlo simulations of future returns were conducted for stress and non-stress periods for a variety of portfolios on the efficient frontier to

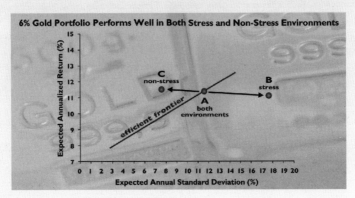

FIGURE 8.5   How gold lowers portfolio risk.

test the consistency of their performance. Based on the results of these simulations, a portfolio with a moderate expected risk exposure of 11.6 percent
(standard deviation) and an expected annual return of 11.4 percent was
selected (point A) for two reasons: (1) This portfolio had relatively consistent
results during both stress and non-stress periods, and (2) the expected returns
were near the level of returns for a typical 60-percent stock/40-percent bond
portfolio. This efficient portfolio includes a 6-percent allocation to gold.

When stress conditions were simulated on the 6-percent gold portfolio
(point A), the return (point B) was 11.1 percent (only 50 basis points lower
than the expected return of 11.4 percent for point A) and the standard deviation was 17.8 percent. Similarly, when non-stress conditions were simulated
(point C), the return was 11.5 percent (10 basis points higher than expected
in point A) and the standard deviation was 7.6 percent. Thus, the selected
portfolio with 6-percent gold weighting had generally similar returns, regardless of whether the environment was stress (point B) or non-stress (point C)
—a desirable result.

ASSET ALLOCATION

Three main problems are associated with traditional methods of asset
allocation:

1. *Historical returns are not normally distributed.*   Almost all asset allocation studies that use mean-variance optimization assume that the
   returns of the assets are normally or log-normally distributed and, con-

sequently, can be described by their mean and standard deviation. Yet, historical returns, in reality, are *not* normally distributed.

2. *Financial stress.* Traditional asset allocation often does not work during periods of financial stress when it is most needed.

3. *Unanticipated inflation.* Traditional portfolios do not perform well during these periods.

Including gold in equity portfolios addresses these three problems. Gold has been shown to reduce both negative skewedness—that is, portfolio underperformance—and the number of outliers by making the portfolio's distribution more normal (see Point 1 previously). Finally, gold improves portfolio performance during periods of stress and unanticipated inflation (see Points 2 and 3).

Therefore, gold can be used to create portfolios that will have less surprise and perform more in line with the investor's expectations created by the asset allocation process.

To illustrate the beneficial effect that low volatility can have on portfolio returns, the returns of two hypothetical portfolios are compared in Figure 8.6. The arithmetic average annual return for both portfolios is the same—that is, 10 percent. However, the standard deviation of the portfolio on the left is lower (1.10 percent) than that of the portfolio on the right (16.43 percent). This means that the low-volatility portfolio's compound annualized return of 10 percent is greater than the high-volatility portfolio's return of 9 percent. Accordingly, an initial $10,000 investment in the less-volatile portfolio yields nearly $1,000 more by the end of the sixth year than the more volatile portfolio—that is, $17,711 versus $16,746.

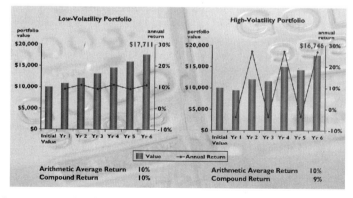

FIGURE 8.6 Lower volatility leads to higher returns through compounding.

COMPETITIVE EDGE

Gold is competitive with conventional diversifiers such as bonds, put options on the S&P 500 Index, and Treasury bills for several reasons:

- Gold serves as an excellent source of liquidity—that is, the ease with which an investor can move out of gold into cash without incurring a loss of value. In this sense, gold can even be considered a proxy for cash.
- Gold is an international commodity that can be readily bought and sold 24 hours a day in one or more markets around the world. This cannot be said of most investments, including equities of the world's largest corporations.
- Bullion transactions generally feature narrow bid/offer spreads.
- Gold contracts can be bought and sold easily on a number of exchanges.
- Gold can be converted into cash in a relatively short period of time, much faster than alternative investments such as real estate, venture capital, or timberland.

Gold's role as a source of liquidity in a portfolio was powerfully demonstrated during the stock market crash in October 1987. All sectors of the equity market (including gold equities) declined sharply at that time. Meanwhile, bullion maintained its value throughout that episode, acting as the insurance policy that it is designed to be in a portfolio.

PRUDENT INVESTMENT

U.S. regulations issued under the Employee Retirement Income Security Act (ERISA), including the "prudent man rule," endorse the total portfolio theory, under which each investment is viewed in light of the entire portfolio held by a pension fund. Gold can be considered as a potentially valuable investment in its role as a risk reducer.

In enacting the ERISA regulations, the Department of Labor has specifically refused to prohibit investments in precious metals. In fact, there have been no reported cases in which investment in precious metals by ERISA plans has been challenged.

Thus, an investment in gold can be considered prudent and permissible under ERISA if the elements of the prudence standard are satisfied.

INVESTMENT CHOICES

Gold bullion is available through brokerage firms and banks throughout the United States. Investors can choose the methods of purchase and storage of gold bullion that best meet the particular institution's needs. Investors can take direct possession (physical delivery) or they can buy through a storage program. In the latter case, the broker, banker, or dealer uses a secure, third-party depository to hold and protect the gold for a small fee.

With a storage account, the investor holds title to a specified amount of gold, which gives him/her the right to demand physical delivery at any time. With most storage accounts, investors are allowed to buy and sell gold over the phone, and they receive a complete record of all transactions for tax and portfolio management purposes. Investors holding a minimum of 10,000 oz. of bullion also have the option of earning a modest return through leasing programs. Like other interest rates, gold lease rates vary, based on market circumstances and the length of maturity of the financial instrument.

Now is a particularly good time to be looking at including gold in an investment portfolio. Since 1999, the U.S. dollar has softened, much of the U.S. stock market has weakened, and the inflation rate has stopped declining. Meanwhile, the price of gold has begun to turn up from a very low level.

Accordingly, portfolio managers are focusing more on "preservation of wealth" strategies rather than aggressively seeking capital gains as they have done in recent years. They are increasingly recognizing the need to diversify their portfolios into alternative assets, including gold. To hold all one's investments in conventional assets, such as stocks and bonds, is to run the risk of experiencing bad portfolio performance due to the unbalanced structure of the portfolio.

NOTES

[1] A Monte Carlo simulation using GARCH techniques was conducted assuming the selected portfolio experienced 5,000 five-year periods of stress and non-stress.

CHAPTER 9

Private Equity: Funds of Funds

By Geoffrey Hirt, Thomas Galuhn, Paul Rice

Private equity encompasses all types of equity investments in non-public companies. A fund of funds approach is one way to create in your portfolio a more comprehensive, diversified private equity asset class consisting of indirect investments in hundreds of companies representing some or all of the categories of private equity.

INTRODUCTION

Private equity is a comprehensive term that represents all types of equity investments in non-public companies. Traditionally, private equity is associated with several broad categories of investments, including venture capital, leveraged buyouts (LBOs), and mezzanine debt, and occasionally a category called special situations.

Venture capital usually is associated with investments in early stage companies in industries such as information technology, telecommunications, biotechnology, and other technology categories. Early stage companies are in the product development process and preparing their initial marketing, manufacturing, and sales plans. Given the life cycle of the firm, venture capital can also be considered middle stage and later stage, with later stage referring to a company that is already producing and shipping products. Later stage companies are often within one or two years of an initial public offering (IPO).

LBOs are another significant category of private equity and can be divided into mid-cap and large-cap buyouts. LBOs can take place with the acquisition of a company or a division of a large corporation that is either a public or private company. In a good market for LBOs, debt is plentiful and a typical LBO may use 90 percent debt and 10 percent equity. However, this debt-to-equity mix will change with the tone of the marketplace; in a tight market, LBOs may have to employ as much as 40 percent equity to complete a transaction. Exit strategies range from taking the company public with an IPO, finding a merger partner, or a buyback from the original owners.

The last category is mezzanine debt, which refers to the use of debt in combination with the equity group to fund the specific acquisition. Mezzanine capital uses subordinated debt but often includes warrants attached to the debt to increase the total return potential of the investment.

Although venture capital is only one part of the private equity category, it is interesting to give some perspective on this segment of the market. Venture capital investing was at record levels during the year 2000. Venture Economics and the National Venture Capital Association stated that venture funds invested a total of $103 billion into private companies during the year 2000, up from $59.4 billion in 1999. These investments included 5,380 companies in 2000 versus 3,967 companies in 1999. However, the fourth quarter of 2000 saw the first decline since the first quarter of 1998, and this trend continued into the first quarter of 2002. Regardless of the cyclical nature of private equity investment, there are several ways to make investments in this asset category and many reasons to add this asset class to your portfolio.

Direct Investments

Direct private equity refers to making equity investments directly into individual companies, both domestically and internationally. These investments can span the spectrum from seed capital through later stage private equity acquisition financing. The minimum staff requirement to make successful direct equity investments is quite large. Also, it is difficult to achieve proper diversification through a direct investment process.

Private Equity Partnerships

Private equity partnerships are commingled funds that invest in a diversified pool of specific direct investments. Most partnership funds usually have a very specific investment strategy, such as early, middle, or later stage venture capital, while some multistage partnerships invest across stages.

Some are also leveraged buyout partnerships that have well-defined acquisition strategies. These partnerships usually invest in middle size companies known as mid-caps or large companies known as large-caps. Some buyout partnerships will do both large-cap and mid-cap deals, and these are classified as diversified buyout funds. Some firms focus on foreign private equity in geographic regions such as Europe or Asia or even specific coun-tries such as Germany. Others focus only domestically, and some do both international and domestic investing.

Private equity partnerships have several advantages. By specializing in one category of private equity, direct equity partnerships are able to develop a knowledge base that enables them to do a superior job of analyzing and managing potential investments. Private equity partnerships have the abil-ity to create an attractive opportunity set. Top-tier partnerships have the abil-ity to source deals that most investors would not be exposed to on their own. The years of experience in assessing, managing, and doing the due diligence necessary for achieving high returns cannot be ignored. The partnership structure provides the partners limited liability on their investment. It also increases the ability for diversification compared to investors who make their own direct investments.

New investors with a small capital allocation to private equity usually have limited access to high-quality partnership opportunities. Top-tier funds often accept only a limited number of new investors because the current investor base usually continues to increase commitments to the next fund. Many private equity firms have investment size limitations. For example, a middle market fund or an early stage fund may have to limit its size to retain its focus on its market segment.

Investors should understand that they are limited partners who have no discretion over investment decisions. These decisions are left to the general partners, and that is why the track record and potential returns of the part-nership are very important. Additionally, the limited partners have to share investment gains with the general partner.

Typical Private Equity Partnership Investors

Investors who find private equity suitable for their investment needs would include corporate and public pension funds, endowment funds, foundations, insurance companies, banks, foreign investors, wealthy families, and wealthy individual investors. Figure 9.1 illustrates the current investor profile, given estimates based on historical trends reported by Venture Economics, the foremost provider of data to the private equity industry. We can see from the profile that in the year 2000, pension funds comprised 27 percent of the capital provided, with the next largest share comprising 16 pecent provided by individuals and families. Although these numbers may move around from one year to the next, it is clear that pension funds are the dominant investors, and this is expected to continue.

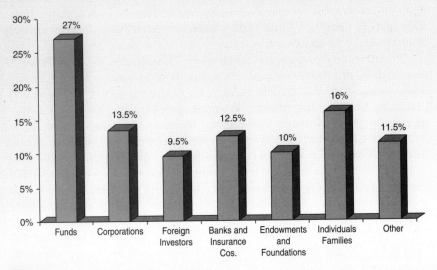

FIGURE 9.1   Investor profile for 2000.

PRIVATE EQUITY FUND OF FUNDS

Many investors may also use a fund of funds approach to develop their private equity investment program. Fund of funds investors usually tend to have a smaller asset base than direct partnership investors and don't have access to the superior performing direct partnerships. They also have limited resources to manage this segment of their portfolio. However, some large investors use selected fund of funds managers to complement their portfolio of direct partnership investments. These investors are effectively outsourcing the management of a segment of their private equity portfolio.

A private equity fund of funds is one way to create a more comprehensive, diversified private equity asset class in your portfolio. With a fund of funds, the manager makes investments in many private equity partnerships. A fund of funds can create a well-diversified portfolio consisting of indirect investments in hundreds of companies representing some or all of the categories of private equity.

Characteristics of Fund of Funds

One of the major advantages of a high-quality private equity fund of funds can be summed up as access to high-quality funds with proven managers, maximum diversification, and cost effectiveness. The major disadvantage to some investors is that there is an additional fee to the fund of funds manager over and above the fees paid to the direct private equity partnership.

The additional fee has to be considered in context. Can the fund of funds provide access to the top quartile of fund investment opportunities? What would be the cost of administering a private equity strategy on your own? Can you hire and *retain* in-house staff that compares favorably with those managers found at the fund of funds partnerships? Only after you consider these issues can you decide whether the additional fee of $3/4$ to $1^1/4$ percent is an appropriate cost. As with all asset management fees, the larger your commitment, the smaller your overall fee. Although 1 to $1^1/4$ percent is a typical fee, total fees can drop to a blended fee of 75 to 85 basis points for a significant investor in a fund of funds.

Access to High-Quality Funds Is Important

A major advantage that experienced fund of funds managers have is the ability to access top-performing, direct-equity partnerships. This access is perhaps most important in creating superior returns for the private equity asset class. If we distinguish between tier one (top quartile firms) and tier two firms, we find that rates of return are wide. This is an extremely important point to consider. In examining Figure 9.2, we can see that between 1969 and 1999, the top quartile partnerships in venture capital and buyouts and all private equity more than doubled the median return. Those partnerships in the lower quartile generated a rate of return less than the Treasury bill rate over the same time period.

Figure 9.2 shows that venture capital funds had the highest performance over this time period, generating 30.5 percent in the top quartile versus a median of 11.6 percent and 2.1 percent in the bottom quartile. The top quartile of buyout funds returned 25.8 percent over this 30-year period, whereas the median returned 11.1 percent and the bottom quartile had no return at all. When we look at all private equity, we see the top quartile returned 27.9 percent; the median was 11.5 percent, and the bottom quartile returned 1.5 percent. If you are going to invest with a fund of funds, make sure they have access to partnerships in the top quartile.

Diversification Benefits for a Fund of Funds

Diversification for a fund of funds is much easier than for an individual partnership. Not only can a fund of funds specify a mix of venture capital, buyout funds, and mezzanine funds, but it also can diversify by industry sector.

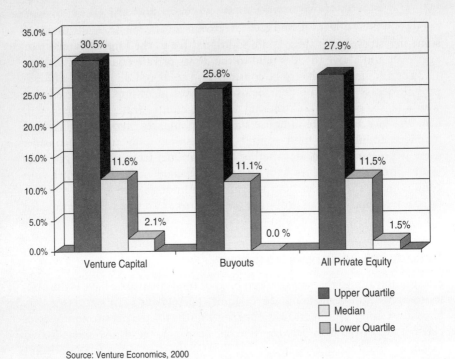

Source: Venture Economics, 2000

FIGURE 9.2 Access to top partnerships is critical (difference between upper and lower quartile performance, 1969 to 1999).

One partnership may specialize in biotechnology, whereas another may focus on computer hardware or software. Each industry sector needs industry analysts and executives with experience in that sector.

There also are a large number of privately owned companies compared to publicly owned companies. Dun & Bradstreet estimates that more than 150,000 companies in the United States have revenues of $10 million or more, and of these about 85 percent are privately owned companies. Watson Wyatt, a consulting firm, estimates that the private equity markets are seven times larger than the public equity markets. That leaves an extremely large number of companies available to private equity investors and provides an opportunity for a diversified portfolio across many different U.S. industries.

Small pension funds or financial institutions investing in a fund of funds can achieve better diversification than they could if they managed their own private equity investments. For example, fund of funds investing in 25 private equity partnerships may have investments in more than 400 private companies, whereas on their own, they could never invest in that many companies. In addition, a large fund of funds probably has more influence with the partnerships than a small investor would have.

Administration and Cost Effectiveness

The minimum investment for a fund of funds catering to institutional investors often starts at $2 million or more; for the most part, fund managers would prefer larger commitments such as $25 million or more. If we take a look at a typical investor, be it a pension fund, endowment, or insurance company, the relevant question is what size does it have to be before it makes sense to manage its own private equity allocation?

Although the minimum cost of entry to establish the proper staffing is important, size may not be the major issue for the potential investor thinking about going it alone. The ability to acquire people with the skills necessary to outperform fund managers who have honed their skills over many years may be difficult. This industry has a steep learning curve, and the potential that new fund managers will make mistakes that penalize their performance always exists. Traditionally, public pension funds have not been able to compete financially for skilled managers with private fund of funds firms. In fact, during the 1990s a flight from public pension funds to private equity funds occurred by managers of alternative investments. So, in the end, a pension fund manager has to decide to either go it alone or engage a fund of funds manager.

PRIVATE EQUITY RETURNS

The returns on private equity fund of funds depend on the composition of the portfolio. Depending upon the diversification and weights assigned to the various categories of private equity, the returns could be quite different. The returns used in this section are from Venture Economics, a well-known source of data on the venture capital industry.

Rate of Return Measures

Although returns for security market portfolios are generally time-weighted to reflect the timing of the cash flow in and out of the portfolio, private equity returns are internal rate of return (IRR) calculations. IRRs are determined by the amount and timing of cash inflows and outflows and include the residual value of investments at the end of the period. IRRs for most private equity partnerships should be expected to be very low, or even negative in the early years of a partnership because value is built up over longer time periods.

Neither the IRR or time-weighted rate of return is a better measure than the other, but they are different enough to make comparisons between securities market returns and private equity returns less than directly comparable. It is important to realize that the returns used for private equity funds are net returns to the limited partners after all management fees and general partners' profit split. Because the life of private equity funds runs 7 to 10 years or more in some cases, returns are also examined for periods of 1 year, 3 years, 5 years, 10 years, and 20 years. If we want to know the cumulative rate of return since inception of the fund, we use the net asset value of the fund as the terminal value or final positive cash flow.

Historical Rate of Return

Table 9.1 shows the performance of private equity funds up to December 31, 2000, over five different time periods. The returns can vary quite a bit from year to year, but our feeling is that, because this is a long-term investment strategy, investors should focus on the 5- to 20-year returns rather than on the volatile 1-year returns. When the public markets are strong and stock indexes, such as the NASDAQ Composite and Russell 2000 Index of small-cap companies, are at high levels, IPOs are met with enthusiasm and values of companies going public are high. For example, the year 1999 had some record IPO prices for companies going public in the telecommunications, Internet, and other technology areas.

One thing that stands out in Table 9.1 is the stability of returns for private equity compared to the returns for venture capital. Notice the high variability of returns for venture capital as opposed to buyout funds and mezzanine debt. This one-year return phenomenon is even more pronounced in early-stage venture capital than any of the other categories. Extremely high returns in one year can create an upward bias in the long-term average returns.

Although the long-term returns are not that much different for venture capital versus private equity, the standard deviation of returns for venture capital is much higher than the standard deviation for private equity. The lower standard deviation for private equity reflects the lower risk achieved by including venture capital, buyout funds, and mezzanine debt in a private equity portfolio. Buyout funds have very low correlation to venture capital, and their inclusion in the portfolio lowers the standard deviation of returns.

Even though private equity funds take a long-term view of creating value, the whims and tastes of the public market affect the capital flows into the industry and the ability of the partnership to exit its investments at high valuations. Returns are based on the ability to exit the investment at the right time or at high valuations. The stock markets of 1999 and early 2000 made exits through IPOs very rewarding, but by April 2000, the stock market bubble had burst and IPOs dried up well into the first quarter of 2002.

Returns for Hypothetical Portfolio Mixes

As we stated earlier, it is difficult to compare returns for private equity fund of funds because of the various weights allocated to the different strategies and sectors. No two fund of funds are exactly the same because the percentage of assets a manager may allocate to any one category will not be equal. Weighting the categories is not a science. The weights that managers assign to their fund of funds categories will be based on future expectations of market returns for each category and the risk/return tradeoffs that managers make in structuring their fund of funds portfolio. Managers rely on their experience and research skills to choose the weights for their portfolios.

Let's look at a matrix of possible returns based on data previously shown in this chapter. Using data from Table 9.1, we construct three different hypothetical portfolios in Table 9.2 based on 10-year returns with the five categories weighted differently. In Fund of Funds AAA the managers choose to place more money in buyout and mezzanine debt and less money in venture capital. Fund of Funds BBB takes an equal-weighted approach to the five

TABLE 9.1 Performance of Private Equity Funds (as of December 31, 2000)

Fund Type	Net IRR to Investors for Investment Horizon* Ending 12/31/00 for Private Equity Funds				
	1YR	3YR	5YR	10YR	20YR
Early/Seed VC	40.7	89.4	63.5	35.1	23.5
Balanced VC	33.3	61.3	42.7	26.8	17.4
Later Stage Focused	18.3	31.0	30.8	25.0	18.1
All Venture	32.5	62.5	46.8	29.4	19.6
Buyout Funds	11.2	14.7	17.4	16.5	18.5
Mezzanine Debt	15.7	11.1	11.6	12.6	11.9
All Private Equity	19.0	30.1	28.1	22.0	19.2

*Net to investors after fees and profit split
Source: Venture Economics/National Venture Capital Association

TABLE 9.2 Hypothetical Portfolio Returns for Various Weightings

Type of Investment	Data from Table 3 10-Year Returns	Fund of Fund AAA Weights	Fund of Fund AAA Returns	Fund of Fund BBB Weights	Fund of Fund BBB Returns	Fund of Fund CCC Weights	Fund of Fund CCC Returns
Early/Seed Focused	35.10%	0.05	1.76%	0.20	7.02%	0.30	10.53%
Balanced Focused	26.80%	0.25	6.70%	0.20	5.36%	0.30	8.04%
Later Stage Focused	25.00%	0.20	5.00%	0.20	5.00%	0.20	5.00%
Buyout Funds	16.50%	0.25	4.13%	0.20	3.30%	0.10	1.65%
Mezzanine Debt	12.60%	0.25	3.15%	0.20	2.52%	0.10	1.26%
Hypothetical Portfolio Returns for Various Weightings			20.73%		23.20%		26.48%

Data for 10-year returns from Venture Economics/National Venture Capital Association categories. Fund of Funds CCC chooses to allocate more money to venture capital, especially Early/Seed Focused and Balanced Focused, and less to Buyouts and Mezzanine. All three firms choose the same allocation to Later Stage Focused.

Over this 10-year time period we can see that the allocations make a big difference in returns. Fund CCC outperforms Fund BBB by 3.28 percent, and Fund BBB outperforms Fund AAA by 2.47 percent. Fund CCC outperforms Fund AAA by 5.75 percent. This hypothetical example demonstrates why it is difficult to compare returns for different fund of funds.

One could argue that, if we could find fund of funds that allocated their assets equally their returns would be comparable. Even this is not true because the returns of each partnership may not be at the average assumed in Table 9.2. What if we take three funds, use data from Figure 9.2 shown earlier, and assume that one fund of funds has access to managers that perform in the top quartile, another in the middle quartile, and another in the bottom quartile? What would the returns look like in this case?

If you return to Figure 9.2, you can see that for all private equity the top quartile returned 27.9 percent for the 30-year period 1969 to 1999, the median return was 11.5 percent, and the lower quartile was 1.5 percent. Fund of fund returns are a function of two variables: (1) access to superior fund managers and (2) the weights applied to various categories of private equity.

Perhaps this hypothetical example also demonstrates why Mesirow Financial thinks that fund of funds should be fully diversified at all times and should not play the timing game and place big bets on individual categories. Investors should be using fund of funds for diversification with traditional assets.

MEANINGFUL ALLOCATION TO PRIVATE EQUITY ASSET CLASS

What percentage of your portfolio should be allocated to private equity? One of the traps that investors fall into is the unwillingness to allocate a large enough percentage of the portfolio to private equity capital to influence the return on the entire portfolio? A 1999 report by Goldman Sachs and Frank Russell Company examined corporate and public pension funds. Corporate pension funds allocated 7.3 percent of their portfolio to private equity, and public pension funds allocated 5.6 percent of their portfolio to private equity.

Private equity falls into the category of alternative investments for many pension funds. This category also includes real estate and foreign securities. Some pension funds create a separate allocation to foreign investing, and others don't. The problem in any portfolio is that if the portfolio manager allocates only 1 percent to an asset class and the returns are 200 percent, the asset class doesn't really increase total portfolio returns by enough to make that 1 percent allocation meaningful. We would suggest that a minimum allocation to private equity would be 3 to 8 percent. One of the problems during the 1990s was that private equity performance was so strong, relative to other asset classes, that private equity moved to the upper bound of allowable allocations for many pension funds, and they couldn't even reinvest their capital distributions in this asset class. The percentage allocated to private equity cannot be considered in a vacuum. You must also consider what private equity does to reduce the overall risk of your portfolio.

RISK ATTRIBUTES OF PRIVATE EQUITY

Several risk attributes must be considered when investing in private equity. First, private equity is not highly correlated to many other asset classes found in most institutional portfolios. Second, because private equity has a long-term focus, liquidity is a risk that must also be considered. Exit strategies can affect the return, the liquidity, and the ability to reinvest capital in a timely manner.

Risk Reduction through Diversification

Private equity as an asset class generally has a low correlation to other assets. Using Venture Economics data for 10 years ending March 2000, we get the correlations depicted in Figure 9.3. When we look at the two categories of venture capital and buyouts and the combined category of all private equity, we get quite different correlations. Buyouts in general have a lower correlation than venture capital. When buyouts and venture capital are combined into all private equity, the resulting correlation to all other assets in Figure 9.3 is less than 0.5.

All three categories (venture capital, buyouts, and all private equity) are negatively correlated to 90-day Treasury bills and the Lehman Brothers Aggregate Bond Index. A security with negative correlation to a portfolio will reduce significantly the total portfolio risk when added to that portfolio. Buyouts have a very low correlation to all the other asset classes found in Figure 9.3, being the most highly correlated to the Russell 2000 Growth Index with a correlation of 0.18. The other asset classes in Figure 9.3 also include high-yield bonds, real estate investment trusts, Morgan Stanley Capital International's European, Asian, and Far East Index (EAFE), the

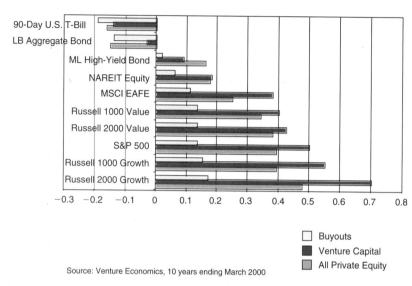

Source: Venture Economics, 10 years ending March 2000

- ☐ Buyouts
- ◼ Venture Capital
- ▨ All Private Equity

FIGURE 9.3 Low correlation to other classes.

Russell 1000 Large-Cap Index, the Russell 2000 Small-Cap Index, the Standard & Poor's 500 Index, and the Russell 1000 Growth Index.

Although venture capital is also negatively correlated with 90-day Treasury bills and the Lehman Brothers Aggregate Bond Index, it is much more highly correlated to the other asset classes than the buyout category. Venture capital is 40 percent correlated to the Russell 1000 Large-Cap Index. A correlation of 0.40 will still achieve a significant reduction in the overall risk when added to a portfolio of large-cap common stocks. If a large enough allocation were made to venture capital, the standard deviation of returns of the total portfolio would be reduced.

It is interesting but not surprising that venture capital is most highly correlated to small-cap, mid-cap, and large-cap growth stocks as represented by the Russell 1000 Growth Index and the Russell 2000 Growth Index. After all, returns on venture capital companies are linked to the new issues market. When the returns on publicly traded growth stocks are high, venture capitalists are able to sell IPOs from their portfolio of investments. We must point out, however, that the highest correlation of 0.70 for venture capital to the Russell 2000 Growth Index will still reduce the risk if added to a growth stock portfolio.

The very significant point that comes from the correlations in Figure 9.3 is that it reinforces what we know from modern portfolio theory about diversification. Modern portfolio theory tells us that risky assets can be combined into a portfolio and reduce risk in that portfolio if the assets are correlated at less than one. The lower the correlation, the better the total risk reduction. Clearly, a fund of funds that invests in buyouts and venture capital could be added to a traditional portfolio of stocks and bonds and reduce the risk (standard deviation of returns) while enhancing the overall portfolio returns. If the correlation between these assets is stable over time, it would make sense to have both buyouts and venture capital in the portfolio through a fund of funds strategy.

LIQUIDITY AND THE SELF-LIQUIDATING PROCESS

Private equity partnerships are formed with the understanding that the partners will contribute cash to the partnership on an as-needed basis. The limited partners put no money down but make a commitment that, as investments are made and capital is called, they will deliver the capital within 10 days. Depending on the economic environment and the ability of the partnership to find suitable investments, the capital investment process can take two to three years with occasional capital calls occurring in the fourth year.

This is demonstrated in Figure 9.4, which depicts a hypothetical estimate of the typical cash flow pattern on a $20 million investment into a fund of funds. Notice that even though a small investment is made in year one, it may be possible that some cash distributions may occur in year two even as the partner is contributing more capital. Eventually, the capital contributions end in year four and the distributions continue until year 13. The figure shows cumulative contributions and cumulative distributions. The self-liquidating process as depicted in Figure 9.4 depends on the available exit strategies of each partnership. The exit could be an IPO, a merger/acquisition, or a buyback.

COSTS OF INVESTING IN PRIVATE EQUITY FUND OF FUNDS

Fees for private equity fund of funds generally have three components:

- A management fee
- A carried interest
- A hurdle rate

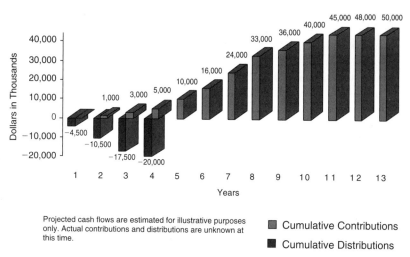

FIGURE 9.4 Cash flow commitment ($20MM commitment).

The management fee is assessed to investors based on the amount of capital they have committed to the fund. Although the fee generally ranges from 0.75 to 1.25 percent, the median and average fee is 1 percent. Slight differences depend on the type of organization running the fund of funds and the makeup of the clients. In general, high net worth individuals pay a slightly higher fee than large institutional investors do, and they occasionally have to pay a placement fee to enter the fund. This may occur because institutional investors have more bargaining power and alternatives than individuals. The management fee charged to limited partners is the same for all clients making equal dollar commitments, but the fund manager has the ability to discount the fee to investors making a large commitment to the fund.

In addition to the 1 percent management fee, some funds charge a *carried interest* fee: in other words, a percentage of the profits. According to Asset Alternatives Inc., about two-thirds of fund of funds in their survey charged a carried interest, with the median being 5 percent of profits and the average being 6.78 percent. Because fund of funds partnerships invest in private equity partnerships that charge a carried interest, it doesn't make much sense to the limited partners in a fund of funds to add a second carried interest on top of their management fee. This behavior will reduce returns to the limited partners and will not induce higher returns from the fund of funds because they have no control over the portfolio companies in which their private equity partnerships invest.

We would not recommend paying a carried interest, but if one is required, the limited partner should make sure a *hurdle rate*—minimum rate of return—is included. Most fund of funds that do charge a carried interest have to generate a hurdle rate before the carried interest goes into effect. In the Asset Alternatives Inc. survey, the hurdle rates are clustered between 8 and 10 percent, but a good number of funds operate with a 15 percent hurdle rate. Hurdle rates can protect an investor's carried interest fee when returns are less than the minimum required return. On the other hand, any fee will lower the rate of return to the investor. Carried interest fees, even with hurdle rates, may only be worth paying for those funds that have demonstrated a capability to access the top quartile of direct private equity partnerships.

ADMINISTRATIVE RESPONSIBILITIES

The general partner manages the assets of the fund of funds and issues quarterly and annual reports describing the activities and performance of the fund of funds' portfolio. Table 9.3 is an example of the normal reporting process and the timeline that exists because of the two layers of partnerships—the direct private equity partnership and the fund of funds partnership.

The quarterly and annual reports from the direct private equity partnership managers generally include the following items:

- News highlights of the activities of the partnership
- Unaudited financial statements of the partnership
- Capital account report showing the fund of funds' investment value
- Summary of portfolio company investments
- Schedule K-1 for tax reporting (annual)
- Audited financial statements (annual)

In addition to reporting responsibilities, the general partner manages the assets of the fund of funds. Assets may include cash on hand, partnership investments, and public or private stock securities received as distributions from the partnerships. The general partner manages the cash, trading, and contractual activities of the fund of funds. These activities include execution of partnership agreements and related documents for investment in the direct private equity partnerships, responding to amendments and special requests by the partnerships, and the handling of capital calls and distributions (cash and stock) of the partnerships. It is the general partner's responsibility to administer the activities of the fund of funds in the best interest of all partners.

Care must be taken to ensure efficient handling of cash and dissemination of information. Timely capital calls and distributions plus adequate reporting reassure the limited partners that the fund of funds is well run.

REGULATORY AND TAX ISSUES

Securities Laws

Limited partnership interests in a private equity fund of funds are generally not public offerings of securities and, therefore, are not registered under the Securities Act or the securities laws of any state, relying instead upon exemptions from registration available for non-public offerings. The investors or limited partners, however, must meet certain qualifications to invest, thus preserving the fund's exempt status. Limited partners may be accredited investors or qualified purchasers. Up to 99 accredited investors or up to 499 qualified purchasers are allowed in any one fund.

If investment is made by parties subject to the Employment Retirement Income Security Act (ERISA) or a comparable state regulation, as corporate and government pension plans generally are, limitations may be placed on the conduct and operations of the fund of funds as the fund would be deemed to hold plan assets. In this case, the general partner of the fund must provide an investment manager that is registered as an investment adviser under the Investment Advisers Act of 1940 to perform as fiduciary to the fund.

TABLE 9.3 Reporting Process

Report as of	Direct Private Equity Partnership Reports Received	Fund of Funds Report Issued
Quarter ended March	May	June
Quarter ended June	August	September
Quarter ended September	November	December
Year ended December	April	May

Federal Income Tax Considerations

As a general rule, the tax considerations relevant to each specific partner depend upon their individual circumstances. Because a fund of funds is usually formed as a limited partnership, the fund serves as a pass-through entity for the partners. A limited partnership's taxable income, gain and loss are not recognized at the partnership level but are passed on to all partners of the fund.

State and Local Tax Considerations

Partners may become subject to state and local income or franchise taxes in the jurisdictions in which a fund acquires real estate or otherwise is considered to be engaged in a trade or business and may be required to file appropriate returns.

DATABASES

The securities industry has numerous providers of data, but several specialize in providing information about the venture capital and private equity industry. Venture Economics, a division of Securities Data Co., is perhaps the foremost provider of data to the industry. It partners with the National Association of Venture Capital to produce an annual yearbook as well as computerized industry databases. Asset Alternatives Inc. is another provider of data, newsletters, directories, and research reports. Frank Russell Company also publishes data on alternative investments.

Asset Alternatives Inc.
170 Linden Street, Second Floor
Wellesley, MA 02482-7919
www.assetnews.com

Venture Economics, Inc.
41 Farnsworth Street
Boston, MA 022210-1223

A Division of Securities Data Co.
Frank Russell Company
1313 Broadway Plaza
Tacoma, WA 98401

REFERENCES

Galuhn, Thomas and Paul Rice, internal documents from Mesirow Financial Private Equity Division.

National Venture Capital Association Yearbook 2000. Boston: Venture Economics, 2000.

Pease, Robert. *Private Equity Funds of Funds, State of the Market.* Wellesley, MA: Asset Alternatives Inc., 2000.

CHAPTER 10

Microcap Stocks

**By John R. Lefebvre, Jr.
and Ralph A. Rieves**

Microcap, one of the newest terms in the language of investing, refers to stocks with market capitalizations of less than $250 million that have attracted renewed interest because of the burgeoning of IPOs and the refinement of market systems for trading smaller capitalized stocks.

INTRODUCTION

The increase in the issues of emerging company stocks since 1996 has regenerated interest in these smallest capitalized equity issues. Some academics and investment professionals have argued that the risk/return characteristics of these microcaps qualify them as distinct alternatives and portfolio enhancements to large market cap investment programs.

The purpose of this chapter is to revisit that argument. We will also discuss whether new market structures and recent regulations have changed how these stocks are valued, issued, and traded. In the course of this discussion, we will touch on that most sensitive issue of modern investment theory: investment manager skill.

NEWEST ALTERNATIVE

Microcap is one of the newest terms in the language of investing. The authors first encountered the word when it was used by John Marquise (founder of the American Association of Individual Investors) on "Adam Smith's" Money World in 1996. The first conference for institutional investors on these stocks was also held in 1996. The term is so new that there is more than one accepted spelling. We use the spelling that has been consistently used by the Bloomberg Press, a division of the financial data and common-actions company, Bloomberg, L. P.

We accept the Frank Russell Company classification of microcap stocks as those having market capitalizations of less than $250 million. The median market cap for this category is $120 million. The focus of this chapter is only on the stocks of emerging companies in the United States, the micro-cap growth stocks. The equities of "reemerging" microcap stocks are most likely to have the characteristics of the distressed securities discussed in the chapter on this topic in this book.

We have also omitted from this chapter the over-the-counter bulletin board (OTCBB) stocks. We consider these speculative stocks inappropriate for any reasoned investment strategy.

EVOLUTION OF MICROCAP GROWTH INVESTING

Among the many changes and events occurring in the capital markets in the 1990s, two factors created the renewed interest in this unique class of common stocks: (1) the burgeoning of initial public offerings (IPOs) and (2) the refinement of market systems for trading smaller capitalized stocks.

Burgeoning IPOs

A convergence of situations and events in the 1990s created one of the most favorable environments for investing in stocks in the history of capital markets. This happy set of circumstances has been the subject of hundreds of articles and, recently, dozens of books. Key factors were the demand for stocks and stock funds by members of defined contribution retirement plans, a reduction in capital gains taxes, and low inflation rates. What distinguished that bull market from previous sustained periods of enthusiasm was the great demand for small-capitalization stocks.

The rapid advances in information and biological technology were being created, for the most part, among small groups of academics, innovators, and inventors. Few were working within the confines of the established corporations that have been the dominant forces in business and industry. These new enterprises needed capital. Because there were increasing demands for new investment opportunities, the time was right for acquiring capital. Most of the capital was acquired from venture investors whose aims were to eventually take the firms public for more money than they put up. Recent history records that many of those companies did go public, resulting in an exploding secondary market for those companies' stocks.

New and Improved Market Systems

The National Association of Securities Dealers Automated Quotations (Nasdaq) system was established in 1971. It quickly became the predominant negotiated marketplace for stocks. The success of the system required continued refinements. In 1982 the National Market System evolved from the original structure to facilitate the trading of stocks of emerging companies that met certain requirements.

The American Stock Exchange (AMEX) also provided the opportunity to selected emerging companies to list their securities if they met the same standards. In addition to meeting these standards, companies were required to follow the filing and disclosure dictates of the Securities and Exchange Commission (SEC) with respect to financial information.

Investors now had marketplaces in which they could trade the smaller capitalized stocks of these emerging companies. They were also assured that the financial information about these companies would be available as readily as the information about the larger capitalized issues. Because seasoned stocks of the established companies were trading at record highs in the late 1990s, investors had to look at the stocks of these newer and smaller companies for the prospects of higher returns.

The demand for these stocks drove their prices up and attracted more money. Thus, an alternative to seasoned equities evolved for institutional investors. The dramatic increase in microcap investing among the professional investors raised the question about whether the historical risk/return relationships were still appropriate for measuring the performance of these particular equities.

MICROCAP RISK AND RETURN

The fact that dividends are not a factor simplifies our discussion about the returns from microcap stocks.

On the most commonly used graph that plots risk and return for common stocks, analysts sometimes like to divide the graph into four equal compass quadrants. Microcap equities are unquestionably found in the "Northeast" quadrant (see Figure 10.1). If Figure 10.1 were an approximation of a map of the continental United States, the argument would be whether these stocks are clustered around Albany, New York, or Bangor, Maine. This depends on what issues are included in the category. If one includes the most recent Center for Research in Securities Prices (CRSP) data for their deciles 9 and 10, then Bangor is the spot. The CRSP deciles are created by taking all of the New York Stock Exchange (NYSE) stocks (other than ADRs, REITs, and closed-end funds) and dividing them into 10 groups ranked by market cap. Decile "1" is composed of the largest companies. The AMEX and Nasdaq stocks are then added to the appropriate deciles.

If one were to segment deciles 9 and 10 into the style classes of growth or value, then the microcap growth stocks are likely to be clustered northeast of Bangor, and the value microcap stocks would likely be clustered somewhere closer to Albany. We have used the imprecise term "likely" because categorizing and characterizing the risk and reward relationships among microcap stocks is a very recent research activity. Academics and investment managers are revisiting the research because of the emergence of all those listed microcap stocks in the 1990s. The research activity has been complicated by the changing market valuations that have occurred since the fall of 2000 and by the effects of new regulations governing trading and reporting.

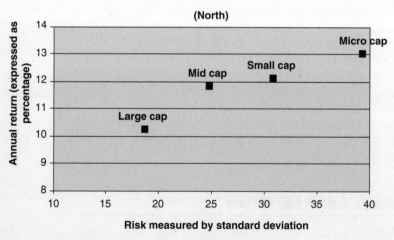

Source: Ibbotson Associates/The Emerging Companies Research Institute

FIGURE 10.1 Risk and return over 14 years (period ending Dec. 31, 1998).

Revisiting The Research

In the late 1970s, Rolf W. Banz at the University of Chicago began studying the returns of stocks based on their market capitalization. His research suggested that, even after adjusting for risk, small company stocks seemed to do better than the stocks of large companies. Banz and Marc R. Reinganum subsequently published papers in the March 1981 issue of the *Journal of Financial Economics*[1,2] that argued that those stocks in the smallest cap CRSP deciles generated returns more than 5 percent higher than returns of the larger cap stocks over the same periods. They construed this excess return as the risk premium for holding the smaller capitalized stocks. This observation was discussed among academics in the context of the Capital Asset Pricing Model (CAPM) and became known as the size effect.

The risk/return aspects of the size effect have been debated frequently over the last 20 years. There is always the question of the actual costs of buying or selling the smallest capitalized stocks. These thinly issued stocks are in relatively short supply, and an investor is always at a disadvantage when posting a buy or sell order for one of these stocks. Critics of the conclusions of the size effect postulate argue that these inherent transaction costs cancel out any supposed risk premium.

Transaction Costs

It is undisputed that the costs of transactions involving the smallest cap stocks are much higher than costs associated with the trading of the larger cap stocks. Not only market cap size but also investment manager style will impact transaction costs. Other than brokerage commissions, what other transaction costs are there? Wayne Wagner and Steven Glass of The Plexus Group, a Los Angeles research and consulting firm, identified and explained those other transaction costs in an article in *The Journal of Investment Consulting*[3]:

- Market impact cost is measured by taking the difference in the quoted price of a stock when the manager placed an order and when the order was executed.
- Delay cost occurs when the investor tries to wait for the "best price" to make a trade with someone who is monitoring the stock closely. The odds are about even that the experienced investor or trader will not get a better price. In the worst case, the order gets canceled.
- Opportunity cost is the extreme of the delay cost. This is the cost of missing out or just partially covering the order.

TABLE 10.1 Cost Patterns by Manager Style

| Style | Cost Components (in Basis Points) | | | | | |
	Delay (Manager Timing)	Delay (Trader Timing)	Market Impact	Commission	Opportunity (Missed Trades)	Total
Large cap value	1	13	8	15	28	65
Large cap growth	82	32	21	10	14	159
Index/passive	31	61	25	9	12	138
Small cap value	5	63	40	20	32	160
Small cap growth	136	72	57	18	29	312

Source: Plexus Group

These costs, as they relate to market cap and style strategies, are summarized in Table 10.1 with the cost components computed in basis points (one basis point is equal to 0.01 percent). Growth style managers investing in small cap companies encounter higher transaction costs than any other investment style, and microcap growth managers face the highest costs of all. (Plexus Group has developed an inclusive transaction cost database and some internally generated benchmarks. Readers who require extensive and refined cost data should visit **www.plexusgroup.com** to find out how this data can be obtained.)

This table compares the average transaction costs (in basis points) incurred with respect to manager styles. Note the range of average costs across these styles. Not surprisingly, large cap value managers (who are shoppers by definition) enjoy a trading costs advantage. The higher costs incurred by large cap growth managers reflect their reactions to news and recommendations. Indexers will incur most of their costs at the trading desk. Small cap value and growth managers will always encounter higher costs because of the problems associated with lesser liquidity.

Survivorship Bias

In addition to the transaction cost argument, there is also a survivorship bias in the discussion of the size effect, just as there is when discussing investment manager performance. CRSP appears to ignore delisted stocks when making its calculations. The omission of the delisted stocks misstates relative performance figures.

REVISITING THE DIVERSIFICATION ARGUMENT

Microcap enthusiasts argue that most microcap stocks are inefficiently priced almost all the time; therefore, they reason that these stocks provide real diversification in a stock portfolio of different market caps. This presupposes some significant variance in market performance from the larger cap stocks. Is there any evidence of this for just microcap growth stocks? How valid is the evidence over several market cycles and macroeconomic cycles? Does past performance guarantee anything, particularly in the light of recent regulations governing financial disclosure and dictating trading procedures?

For the 30-year period ending December 30, 2000, small company stocks (CRSP deciles 6 through 10) returned 150 basis points over the stocks of the large companies (CRSP deciles 1 through 5), including reinvested dividends but not before transaction costs. One can therefore infer that the absolute returns difference could be negligible.

For the 25-year period ending December 31, 1998, CRSP 9 and 10 had an annual return of 13.8 percent. The S&P 500 Index annual return over the same period was 12.3 percent. Again, the difference was in favor of the smallest stock issues by 150 basis points, including reinvested dividends, but not before transactions costs.

Only when the comparisons are broken down into smaller time segments does the argument for cap size diversification appear to have merit (see Table 10.2).

TABLE 10.2 Comparison of Returns Between CRSP Deciles 1/2 and 9/10 Over Market Cycles from 1969 to 1999

Time Period	Returns from Deciles 1/2	Returns from Deciles 9/10	The Better Return by Percentage Points
1969–1974	−17%	−70%	Deciles 1/2 by 53%
1975–1983	+247.5%	+1,197.5%	Deciles 9/10 by 950%
1984–1990	+159%	−15%	Deciles 1/2 by 174%
1991–1994	+52%	+127.5%	Deciles 9/10 by 75.5%
1995–1999	+201%	+80%	Deciles 1/2 by 121%

Source: The Emerging Companies Research Institute using data from The Center for Research in Securities Prices.

There is almost no research available on what caused this divergence, but some observations about the behavior of investors and the nature of microcap stocks may help explain some of the performance. Microcaps are the last stocks to move in the direction of a market cycle. They will be the last stocks to rally because investors turn to microcaps when they suspect that the higher caps are becoming overvalued. They are the last stocks to be sold in a major downturn because investors are loath to sell their less liquid stocks in the face of a buyer's market. As Daniel P. Coker points out in his excellent book, this late-in-the-cycle downturn " . . . is due more to avoidance than to actual selling . . ."[4]

Alert readers will note that the relative performance periods in Table 10.2 are of unequal length. This is an attempt to smooth out those periodic "bursts" of extreme highs and lows that have occurred in the overall U.S. market from 1969 through 1999.

Some readers will want to deconstruct these performance periods to determine the existence of an alleged anomaly known as the "January Effect," wherein small cap stocks go up every January. Don't waste your time. If there were such a distinct pattern, it hasn't existed for the last decade. There is no "January Effect." None. End of discussion.

Critical readers will point out that, because of disparate market caps and share floats, it would be difficult to proportion a portfolio equally between microcaps and larger cap stocks—and impossible to shift funds from one class to another. They are correct. The strategic use of microcaps therefore is to allocate a relatively small proportion of microcap holdings within a diversified investment program. The degree of that proportion depends on each investor's risk tolerance, and you have to remember high transaction costs when you want to rebalance. Never try to be market timer or a "style tilter." Never.

Critical and alert readers will point out that the CRSP data is for all stocks, and there is no breakdown between value stocks and those stocks we set out to discuss: microcap growth stocks. Where are the data and the indexes with respect to investment styles? What are the best index funds if we want to use them instead of stocks in our allocation strategy?

MICROCAP SEGMENTATION AND BENCHMARKS

Microcaps command very little attention from that largest of institutional pools, public, and private defined-benefit pension plans. Consequently, consultants, investment managers, or brokers have not been motivated to underwrite or undertake any sustained compilation of segmented microcap benchmarks. There have been attempts by some Web sites to construct microcap growth stock indexes. They have not been successful. Delistings and bankruptcies compounded the difficulties in developing a representative group of stocks in any meaningful and representative quantity.

Experienced microcap investors will tell you that most microcap stocks are considered growth stocks. They have discovered that the small number of value plays are really a variation on vulture investing. The other micro-cap issues either demonstrate sustained growth or they fail. So a benchmark comprised of all microcaps is a close proxy for microcap growth stocks (allowing for some survivorship bias). Does such a benchmark exist?

Less than 10 percent of the companies comprising the Russell 2,000 Index fall into the CRSP 9 and 10 deciles. The only near aggregate available for benchmarking is the Dimensional Fund Advisors mutual fund, the DFA 9 to 10 Small Company Fund. This fund invests in the smallest 20 percent of all publicly traded stocks, approximating the stocks in the CRSP 9 to 10. The fund's median market cap runs less than $130 million. It is not, however, a true index fund. The fund has some latitude in which stocks it buys and sells within the 9 to 10 universe. The fund is intended for major institutional investors who want an efficient means with which to capture size effect. The minimum purchase is $2 million.

There is no readily available microcap benchmark for the individual investor. This is not necessarily a disappointing state of affairs. There would be a dilemma for an investor in a benchmarked microcap fund. In a true index fund, stocks would get sold out of the portfolio once their market cap outgrew the micro stage. The fund could be subject to a lot of turnover and the related transaction costs. Most important, though, the investor would miss out on any subsequent increases in value of the stocks sold.

The alert and critical readers are now questioning the relevancy of this benchmark talk. "If the whole point of this chapter is a discussion of the relative performance and divergence between microcaps and large caps, why waste any more time talking about benchmarks that don't exist?" They're right again. We should discuss more pertinent systemic issues such as recent SEC regulations and their impact.

RECENT REGULATORY IMPACT

The adage about past performance is relevant to the discussions in this chapter but not just in the usual "mean reversion" context. Investment professionals now are working in an environment that has been changed fundamentally. Recent regulations are having a critical impact on the manner in which equities are traded and valued, particularly microcaps.

Where Are the Market Makers?

The SEC issued a new set of rules in 1997 that changed the way orders were handled by the Nasdaq systems. The rules were intended to correct some practices that were allegedly increasing investors' trading costs. After the new rules were implemented, securities dealers who had provided the liquidity with their trading desks soon discovered that it was impossible to make any money trading the smallest of caps under the new rules. These securities dealers subsequently shut down their trading operations and ceased making "retail" markets in the Nasdaq Small Cap Issues system.

A few large (extremely well-capitalized) dealer firms had been functioning as warehousing wholesalers to the smaller dealers. When those dealers ceased making markets, the wholesalers became the only game in town. The new rules didn't permit those few large dealers to make any money on transactions either. However, these firms may have found a better way to make money from their well-capitalized advantage: They can glean information from the flow of all those buy and sell orders that come to them.

There is now an oligopolic structure standing astride the Nasdaq Small Cap Issues system that is not providing the necessary liquidity for that system's listed stocks. Investment bankers who underwrite IPOs that would have been listed on the Small Cap Issues system are now arranging to have those stocks listed on the AMEX. There also have been many instances wherein companies have left the Small Cap System for the AMEX.

Conventional wisdom has held that the auction markets (exchange floors) exist for seasoned (higher capitalized) issues and that negotiated markets have accommodated the smaller publicly listed issues. Such arrangements are no longer the case. Will the move toward trading qualified microcaps on the AMEX enhance their liquidity and reduce transaction costs? Will another exchange decide to challenge the AMEX microcap franchise? For investors interested in microcap growth stocks as alternative investments, these questions are relevant, pertinent, and crucial.

Regulation FD

In October 2000, the SEC instituted a new rule governing the disclosure by corporations of their operating and financial information: Regulation fair disclosure (FD). This new rule is a deliberate effort by the SEC to "level the playing field" for individuals and institutions.

Regulation FD was a response to the practice of issuers selectively sharing material, nonpublic information with certain institutional clients and analysts before disseminating their findings to the public at large. This practice was thought to put all excluded investors at a disadvantage.

Regulation FD requires that, when a public company has material, non-public information to discuss in a selective forum, it must first disclose that information publicly through a news release, an 8-K filing, or simultaneously through a fully accessible, nonexclusionary Webcast or telephonic means. Not surprisingly, Regulation FD has had some unforeseen consequences with respect to fundamental research conducted by individual investors and buy-side investment managers who use a "pick-and-shovel" approach to security analysis.

When a diligent money manager or enterprising individual calls a company to confirm some material information obtained through the investor's own initiative, the company response is: "Our lawyers told us we can't respond to your question until we disclose our complete response through a fully accessible medium. Sorry, goodbye." From conversations with several microcap investment managers, we have confirmed that this response, or a paraphrase, is always the case. From conversations with some of the top securities lawyers in the nation, we have learned that this response is the most appropriate. No guidance from the target company, however indirect, is advisable. This prevailing condition leaves the diligent investor with two alternatives: (1) sustained queries among the target company's suppliers, customers, distributors, and competitors or (2) "the hell with 'em."

The sustained queries become indirect, but identifiable, additional costs of investing—the unintended consequence of a well-intentioned mandate. The alternative response could result in an opportunity cost. The microcap market is inherently imperfect because information within this area of investment activity is not widely disseminated. Regulation FD compounds this situation. Indisputably, investor skill has become a more significant factor. Tenacious research is a comparative and competitive advantage.

SECURITY ANALYSIS

Up to this point we have discussed microcap growth stocks in the context of market risk. The critical features in any portfolio are the risks specific to each of the companies whose stocks are owned. Not too long ago, vigorous debates about the valuations of emerging company stocks dominated the financial news. When reviewing the comments by market professionals and academics about this matter, one can come to either of two conclusions: (1) Each party had a responsible point of view, or (2) some of the debaters didn't have a clue. In our opinion some of the most responsible arguments are those of Baruch Lev, who teaches at the Stern School of Business at New York University (NYU), Robert G. Eccles of Advisory Capital Partners in Jupiter, Florida, and Andy Kessler, a partner at Velocity Capital Management in Palo Alto, California.

Arguments withstanding or not, microcap investors should begin their due diligence by studying the operating, financial, and accounting measures that are the practical day-to-day concerns about the specific risks of owning microcap growth stocks. We will discuss qualitative aspects at the end of this section.

The Income Statement

The most frequently mentioned valuation measure in the popular media is earnings. No experienced investor accepts earnings as a "first-cut" measure of appeal, regardless of the size of the subject stock's market cap. The experienced response is always, "How were the earnings computed?" This quality of earnings issue will be discussed but not in the context of earnings per share (EPS).

Earnings measured in shares outstanding of an emerging company's stock are not relevant to meaningful analysis. An emerging company has a relatively small number of equity shares outstanding, (and an even smaller proportion in the float). So, what if an increase in the number of outstanding shares would decrease EPS? It's the earnings and their sustainability that count. An increase in the float (such as from exercised options) will always enhance the appeal of a microcap stock due to increased liquidity, and so would an increase in the shares authorized for public trading.

There are two concerns with respect to microcap company earnings: Can an increase in earnings be sustained? How were the earnings computed?

With respect to sustaining earnings, here are two typical comments from money managers about any report of a decrease in earnings by a microcap company:

1. "Don't tell me that a microcap company can have a bad quarter once in a while and then bounce back. Phooey! When a company's profits turn south, it takes a long time to reverse course."
2. "An earnings surprise in a microcap stock is the beginning of a long period of underperformance—maybe the beginning of the end."

Whether or not you subscribe to such severe interpretations, the fact that others do creates a substantial headwind for a buy decision. Hurray for you contrarians! Just don't underestimate the effects of consensus risk.

The "quality of earnings" issue is the other concern in the analysis of an emerging company. Yes, there is always the probability of some chicanery in a company's financial reporting, but that probability is of relatively small concern. Ninety-nine percent of listed emerging companies won't engage in it for the same reasons that 99 percent of the higher capitalized companies won't. The consequences from having the abuses being discovered are too severe.

Time spent trying to detect crime puts the investor/analyst at a severe cost disadvantage. Just focus on the presentations in the SEC forms 10-Q and 10-K. The methods permitted for the reporting of revenues and expenses will provide challenge enough.

Revenues In July 2000, the Financial Accounting Standards Board (FASB) issued new revenue recognition rules, most notably mandating distinctions between gross and net revenues. Gross revenue is the amount invoiced. Net revenue is how much the company retains after paying a wholesaler or manufacturer for the invoiced products. The experienced investor recognizes this as a cost of goods sold (COGS) issue. Past practice for "old economy" firms was to report in their gross income computations a deduction of the direct (actual) costs of goods sold. To compute revenues otherwise would overstate them substantially. A lot of microcap companies within the high-tech sector have computed otherwise. How was this permissible?

The question of permissibility was succinctly treated in an article by Julia Lawlor in the December 4, 2000, issue of *Red Herring*[5]. Many e-merchants operate as agents, rather than principals, in a transaction. No brick-and-mortar travel agency would book as revenue the cost to its customers of the travel and lodging it reserved, just the commissions earned. Priceline.com booked as revenue the full price of the reservations it arranged for customers. Lawlor cites the Priceline.com justification: " . . . although it doesn't take title to the product until after the customer has made a nonrefundable purchase by credit card, it assumes the risk if the customer's credit is bad, the charge is disputed or the supplier goes out of business . . ." The diligent investor understands that "disputed" might be the only operative word in the that rationale.

Lawlor also addresses the practices among emerging biotech firms: " . . . Historically, biotech companies have gotten upfront fees when they have affiliated with big pharmaceutical companies for joint research and development arrangements. The fees are booked immediately as revenue, under the assumption that the payment is for research the companyhas already completed. But the SEC says the payments should be spread out over the term of the agreement." The industry has been challenging the SEC's view.

As Andy Kessler reminds us, chief financial officers love to tweak. They are tempted to smooth out "lumpy" revenues. Revenues actually received from a larger-than-usual sale in the last few weeks of one quarter may not be reported for that quarter but apportioned over a couple of subsequent quarters. This has probably occurred a few times among a lot of firms, big or small. If you discover that this practice is frequent and common at one of your target companies, then remove the company from further consideration. Another tactic of concern is the flip side of the booking issue: Watch that a company doesn't report all the revenue stipulated in a long-term contract as revenue received now.

The key questions remain. Did real money come into the company as the result of a sale? Is any of that money owed to the actual selling principal in the transaction? Did the company put that money into their operating account at the bank? Should some of the money have gone into a reserve account?

A decrease in revenue growth can be interpreted as negatively as the previous responses to earnings decreases. A couple of quarters of increased earnings but flat revenues should be cause for concern. Any evolving company should be enjoying economies from moving further up the learning curve. What is happening to the top line? Look closely at unit volume, the aging of receivables, and the retention rate of existing customers. Determine how quickly new customers are being acquired and, more important, how much revenue is from new products or services. Research conducted by Eccles and PricewaterhouseCoopers provides evidence of a direct link between revenues from new products and market cap growth.

Rapid revenue growth is a critical element in valuing emerging companies.

Expenses and Amortization   The accrual questions about what should be charged as direct expenses and what should be capitalized are common to any listed company. These concerns have been around as long as there have been federal agencies. Consider how expenses are viewed from the perspective of the SEC and then from the perspective of the Internal Revenue Service.

Investors' preoccupation with earnings has aggravated a legitimate concern. Generally accepted practices discipline the reporting process. Still, there is incongruity with respect to accruals. NYU's Lev is continually addressing accounting incongruities in his teaching, writing, and research. His intriguing and well-reasoned insights are the subject of several articles, the best of which was written by *Barron's* Jonathan R. Laing[6].

Lev argues that traditional methods do not accurately account for intangibles such as research and development, innovation, brand positioning, or employee training. Lev's point is that, like the purchase of machinery, these expenditures are investments, not expenses. Lev's arguments should be considered when you deconstruct a company's financial statements; however, stay focused on the tangible expenses.

Look for clear evidence of a return on specific expenses such as productivity gains relative to personnel costs and sales increases from higher marketing costs. Be concerned if there is a pattern of expenses increasing at a faster rate than revenues. One microcap investment manager remarked to us, "I'm very partial to inverted burn rates." Before analyzing operating expenses of a microcap company, put on some kilts and pretend that you are Scotch.

The Balance Sheet

At some point in the early life of an emerging company, the balance sheet ought to reflect a march to value. A company that has operated for more than five years as a publicly traded corporation should have an overall ratio of at least 1.25:1 in the amount of assets to liabilities. Pay attention to the nature of the assets, particularly accounts receivable.

Look closely at the total capital structure and the underlying debt instruments. With respect to long-term debt, look for early call provisions and for any conversion terms.

Calculate *enterprise value*. It's a reliable number to keep in your head. Most investors calculate enterprise value by adding common stock market capitalization to debt and preferred shares and subtracting cash and equivalents. This is the calculation as described at Investopedia.com. Changes in enterprise value can be a better measure of circumstances than just looking at changes in market capitalization.

The best measures remain an increase in stockholder equity and cash equivalents on hand. Where is the cash? Where did it come from? Where did it go?

MERGER AND ACQUISITION CONSIDERATIONS

There is an estimate floating around Wall Street that, for every company that goes public, six get merged. Some of those who invest in microcap stocks do so with the expectation that the returns will come from takeovers.

Experienced investors are skeptical about such prospects. What are the benefits of such an outcome: Economies of scale? Increased market share? Synergy-driven increases in revenues and decreases in overall expenses? Will the acquiring company lose its focus on the activities that drove its growth? Reemerging companies are most likely to be acquisition targets, that is, target for value plays. In our opinion, the likelihood of being acquired should not be your *primary* reason for buying a microcap growth stock.

BEYOND THE NUMBERS

Lev, Eccles, Carolyn Brancato of The Conference Board[7], Robert H. Herz of PricewaterhouseCoopers, Harold Kahn of Scudder Kemper Investments, and the Cap Gemini Ernst and Young Center for Business Innovation[8] have been at the forefront of the argument that traditional accounting doesn't reflect adequately the real value of a publicly traded company. Eccles and Herz have coauthored a watershed book, *The Value Reporting Revolution*, with Herz's PricewaterhouseCoopers colleagues E. Mary Keegan and David M. H. Phillips[9].

We believe there are investors who do outperform prescribed equity markets' benchmarks over the long run. We believe that this sustained success is in how these investors analyze companies. Winning investors have always looked beyond the numbers reported in those mandated financial reports. Lev, Eccles, et. al. are identifying and categorizing dozens of characteristics and performance measures that create value in an enterprise, yet may be "off the books." Many of those characteristics and measures are appropriate to the analyses of emerging companies, and some are especially pertinent. Investors who aspire to sustained success should study the sources cited at the end of this chapter.

OUR PREJUDICES

We prefer companies in which management has a large ownership stake. We like to see our investments operating businesses with high barriers to entry. Employee turnover rates are of special interest to us. We have long memories for managers who have provided inaccurate information or who have mismanaged other enterprises.

OTHER ISSUES

Taxes

In practicality, their small floats make microcaps long-term holds. Any gains from subsequent sales within taxable portfolios will be taxed at a favorable rate. If circumstances do require you to sell these issues quickly without regard for the forces of supply and demand, you will have the benefit of substantial offsetting losses.

Custody

The custody, transfer, and shareholder-recording procedures for listed stocks in the United States are administered and regulated in the same manner, regardless of market capitalization. Because a microcap company is likely to be understaffed, it may not be dealing in a timely fashion with its custodian and transfer agent. The shareholder records may be in some disarray. Make sure that your ownership is a matter of record with all appropriate institutions and agencies.

Some Good News About Bad Guys

The stocks of the microcap companies that you own are always in relatively short supply. It is unlikely that these companies ever will be targets of a bear raid entailing short-selling tactics because the "shorts" can get killed trying to cover on a runup.

DON'T TRY THIS AT HOME

We think that microcap growth stocks are attractive, alternative vehicles. The appeal of microcap growth stocks is in their divergent performance within market cycles and in their proportionate return to the risks and costs associated with them. These returns are related to some real inefficiencies encountered in the discovery, appraisal, and trading of microcap growth stocks. Yes, we do think that this small universe of equities exists as an opportunist's market, particularly in the altered regulatory environment.

However, an enormous amount of time is required to master the knowledge and techniques necessary to turn those inefficiencies into high returns. In our experience, trading skills are of equal importance with analytic and portfolio construction skills. Many times the trading skills are paramount. Wall Street jokes that microcaps trade by appointment. For that reason, we recommend searching for investment managers who have had extensive experience in this investment style. We will not, however, recommend any specific managers.

We can remind readers of an approach to a manager search that is a favorite of ours. We assume that the reader—for reasons of control, costs, and tax planning—would prefer an individually managed account to a microcap growth mutual fund. We have discovered that the most experienced practitioners of this style do manage both mutual funds and individual accounts. So, you can easily find a manager in *Morningstar's* small cap growth mutual fund profiles. The data provided for each fund will inform you as to which fund is truly managed as a microcap growth fund.

When *Morningstar* writes up a mutual fund profile, it always includes a Sharpe ratio. Any college textbook on investments will provide the reader with a refresher on the Sharpe ratio. This performance measure can be used to compare managers' performances among their style peers and among other managers of larger cap portfolios. It is logical that the performance of a manager's individually managed accounts should parallel that of the manager's listed mutual fund.

Did we remember to state that past performance is not necessarily a valid indicator or guarantee of future results?

NOTES

[1]Banz, Rolf W., "The Relationship Between Return and Market Value of Common Stocks," *Journal of Financial Economics* (March 1981).

[2]Reinganum, Marc R., "Misspecification of Capital Asset Pricing: Empirical Anomalies Based on Earnings' Yields and Market Values," *Journal of Financial Economics* (March 1981).

[3]Wagner, Wayne H. and Steven Glass, "Analyzing Transaction Costs: Part I." *The Journal of Investment Consulting* (June 1999).

[4]Coker, Daniel P., *Mastering Microcaps: Strategies, Trends, and Stock Selections*, Princeton: Bloomberg Press, 1999

[5]Lawlor, Julia, "Book Cookery," *Red Herring* (December 4, 2000).

[6]Laing, Jonathan R., "The New Math," *Barron's* (November 20, 2000).

[7]Brancato, Carolyn K., *Institutional Investors and Corporate Governance: Best Practices for Increasing Corporate Value*, Burr Ridge, Illinois: Irwin/McGraw-Hill, 1997.

[8]Interested readers should visit **cbi.cgey.com** to review back issues of *Perspectives on Business Innovation* as well as explore other research under way there.

[9]Eccles, Robert G., Robert H. Herz, E. Mary Keegan, and David M. H. Phillips, *The Value Reporting Revolution: Moving Beyond The Earnings Game*, New York: John Wiley & Sons, Inc., 2001.

CHAPTER 11

High Yield Securities

By Martin S. Fridson, CFA

The high yield asset class has had a colorful and sometimes controversial history over the last 100 years, but the Merrill Lynch High Yield Master Index outperformed intermediate Treasuries from 1985 through 2000 by an annualized total return margin of 10.32 percent to 9.36 percent.

The high yield asset class, as customarily defined, includes public, nonconvertible, corporate bonds rated below investment grade but not in default. In the United States, "public" issues include bonds distributed under Securities and Exchange Commission (SEC) Rule 144a with registration rights attached. The definition excludes convertibles, which perform more in line with their related stocks, as a rule, than with fluctuations in interest rates or default risk premiums.

Noninvestment grade municipal and sovereign bonds are conventionally classified as subsets of categories that include their investment grade peers rather than as part of the high yield asset class. "Below-investment-grade" ordinarily means a rating of Ba1 or lower by Moody's Investors Service or a rating of BB+ or lower by Standard & Poor's. Most authorities count issues with split ratings (Baa3/BB+, for example) as high yield bonds.

The high yield universe also includes nonrated bonds with credit characteristics comparable to those of issues rated Ba/BB or lower. Securities of bankrupt companies, which generally produce no current income, are more the province of "vulture capitalists" who specialize in bankrupt stocks and bonds. Practitioners use the terms "high yield," "noninvestment grade," "subinvestment grade," "below-investment-grade," and "speculative-grade," as well as the pejorative "junk bond," more or less interchangeably.

Managers of high yield portfolios commonly dabble in speculative-quality instruments outside their strictly defined asset class. These include syndicated loans, preferred and preference stocks, "busted" (deep-out-of-the-money) convertibles, and investment grade bonds trading at levels commensurate with lower-rated issues as a consequence of perceived risk of downgrading. At times, high yield managers' portfolios also contain small amounts of equity warrants, issued either as sweeteners in new issues or in the settlement of claims on defaulted issuers.

High yield bonds come into existence in two different ways. "Fallen angels" begin life in the investment grade realm—that is, rated Baa3/BBB-or higher—and enter the noninvestment grade category through downgrading. "Original issue" high yield bonds initially come to market with speculative grade ratings. Most originate in underwritings, with a small percentage spawned by exchange offers for existing issues, settlement of bankruptcy claims, or payment for stock acquired in mergers.

MARKET SIZE AND COMPOSITION

On December 31, 2000, the U.S. dollar-denominated high yield universe consisted of about 3,500 issues of approximately 1,750 issuers, with an aggregate principal amount of about $517 billion. This estimate of the amount outstanding is generally consistent with figures published by Moody's Investors Service and Fitch. Other sources, which put the number considerably higher, apparently include certain instruments mentioned previously in which high yield managers invest but which do not qualify as high yield debt under a strict definition. Also at the end of 2000, there were about 135 issues outstanding in European currencies with a combined principal amount equivalent to about $24 billion.

Table 11.1 shows the distribution of the U.S. high yield universe by rating as of the end of 2000. A more finely graded breakdown of the European universe appears in Table 11.2. With each step down the rating scale, default risk and yields rise. Reserving requirements of insurance companies, charters of mutual funds and contractual requirements of collateralized bond obligations impose ratings-based constraints on the security selections of high yield managers. Many pension plan sponsors establish guidelines based on ratings as well.

The high yield universe can also be broken down by bond structure (see Figure 11.1.) Conventional cash-coupon instruments account for the vast majority (92.1 percent) of outstanding issues. The next largest group (5.6 percent) includes deferred-interest bonds (DIBs) and multicoupon issues. DIBS, or zero-coupon issues, are issued at a steep discount to face value

TABLE 11.1   Ratings Distribution of the U.S. High Yield Market[1]
(December 31, 2000)

Rating	By Principal Amount	By Number of Issues
Split-Rated[2]	2.3%	2.3%
Double-B	28.5	38.1
Single-B	50.4	38.8
Triple-C/Double-C/Single-C	14.4	12.8
Nonrated	4.5	8.0
	100.0%	100.0%

[1]Columns may not sum to 100.0 percent due to rounding error.
[2]Rated below Baa3 by Moody's or below BBB- by Standard & Poor's, but not both.
Source: Merrill Lynch & Co.

TABLE 11.2   Ratings Distribution of the European High Yield Market
(December 31, 2000)

Rating	By Number of Issues
BB1	5.1%
BB2	4.0
BB3	5.7
B1	14.3
B2	26.3
B3	22.3
CCC/CC/C	22.3
Total	100.0%

Source: Merrill Lynch & Co.

and provide a return to investors through gradual appreciation to par at maturity. Multicoupons are DIBs with "back-end coupons"—that is, zeros that turn into cash-pays after an initial noncash-interest-paying period. Floaters (1.9 percent of outstanding issues) have coupons that periodically reset at fixed interest rate spreads over specified reference rates, such as the yield on Treasury bonds of a stated maturity. Finally, payment-in-kind bonds (PIKs) pay interest in the form of newly issued fractional bonds rather than in cash.

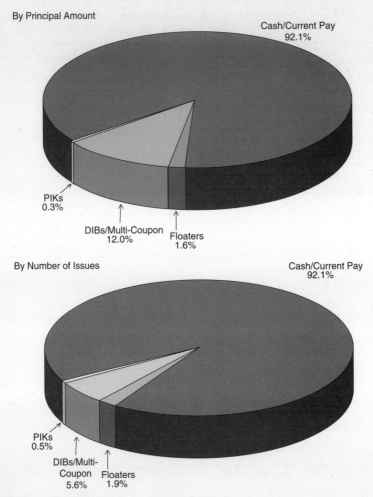

FIGURE 11.1 Bond Structure Distribution of the High Yield Universe, (as of December 31, 2000)
Source: Merrill Lynch & Co.

PUBLIC HIGH YIELD DEBT VERSUS PRIVATE DEBT

From the issuer's perspective, the ability to borrow on an unsecured basis is a major appeal of the high yield market, relative to borrowing privately from banks or other institutional lenders. Secured issues accounted for just 2.6

percent of the issues in the widely used Merrill Lynch High Yield Master II Index as of the end of 2000 (see Figure 11.2). The largest concentration by capital structure priority is the senior unsecured class (79.6 percent), with subordinated issues accounting for the balance (17.7 percent). Recoveries in bankruptcy decline, as a percentage of the holder's claim, with each step down this scale, a fact reflected in the relative risk premiums observed for the three seniority classes.

Buyers of most high yield issues forgo not only a secured interest but also the maintenance covenants customarily contained in private debt indentures, settling instead for incurrence covenants. Under a maintenance covenant, a company is in default if a specified financial ratio, such as debt as a percentage of capital, falls below stated levels. Bondholders typically

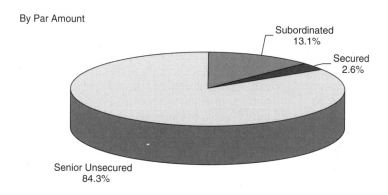

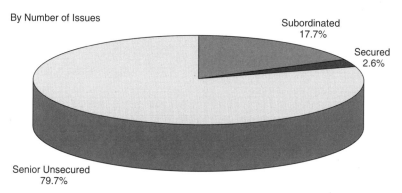

FIGURE 11.2   Seniority Distribution of the Merrill Lynch High Yield Master II Index
Source: Merrill Lynch & Co.

exact concessions, such as more frequent review of operating results, as the price for agreeing to waive the violation—that is, they refrain from demanding immediate repayment of principal to which they are entitled by virtue of the covenant breach. Under an incurrence covenant, by contrast, the issuer is merely precluded from taking certain actions, such as issuing new debt, if the financial test would not be satisfied after giving effect to the proposed action.

Issuers also enjoy greater latitude regarding prepayment in the public high yield market than in the private bond market, although high yield bonds' early redemption penalties are generally more severe than in the syndicated loan market. The most common variety of public high yield bond has a 10-year final maturity, with redemption prohibited for the first five years. Bonds that are nonredeemable before maturity accounted for only 16 percent of the principal amount of the Merrill Lynch High Yield Master II Index as of December 31, 2000. Less than 1 percent of the index's principal amount represents debt puttable by holders.

In principle, investors grant issuers the greater financial flexibility inherent in unsecured debt, incurrence covenants, and limited protection against early redemption in exchange for the investment flexibility afforded by a public market for their securities. If holders of a public high yield issue are unhappy with management's performance, they can vote with their feet—that is, they can sell their positions, an alternative that is available to holders of privately placed bonds to a very limited extent only. The investor's evaluation of the tradeoff between private debt's advantages and the benefit of a secondary market depends on the vibrancy of that market in practice. Particularly pertinent is the high yield sector's liquidity under stressful economic conditions, when the desire to sell is likely to be strongest.

THE NEW ISSUE MARKET

Most original issue high yield bonds are distributed through a marketing process that features a series of "roadshow" presentations by senior management to institutional investors. During the marketing period, the underwriters disseminate preliminary pricing notions, usually expressed in yield-to-maturity terms. As the institutions indicate the extent of their interest, the underwriters adjust the pricing, aiming to clear the market by a sufficient margin, such that the bonds will trade to a small premium in the after-market. In effect, the underwriter conducts an auction before setting the final price. At the point of pricing, the underwriter legally takes title to the securities but quickly resells them to investors at a yield and in amounts determined beforehand. Rarely does a high yield underwriter try to price an issue "ahead of the market," thereby running the risk of being left with a substantial amount of unsold bonds.

During brief periods of exceptionally strong demand for high yield new issues, underwriters typically price a limited number of "drive-by" or "quick-to-market" deals. These transactions dispense with the roadshow, often progressing from initial announcement to pricing in the space of 24 hours. Drive-by offerings sometimes come about as a response to "reverse inquiry"—that is, requests by institutions with large sums of cash to put to work to be shown deals meeting their specifications. The drive-by window is accessible only to large, frequent issuers with credit stories that are already well-known to investors.

Compact underwriting groups, rather than syndicates composed of many investment banks, are the norm in the high yield market. The book-running manager tends to dominate the distribution, with comanager roles often awarded by issuers in consideration of other banking services provided. Institutions, too, encourage the appointment of comanagers, who they hope will make a secondary market in the securities, leading to greater liquidity than would result from a sole manager subsequently acting as sole market-maker.

The high yield underwriting business is fairly concentrated. In 2000, the top six managers accounted for 68 percent of offerings and 76 percent of proceeds. This tight distribution of market share is essentially mandated by costs. To be a credible lead manager, a firm must offer the full line of high-yield-specific services to issuers and institutional investors, including sales, trading, research, advisory services, origination, and restructuring. An infrastructure that vast is difficult to support without the revenues realizable from volume that approaches 10 percent of the total pie. Breaking into the bulge bracket of the top half-dozen or so underwriters is achievable only by a firm that has the patience and financial wherewithal to compensate top-flight personnel in all functional areas for several years, until the nascent effort finally begins to coalesce.

Table 11.3 shows dramatic, but highly variable, growth in high yield underwriting volume over the past quarter-century. From a small trickle prior to 1977, the global primary market grew to $1 billion annually though the early 1980s, with booming energy prices creating large financing demand among independent oil and gas exploration companies. During the heyday of leveraged buyouts, issuance rose to a peak of $33 billion in 1986. As a large proportion of the most extremely leveraged transactions began to default, investment capital left the sector, and new issue activity plummeted in 1990 to just 10 issues with aggregate proceeds of only $1 billion. Many observers proclaimed the high yield primary market dead at that point, mistakenly believing that it was entirely dependent on mergers and acquisitions. In fact, the longer-run growth trend resumed, with merger-related financing accounting for only 20 percent to 30 percent of volume in the late 1990s compared to more than 60 percent in the late 1980s. In the context of rapid economic expansion in the United States, high yield issuance set a new record of $141 billion in 1998.

Since 1992, a significant portion of new high yield bonds have been distributed under SEC Rule 144a, which accounted for 79 percent of the total in 2000. Rule 144a transactions are private placements, but the normal practice in the high yield market is to attach registration rights to the bonds being issued. Once the issue has been registered (or exchanged for registered "clone" securities), the buyers hold an investment essentially indistinguishable from an offering made through a conventional public underwriting. Moreover, the managers of a 144a high yield transaction customarily conduct due diligence no less thorough and provide institutional investors a roadshow no less extensive than they would in a conventional public offering. The difference is that in a 144a-with-registration-rights transaction, the issuer can defer the time-consuming SEC registration process until after the deal. By doing so, the company avoids the risk of incurring registration costs, only to see the financing window close before the deal can be consummated.

THE SECONDARY MARKET

Secondary trading in high yield bonds occurs mainly in an over-the-counter market rather than on a centralized exchange. Broker/dealers serve as market-making intermediaries, trading as principals. They are not bound by rules requiring them, as a condition of representing themselves as market-makers in an issue, to offer or bid for a specified minimum amount at all times. The underwriter of an issue, however, faces meaningful pressure from institutional investors to maintain a secondary market in it. Failure to fulfill this unofficial obligation undercuts a firm's ability to distribute new deals in the future.

Most of the high yield market's 3,500 outstanding bonds do not trade on any given day. Therefore, holders of all but the most liquid issues should not expect to receive a bid "on the wire" if they decide to sell. The more likely response is an indication from a dealer of the range in which the securities can probably be sold, given time to identify likely buyers and provide them updated credit information. Another ramification of the infrequent trading of most high yield bonds is that many of the prices reported for valuation purposes represent appraisals rather than levels at which transactions occurred.

Outside of the over-the-counter activity, fairly regular transactions occur in a changing list of 50 large issues on the Fixed Income Pricing System

TABLE 11.3   Global New Issue Volume, (1977–2000)

Year	Public Number of Issues	Public Principal Amount ($ Millions)	144a Number of Issues	144a Principal Amount ($ Millions)	Total Number of Issues	Total Principal Amount ($ Millions)
1977	61	$1,040.2			61	$1,040.2
1978	82	1,578.5			82	1,578.5
1979	56	1,399.8			56	1,399.8
1980	45	1,429.3			45	1,429.3
1981	34	1,536.3			34	1,536.3
1982	52	2,691.5			52	2,691.5
1983	95	7,765.2			95	7,765.2
1984	131	15,238.9			131	15,238.9
1985	175	15,684.8			175	15,684.8
1986	226	33,261.8			226	33,261.8
1987	190	30,522.2			190	30,522.2
1988	160	31,095.2			160	31,095.2
1989	130	28,753.2			130	28,753.2
1990	10	1,397.0			10	1,397.0
1991	48	9,967.0			48	9,967.0
1992	245	39,755.2	29	$3,810.8	274	43,566.0
1993	341	57,163.7	95	15,096.8	436	72,260.5
1994	191	34,598.8	81	7,733.5	272	42,332.3
1995	152	30,139.1	94	14,242.0	246	44,381.1
1996	142	30,739.4	217	35,172.9	359	65,912.3
1997	103	19,822.0	576	98,885.0	679	118,707.0
1998	116	29,844.0	604	111,044.7	720	140,888.7
1999	60	16,520.0	357	83,157.0	417	99,677.0
2000	32.0	10,621.1	149.0	39,593.6	181.0	50,214.7
Total	$2,877.0	$452,564.2	$2,202.0	$408,736.3	$5,079.0	$861,300.5

Includes nonconvertible, corporate debt rated below investment grade by Moody's or Standard & Poor's. Excludes mortgage- and asset-backed issues, as well as non-144a private placements.
Source: Merrill Lynch & Co.

(FIPS). This trading site, which is managed by the Nasdaq Stock Market, also records interdealer transactions on all other outstanding high yield bonds. In addition, institutions deal directly with one another, as well as with dealer intermediaries, through electronic marketplaces. Selected issues are listed on the New York Stock Exchange and the American Stock Exchanges, where individual investors trade them in odd lots. (Round lots are conventionally defined as par amounts of $1 million or more.)

The development of derivatives in high yield securities has been hampered by the lack of a reliable price stream on most of the underlying cash instruments. Over-the-counter index rate swaps are available in modest size to institutions seeking either to hedge their high yield portfolios or to obtain exposure to the sector without having to select individual issues. No viable instrument exists, however, for aggressive money managers who would like to trade in and out of the high yield market quickly, with minimal transaction costs, in notional amounts of several hundred million dollars or more. At the individual security level, derivatives desks maintain a respectable volume in structures that permit default risk to be traded separately from the instruments' other risks and embedded options.

SOURCES OF INFORMATION

Investors obtain basic financial information on a high yield issuer from the prospectuses published in conjunction with the underwriting and from mandatory SEC quarterly and annual filings made thereafter. Under certain circumstances, privately owned companies that issue public bonds are exempt from SEC filing requirements. Such issuers typically covenant to provide holders with periodic financial reports in the form specified by the SEC, whether or not they are legally required to file.

Brokerage houses active in the high yield market publish extensive credit analysis of individual issuers. Multiple opinions are generally available on the issuers with the largest amounts of debt outstanding, whereas investors usually must rely on the underwriter alone for continuing analysis of the smaller issuers. Institutional investors recognize that underwriting relationships may interfere with the objectivity of the brokerage houses' analysts but see value in the information that those analysts are able to obtain and disseminate by virtue of their connections with issuers.

Bias is less of a concern with third-party providers of credit analysis, which derive at least a portion of their revenues directly from the sale of research. This group includes the bond rating agencies, such as Moody's Investors Service, Standard & Poor's, Fitch and Egan-Jones Credit Ratings, which publish rationales for the ratings they assign. Dominion Bond Rating Service provides similar analysis of Canadian high yield issuers. The agencies are also sources of aggregate credit statistics for industry- and rating-based subgroups within the high yield universe. Other providers of credit opinions on high yield bonds include KDP, based in Montpelier, Vermont, and San Francisco-based KMV. KMV relies on quantitative analysis involving the levels and volatility of issuers' stock prices.

In the area of market data, the above-mentioned rating agencies and New York University's Stern School of Business produce extensive statistics on high yield bond default rates. AMG Data Services (Arcata, California) and the Investment Company Institute (Washington, D.C.) report on capital flows into and out of high yield bond mutual funds. Additionally, brokerage houses' high yield strategy departments compile and analyze data in such areas as new issue quality, historical returns, and yield spreads.

Reviews of market activity over periods ranging from a day to a year represent another type of information provided by brokerage houses' high yield strategy departments. The *Wall Street Journal*'s daily "Credit Markets" column reports regularly on the asset category that it refers to with the pejorative "junk bonds." Thomson Financial's *High Yield Report* covers the sector on a weekly basis. In Europe, *International Financing Review* features a weekly high yield column, whereas The Investment Dealers Association of Canada publishes a semiannual *Higher-Yielding Debt Issuance Report*.

High yield portfolio managers also find value in conferences sponsored by underwriters, which feature management presentations by past issuers of debt that remains outstanding. The New York Society of Security Analysts hosts an annual one-day seminar on the high yield market in June, focusing on broad topics such as the market outlook, new analytical methods, bond covenants, and syndicate practices. For-profit companies and universities also sponsor high yield conferences from time to time. In addition, discriminating investors can sometimes find items of considerable practical value among the articles published in academic and professional journals.

HISTORY

The comparative investment merits of lower-risk and higher-risk bonds were analyzed as far back as 1904, when the London-based Investment Registry & Stock Exchange published a treatise on the subject. In 1909, John Moody introduced bond ratings, classifying some of the period's issues below the speculative grade demarcation line separating Baa from Ba. (The rating agency did not add its 1, 2, 3 modifiers until 1982.) By 1919, Moody was using the term "high yield" to denote bonds rated below that cutoff. During the 1920s and 1930s, Arthur Stone Dewing of Harvard Business School and Harold Fraine, later of the University of Wisconsin, debated the proposition that lesser-quality bonds had produced higher returns over long periods than their gilt-edged counterparts. Dewing's disciple, W. Braddock Hickman, completed a widely cited 1958 book on corporate bond quality that carried on the high yield debate.

In 1970, mutual fund organizations set the stage for the modern high yield market by launching funds specializing in lower-rated bonds. The impact was modest until the mid-1970s, when interest rates fell sharply. Striving to maintain their income, small investors flocked into the high yield funds. This increased demand absorbed the available supply of speculative grade bonds, which had been sharply reduced through retirements and upgrades to investment grade. Investment bankers began to capitalize on the resulting opportunity in 1977. They intensified their focus on underwriting public bonds for noninvestment grade companies, hitherto a minor line of business.

The now-defunct brokerage house Drexel Burnham Lambert is often credited erroneously with the "innovation" of floating new issues for high yield issuers. In reality, Lehman Brothers racked up three offerings during the first quarter of 1977 before Drexel even got out of the starting gate in April. To be sure, Drexel subsequently became the leading high yield under-writer by intensively concentrating its assets and revenues in the area, a risky strategy that contributed to its 1990 bankruptcy. Drexel's high yield chief, Michael Milken, proselytized vigorously for the high yield market, but his evangelical zeal was probably counterproductive among the mainstream pension plan sponsors and insurance companies that he hoped to lure into the asset class. These institutions also viewed as a negative their impression (which was false but encouraged by Drexel) that the high yield market had only one market-maker of any consequence. On the whole, Milken may well have retarded the development of the high yield market before exiting the business and later pleading guilty to six felony charges.

To be fair, the expansion of the high yield market was also impeded during the 1980s by the sector's association with corporate raiders. In retrospect, the U.S. economy probably benefited from the rationalization and efficiency enhancement forced upon many companies by the threat of hostile takeover, many of which relied on high yield financing. At the time, however, it was politically difficult for corporate pension plans to provide financing to the very parties who were attempting to seize control of their employee-beneficiaries' companies, often with an eye toward reducing the headcount. Worries about declining credit standards, which were vindicated by record-high default rates in 1990–1991, reinforced institutional investors' go-slow attitude.

Once the takeover controversy was defused by a general rise in stock prices, institutional policymakers began to consider the high yield asset class more purely on its investment merits. At the end of 1995, high yield bonds boasted a trailing five-year return higher than the stock market's in absolute (not just relative) terms. That anomaly arose from the happenstance that

December 31, 1990, was very nearly the bottom of the high yield market's Great Debacle, which extended from mid-1989 to the first few weeks of 1991. Nevertheless, the past performance figures helped to accelerate the flow of institutional money into the high yield asset class. With money also pouring into high yield mutual funds in record amounts during 1997–1998, demand for high yield bonds outstripped the supply of conventional issuers —that is, low-technology companies characterized by high levels of cash generation and high expected recoveries in the event of default. The investment banks, which had filled a similar gap in the 1980s with leveraged buyouts, began underwriting issues for companies that did not fit the classic profile, notably early-stage telecommunications ventures. Another sharp surge in default rates followed in 2001.

PERFORMANCE

Recorded returns on high yield indexes have long since resolved the Dewing-Fraine-Hickman debate about the relative performance. In absolute terms, the Merrill Lynch High Yield Master Index outperformed intermediate Treasuries from 1985 through 2000 by an annualized total return margin of 10.32 percent to 9.36 percent. High yield bonds also won on a risk-adjusted basis over the period. Figure 11.3 shows that the high yield index plots slightly above the Securities Market Line. By contrast, intermediate Treasuries fall slightly below the line, indicating an inferior risk/reward trade-off. Calculated on a monthly basis, the high yield index's Sharpe ratio (the asset class's total return minus the return on 91-day Treasury bills, all divided by the asset class's standard deviation of returns) was 0.22. That easily beat intermediate Treasuries' 0.13.

A mean-variance analysis, such as the Securities Market Line, is not, strictly speaking, applicable to securities with embedded options. High yield bonds contain such options in the form of provisions for redemption prior to maturity. They consequently generate asymmetrical returns. That is, the call provisions typically cap the upside at about 15 points above par while the loss of principal on defaulting bonds has historically averaged around 60 percent.

Let us conservatively assume that the high yield sector's long-run returns, adjusted for the impact of embedded options, represent only a fair reward for the risk. The asset class nevertheless provides a valuable diversification benefit, which is depicted in Table 11.4. High yield bonds have comparatively low correlations of returns with all other major asset classes. The efficient frontier shown in Figure 11.4 underscores the large potential benefit

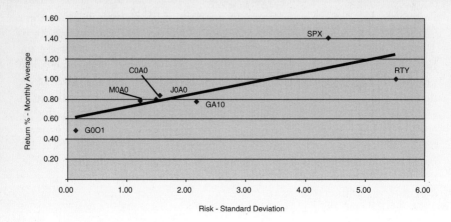

RTY = Russell 2000 Index
SPX = S&P 500 Index
J0A0 = Merrill Lynch High Yield Master Index
C0A0 = Corporate Index
M0A0 = Mortgage Index
GA10 = 10 yr. Treasury Note
G0O1 = 3 mo. Treasury Bill
Sources: Loan Pricing Corporation, Standard & Poor's, Russell Indexes, Merrill Lynch & Co.

FIGURE 11.3   Securities Market Trendline, (1985 to 2000)

of combining high yield debt with better-quality bonds to achieve an optimal risk/return tradeoff. Few institutions are likely to concentrate 70 to 80 percent of their fixed income assets in noninvestment grade corporates, yet even such a radical mix would constitute a portfolio mix superior to 100 percent concentration in default-risk-free Treasuries.

DEFAULT RATES

Discussions of high yield bond performance inevitably turn to the topic of default rates, but it is important to avoid equating the two. Over the short-to-intermediate term, the total return on a high yield index and the default rate on speculative grade bonds may have little apparent connection. During 1991, for example, the high yield sector's total return reached an all-time high, despite the fact that default rates were also at their highest level of the modern era (beginning in 1977). In that case, as in a number of other instances,

TABLE 11.4 Correlation of Monthly Returns (Selected Asset Categories, 1985 to 2000)

	High Yield[1]	Mortgage-Backed[2]	Ten-Year Treasuries	Three-Month Treasuries	Big Stocks[3]	Small Stocks[4]	High Grade Corporates[5]
High Yield	1.000						
Mortgage-Backed	0.419	1.000					
Ten-Year Treasuries	0.340	0.872	1.000				
Three-Month Treasuries	0.009	0.364	0.324	1.000			
Big Stocks	0.508	0.268	0.286	0.017	1.000		
Small stocks	0.571	0.112	0.100	−0.084	0.769	1.000	
High Grade Corporates	0.529	0.900	0.934	0.299	0.373	0.217	1.000

[1]Merrill Lynch High Yield Master Index.
[2]Merrill Lynch Mortgage-Backed Master Index.
[3]Standard & Poor's Index of 500 Common Stocks.
[4]Russell 2000 Index.
[5]Merrill Lynch High Grade Corporate Index.
*First twelve months.
Sources: Merrill Lynch & Co., Russell Indexes, Standard & Poor's.

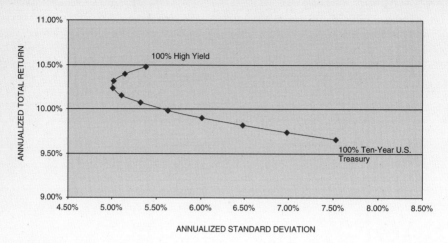

FIGURE 11.4 Efficient Frontier, High Yield Bonds versus Ten-Year Treasuries (Monthly, 1985 to 2000)
Source: Merrill Lynch & Co.

the bulk of the price decline on the period's defaulting issues had already occurred in earlier periods. Bonds do not, as a rule, go directly from par to default. The relevance of default rates to returns therefore is primarily in a longer-run analysis. Over a period of many years, the net return on the high yield asset class will roughly equate to its yield less the default losses.

Many variant default rate calculations are available for investors' use. The authorities agree, by and large, on the number and dollar volume of defaults. Differences arise, however, on such questions as the basis of calculation (issuers or principal amount), the relevant universe (United States and other developed countries only or global, including developing countries) and types of instruments included (nonconvertibles only or nonconvertibles plus convertibles). No calculation is inherently right or wrong; the appropriate measure to use depends on the application. For example, an issuer-based series is probably the most suitable benchmark for a collateralized debt obligation, which typically owns similar amounts of a number of different issues as a function of its diversification requirements. By contrast, the portfolios of multibillion-dollar mutual funds tend to reflect issuers' unequal market weightings, making the principal-amount default rates more relevant.

Moody's reports both an issuer-based and a principal-amount-based default rate monthly, on a trailing-12-months basis. Table 11.5 shows that the two series have diverged significantly in certain years. Nevertheless, they have both recorded means of 3.4 percent over the last three decades.

TABLE 11.5   Moody's Trailing Twelve-Months Default Rate
(Yearly, 1971 to 2000)

Year	Percentage of Principal Amount Outstanding	Percentage of Issuers
1971	1.84	1.47
1972	3.94	1.88
1973	2.60	1.24
1974	2.93	1.32
1975	3.50	1.74
1976	1.44	0.87
1977	5.18	1.34
1978	2.13	1.78
1979	0.30	0.42
1980	1.93	1.61
1981	0.77	0.70
1982	5.52	3.54
1983	1.70	3.83
1984	1.73	3.32
1985	2.35	4.13
1986	1.59	5.67
1987	1.20	4.24
1988	3.17	3.47
1989	6.90	6.03
1990	10.95	9.96
1991	9.55	10.50
1992	3.80	4.85
1993	1.31	3.51
1994	1.04	1.93
1995	3.63	3.29
1996	1.61	1.65
1997	2.95	2.03
1998	3.32	3.47
1999	7.78	5.68
2000	6.21	5.71
Average**	3.43	3.37

**Figures not weighted by amount outstanding each year.
Note: Defaults based on developed and emerging markets rated universe.
Source: Moody's Investors Service.

Investors' returns are affected less directly by the gross default rate than by the default loss rate, which also takes into account recoveries on defaulting bonds. Practitioners customarily calculate recoveries on the basis of trading prices shortly after default. The presumption is that the income-seeking investors attracted to the high yield market liquidate issues upon default, because they generally cease to pay interest at that point. Over the period 1981 to 2000, Moody's reports average recoveries on all seniority classes of 39.1 percent of face value (See Table 11.6). The rating agency's sample includes recoveries on bank loans and preferred stocks, causing its figure to differ somewhat from bond-only recovery rates reported by other sources.

OWNERSHIP

The distribution of ownership of outstanding high yield debt is a major concern of potential new investors in the asset class. They worry particularly about the concentration of holdings in open-end mutual funds, which are prone to sudden, large inflows and outflows of capital. Big inflows can lead to too many dollars chasing too few deals, in turn opening the financing window to extremely low-quality issuers and ensuring a surge in default rates a few years later. When mutual fund managers suffer big outflows, on the other hand, they may be forced to liquidate bonds at less than their intrinsic value to meet redemptions. Other investors must bear the brunt of credit quality deterioration and price volatility generated by the mutual funds' large presence.

High yield bonds are owned by both mutual funds specializing in the category and other types, including general corporate bond funds that allocate a minority of their holdings to the noninvestment grade category. The

TABLE 11.6   Average Recoveries on Default, by Seniority Class,
(1989 to 2000)

Class	Average Recovery (Percent of Face Value)
Bank Loan/Senior Unsecured	64.3%
Bond/Senior Secured	53.9
Bond/Senior Unsecured	47.4
Bond/Senior Subordinated	33.3
Bond/Subordinated	32.3
Preferred Stock	18.4
Total	39.1%

Source: Moody's Investors Service.

tendency of small investors to buy or sell in droves, in response to changes in the outlook for high yield bonds, is concentrated in the specialized high yield funds that represent nearly a pure play. Fortunately, those funds have not increased their share of outstandings over the long run. Since 1984, the holdings of specialized high yield funds have ranged between one-sixth and one-third of the total, on a market value basis, but their share has been trend- less over the full period (See Figure 11.5).

The mutual fund organizations have mitigated the problem of large redemptions to some extent by advertising their high yield funds much less aggressively than in the 1980s. Today's holders are less likely than in those years to be income seekers who do not understand that their net asset value may decline and who will panic when it inevitably does. Nevertheless, pro- longed periods of outflows still occur when the high yield market comes under stress. During 2000, for example, the Investment Company Institute reported five consecutive months of outflows during the first half and another five straight negative months in the second half. One saving grace is that the funds' portfolio managers can endure a fairly high level of with- drawals before being forced to liquidate bonds, thanks to cash generated from coupons and retirements of debt.

To a considerable extent as well, the mutual funds' flow patterns are counterbalanced by different patterns among the high yield sector's other main investors (See Table 11.7. Note that precise figures are unavailable for some categories.) Life insurance companies tend not to sell in response to market fluctuations as a function of their regulatory accounting regime.

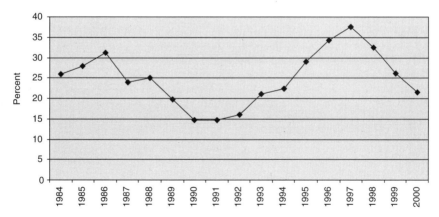

FIGURE 11.5 High Yield Mutual Funds' Share of Outstanding High Yield Debt (Market-Value Basis, 1984 to 2000)

However, some life insurers take advantage of dips to add to their holdings at attractive prices.

Collateralized debt obligations (CDOs), which appeared as early as 1988 but became a significant force only in the second half of the 1990s, have also tended to be buyers during depressed periods. In essence, CDOs are structured financing vehicles that derive their returns from the interest rate differential between their cost of funds and the yield on a diversified portfolio of high yield securities. A sharp price drop ordinarily increases this "funding gap" and therefore the attractiveness of launching new CDOs. Pension funds, which hold the largest share of outstanding high yield debt, have very long-lived liabilities. They do not generally make large asset allocation shifts in response to very short-run market developments, although some engage in moderate market timing.

MANAGER SELECTION AND EVALUATION

Outside management is the preferred path for all but the largest institutional investors who decide to participate in the high yield sector. It is not an asset class that can be managed purely by top-down sector decisions or computer-based security selection. A high yield portfolio requires the attention of not only a full-time, dedicated manager but also a team of experienced credit analysts. Justifying the associated costs is difficult unless they can be spread out over a high yield asset base of several hundred million dollars.

TABLE 11.7 Estimated Distribution of Ownership of High Yield Bonds[1]
(Par Value Basis, 2000)

Mutual Funds	
• High Yield	17.2%
• Other	11.4
Life Insurance Companies	12.4
Collateralized Debt Obligations	13.3
Pension Funds	31.4
Other[2]	14.5
	100.0%

[1]Column total is subject to rounding.
[2]Includes endowments, individuals, dealer inventories, and miscellaneous.
Sources: American Council of Life Insurance, AMG Data Services, Investment Company Institute, Merrill Lynch & Co., Standard & Poor's.

Money managers who focus exclusively on the high yield sector argue that only firms of their kind possess the requisite skills to analyze and trade speculative grade credits. Only past performance records can ultimately determine the validity of this assertion. As a practical matter, clients must also deal with management fees that grow inversely, as a percentage of assets, with asset size. For example, a pension plan sponsor seeking to place $25 million with a high yield manager may find that the proposed allocation falls below the threshold for the minimum percentage fee. The $25 million high yield allocation, however, may represent 10 percent of a $250 million total fixed-income allocation, a figure that may be large enough to qualify for the minimum percentage fee charged by a general fixed-income manager. In that case, the client must determine whether a prospective manager for its entire fixed-income portfolio has a dedicated high yield team with skills equivalent to those of the specialized high yield firms. The client should view with skepticism any claim by a broad-based firm that it can obtain satisfactory credit information on high yield issuers by relying solely on its in-house equity analysts.

Several investment banks offer high yield indexes designed to be used as performance benchmarks. The ratings mixes of these indexes, however, are passive reflections of the ratings mix of actively quoted issues at the time. Only by coincidence would a particular client's risk preferences happen to match that mix, which changes continuously in any case as a result of upgrades, downgrades, and the fluctuating ratings distribution of the new-issue calendar. Accordingly, clients should work with their managers and consultants to design performance benchmarks that match their long-run risk profiles, weighting the rating segments of the index according to their own preferences.

In no event should clients set up a dual system of evaluating managers against both a total return and a default rate benchmark. On the equity side, surely, they do not define performance as a combination of total return and the percentage of stocks that fall by 60 percent (approximately the loss from par on the average defaulting bond). High yield managers can game a default rate performance measure by selling all issues that drop below a certain dollar price or ratings level. Such a strategy will avoid most defaults but may also lead to suboptimal returns through excessive risk aversion. Instead of attempting to micromanage the situation, clients should monitor credit performance in an informal manner but ultimately judge their managers on the basis of returns *over an extended period*. The best-performing high yield manager during a bull market may be the one taking the greatest credit risk and therefore the manager most likely to trail the pack during the next downturn.

VALUING THE SECTOR

Institutions that decide to enter the high yield asset class should make a long-term commitment. Given the lack of a well-developed market in synthetic high yield bonds, the transaction costs of incessantly increasing and decreasing exposure to the sector is prohibitive. That being said, tactical asset allocation can play a productive role if linked to instances of gross under- or over-valuation.

Investment officers should bear in mind that a wider (narrower)-than-average spread versus Treasuries does not necessarily demonstrate that the high yield sector is cheap (rich) at a given point. The spread is a risk premium and *should* be wider (narrower) than average if the sector's risk is temporarily greater (smaller) than it has been historically. A misvaluation is indicated only if the risk premium is out of line with the measurable risk.

Merrill Lynch High Yield Strategy publishes an econometric model of the high yield spread-versus-Treasury based on this premise. The Garman Model explains 89 percent of the variance in the spread, from 1985 onward, on the basis of eight independent variables representing three general categories of risk:

Credit Risk

- The default rate on speculative grade bonds
- The capacity utilization rate

Illiquidity Risk

- High yield bond mutual fund flows
- Cash percentages of the high yield mutual funds
- Post-Russian-default period (Dummy variable for period beginning August 1998)

Monetary Conditions

- Inflation
- Money supply growth
- Slope of U.S. Treasury yield curve

On three occasions, the observed spread-versus-Treasuries result has diverged from the value estimated by this model by two standard deviations (100 basis points) or more. Dramatic rallies followed each of these events —in early 1991, late 1998, and early 2000. A number of institutions have capitalized on this fully transparent model, which Merrill Lynch High Yield Strategy updates monthly.

CHAPTER 12

Energy

By Jeffrey E. Modesitt

Energy awareness is once again forcing itself into the astute investor's consciousness as investors look beyond "Big Oil" and "Big Gas" to possible alternatives including junior exploration and development companies, limited partnerships, and direct investments, especially in natural gas. They are risky but potentially lucrative if you can find the best opportunities.

In 1973, at the beginning of the embargo years, U.S. energy consumption represented an estimated 2.1 percent of Gross Domestic Product (GDP).[1] The embargo years produced intense conservation efforts, multiple research projects to develop a number of alternative energy sources, and a national awareness of the United States's long-term energy dependencies. Almost 30 years later, the United States is more dependent on energy imports than ever before, treats conservation as a disease primarily afflicting environmentalists, and has upped its energy consumption as a percentage of GDP to more than 6 percent. The steadiness of energy supplies at reasonable prices is critical to the United States, yet between the oil embargo years and the new millennium, energy investments beyond "Big Oil" were rarely the focus of investor interest.

Energy awareness, however, is once again forcing itself into the astute investor's consciousness. This time, the culprit is not the Organization of Petroleum Exporting Countries (OPEC), gas-guzzling cars, or frigid weather in the northeastern United States. The most identifiable culprit, because it is the newest and most unexpected, is the Internet and related communication technologies.[2] Businesses are looking at this new paradigm to lead them to unprecedented efficiencies in the years ahead. Ironically, these same communication efficiencies are leading to energy deficiencies, particularly for natural gas and electric-generating capacity.

INVESTMENT OPPORTUNITY

Energy is now and will continue to be an interesting investment focus for those who take the time to understand the industry and its economic environment. Investing in "Big Oil," which is also "Big Gas," is not the only way to participate in this boom. Possible alternatives include junior exploration and development companies, limited partnerships, and direct investments. These alternative investments are inherently risky but potentially very lucrative. Finding the best is, as always, a function of knowing what to look for. This chapter attempts to provide a framework for understanding the domestic energy industry and, more specifically, the oil and gas sector.

This is not the world of the 1970s' embargo years when oil dominated the investment horizon. For the last decade, the energy industry, although huge and incredibly diverse, has been almost invisible to the investment community. When we do think of energy, most of us tend to think in terms of oil, but whether the source of energy output is oil, natural gas, wind, solar, hydrogen, biomass, or coal, an understanding of basic terms and valuation techniques utilized in the proper economic context is critical to successful energy investing. Although many of the analytic terms used in this chapter will be familiar to most investors, the application and weight of the analytic tools differ substantially from most investment sectors other than those involving natural resources.

This chapter focuses predominately on natural gas and its increasingly important role in economies around the world. No other fuel source has the near-term potential to supply the increased demand generated by the Internet and its related communication technologies. Other energy sources, such as wind and solar power, are becoming increasingly competitive, but together all the so-called "alternative" energy technologies supply only 8 percent of U.S. demand.[3] Many of these alternative technologies are and will continue to be hope for the future, but the boom years for natural gas have already started and afford an investor looking for above-average growth potential a potentially fertile hunting ground.

Equally important, this chapter tries to outline and explain the investment paradigm investors must enter and understand to be successful. Understanding the energy exigencies of our world is the first step in becoming a successful energy investor. The importance of establishing a valid reason to invest should be crystal-clear, particularly following the dot.com debacle of the last few years. Many dot.com investment losses could easily have been avoided by simply answering three questions:

1. Why does an investment make sense in terms of fulfilling a demand?
2. How can the product or service make money?
3. When can a return be expected?

It is not only valid to ask these same three questions of any energy investment under consideration, but essential. Let us start with the "why."

GAS DEMAND

Natural-gas pricing has always been cyclical, very much dependent on weather patterns, and, until the mid-1980s, highly regulated. Demand for natural gas in the northern states peaks in the cold winter months, and the hotter southern states require increased supplies in the summer months for air conditioning. Several dynamics are changing this historical paradigm.

In 1973, the United States used 22 trillion cubic feet (TCF) of gas.[4] By 1986, natural-gas demand had dropped to 16.2 TCF.[5] The drop in demand resulted from increased energy efficiencies that flowed from the embargo years, a poor economy, and escalating natural-gas prices. In 1970, the average wellhead price of natural gas in the United States was $0.17.[6] By 1984, the price peaked at $2.66. With gas prices at record levels, demand languished and excess capacity built up quickly, creating what has become known as the "gas bubble."

From the consumers' perspective, the trend was beneficial. An excess of gas ultimately meant lower prices. Utilities also liked the situation. Environmental concerns focused tremendous negative press on coal, the largest fuel source for electric generation. Replacing coal and oil with natural gas as the fuel of choice for new electric-generating capacity made terrific sense. Not only was natural gas an environmentally superior fuel, but excess natural gas capacity, together with increasingly efficient combined-cycle (natural gas and steam) turbine and cogeneration (waste heat) technologies, made both small- and large-scale developments economically competitive with coal-fired plants.[7] The trend toward gas-fired generation gathered speed in the 1980s. In the late 1990s, natural-gas utilization continued to accelerate, as natural-gas prices were often less than $1.50 per thousand cubic feet (MCF). As a result, natural-gas demand increased about 36 percent since 1985, and the "gas bubble" of the previous two decades evaporated.[8]

Currently, there are more than 250 power plants under construction or in the development stage in the United States. Ninety-eight percent of these will be gas-fired.[9] That number is extraordinary but pales in comparison to the 1,900 power plants that Vice President Dick Cheney claims will be required over the next two decades.[10]

Building two power plants a week for 20 years may be possible, but finding long-term natural-gas supplies will require a Herculean effort. This will assure a strong natural gas market for the next four or five decades, assuming normal ranges of economic activity and the availability of no new, rapidly deployable energy technologies. Demand from the electric-power-generating sector alone is likely to increase from 5.5 to 10.3 TCF over the next 10 to 15 years.[11] In part, this additional natural-gas demand will be created by the United States's continuing evolution toward becoming a "wired" society. Not only does the information-age infrastructure consume huge amounts of electric power on a year-round basis, but also each personal computer is estimated to increase an individual household's electric demand up to 5 percent.[12] U.S. electric demand attributable to Internet usage is now estimated to be 7 to 10 percent. It is projected to reach 50 percent between 2010 and 2015.

Because of the surprising increases in demand, natural-gas prices in many areas have risen to more than $9 per MCF in recent years, and spot market prices rocketed to over $50 in southern California during December 2000.[13] Natural-gas consumption in the United States was 22.8 TCF in 2000 and is projected to increase 3.4 percent per year between 2001 and 2002,[14] whereas production is expected to increase 2.1 percent to 18.7 TCF.[15] The balance of demand is expected to be met predominately by imports from Canada.

Increased prices will generate more exploration activity both in the United States and Canada, yet this may not be enough to balance the U.S. supply/demand equation. Remember, oil and natural gas are depleting resources. The typical productive life of a well is about seven years or less. Half of a well's production usually occurs in the first year or two, and during these first years, the rate of production can decrease dramatically. When rapid economic growth occurs, the energy sector must find enough resources to replace established reserves and create adequate additional reserves to meet new demand. Currently, the United States is experiencing rapid declines in some of its largest and most prolific production areas, most specifically, the Gulf Coast. Production from many of the offshore Gulf fields is declining at rates of 25 percent or more per year.[16] The combination of extraordinary growth in the demand for natural gas and the need to replace a significant amount of produced reserves creates an exceptional opportunity for the energy sector and interested investors.

Other important factors exacerbate the problem and reduce the number of viable solutions. For example, demand for natural gas will continue to increase as old nuclear and coal-fired facilities are decommissioned. New nuclear capacity is almost totally out of the question in the foreseeable future. New coal-fired generating facilities would also be difficult to permit under current environmental laws. New clean-coal technologies are available, but mining coal remains a hotly contested topic. Even if new coal-fired or nuclear facilities could be permitted, the development time might easily reach five to seven years or more. Given this scenario, natural gas is the only fuel that has a chance of supporting near- to intermediate-term increases in power generation on the scale necessary to meet projected demand for electric power. In short, there are only two near-term solutions to the electric-power-demand quandary: Either find additional sources of natural gas or reduce electric demand.

Here the astute investor suggests that the most obvious solution has been ignored: Simply use more oil to generate electricity. A number of generating facilities are capable of fuel switching, and, in those cases, oil is a viable alternative. Practically, however, natural gas is the more logical choice for three reasons:

1. Electric-generating technologies have focused on natural gas as the environmental fuel of choice.
2. Natural gas is a far more abundant resource within North America.
3. The long-term international outlook for oil suggests that the United States will have a difficult time increasing the share it consumes. Depending on an uncertain source of energy for our electric generation would be very foolhardy, indeed, particularly as much of the world's oil reserves are in politically unstable areas.

U.S. OIL REALITIES

The United States is a mature oil province. Millions of wells have been drilled in the United States and its coastal waters, making it geologically the most thoroughly explored country in the world. Drilling continues to produce new discoveries every year, but few are "elephants," or giant oil discoveries. Studies indicate that the bulk of recent increases to the United States proved reserve category actually results from improvements in enhanced oil-recovery technologies that extend the useful lives of old fields.[17] Many of this country's largest fields were discovered prior to 1940. Not only are domestic reserves declining alarmingly, but the rate of production is also on a steep downtrend. The 1947 to 2001 United States Domestic Oil Production chart illustrates the point very effectively.

As you can see in Figure 12.1, U.S. domestic oil production reached its peak capacity of 9.6 million barrels per day in 1970.[18] The Middle Eastern

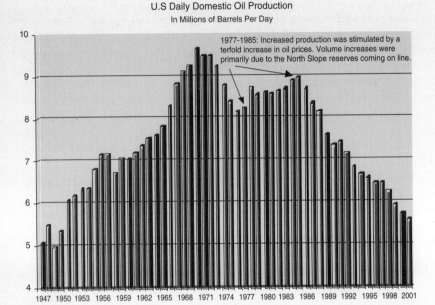

FIGURE 12.1   U.S. daily domestic oil production.

oil-producing countries understood this reality, and that knowledge was a prime factor leading to the oil crises of the 1970s. The United States could no longer defend low oil prices by increasing its production but would have to rely on imports to supply an increasing portion of its domestic demand. By 1977, production dropped to almost 8 million barrels per day. A tenfold increase in the price of oil and the commencement of production from Alaska's huge Prudhoe Bay field only managed to stabilize domestic production until about 1984. Since that time, domestic crude oil production has decreased to less than 6 million barrels per day.

The hope of achieving oil supply self-sufficiency is an impossibility given current economic activity and transportation technologies. The largest U.S. reserve additions since Prudhoe Bay are located in Southern California's coastal waters. These were discovered in the early 1980s, and production schedules are uncertain due to governmental interference. When and if produced, these reserves would supply total U.S. oil demand for about three months. Similar statistics would apply to the Arctic oil reserve, thought by many to be the United States' way toward energy independence.

It is a major challenge for the United States oil industry to simply slow the rate of domestic oil production decline. If prices drop below $25 per barrel, U.S. oil production could well decrease to 3 or 4 million barrels per day during the next 10 years. During 2000, consumption was 19.5 million barrels per day.[19]

It is easy to see why serious consideration of the use of oil to fuel up to 1,900 new electric-generating facilities would be irresponsible. An understanding of the world oil situation clarifies the situation even further.

WORLD OIL ECONOMICS

According to the Energy Information Administration (EIA), the United States has 4.6 percent of the world's population, uses 26 percent of crude oil produced, and contributes 28 percent of the world's economic output. Proven oil reserves have only 21.765 billion barrels. Yearly demand is more than 7 billion barrels, of which about 57 percent is imported.[20]

Oil has been so omnipresent and omnipotent as the king of energy that little thought has been given to other energy sources. Oil does not depend solely on a fixed pipeline infrastructure to deliver the product to market. Pipelines, supertankers, and trucks can economically move oil. This characteristic contributes to OPEC's ability to control world oil markets so effectively. Oil remains the dominant transportation fuel with 97 percent of U.S. vehicles being gasoline-powered.[21] Oil also continues to be the primary fuel source for industrial uses.

For the last two decades, unofficial U.S. energy policy has attempted to stabilize the Middle Eastern countries and to make sure oil continues to flow in the open market. More than one war has been fought in the Middle East to accomplish this goal. In terms of modern-day supply, however, oil has rarely been a scarce commodity. It simply and perversely, from a U.S. perspective, tends to be found in politically uncomfortable, remote, or naturally dangerous areas. OPEC, and most specifically Saudi Arabia, controls the world price of oil. Supplies are relatively secure and will be made available to the limit of productive capacity at prices determined by OPEC. Who will get the production is another and potentially more difficult problem as we look to the future.

A QUESTION OF ALLOCATION

China and India have more than 37.4 percent of the world's population,[22] use about 9 percent of the world's oil supply, and have modest oil reserves.[23] [24] Both of these countries are likely to compete over time for additional energy resources—the same resources the United States depends on for its energy supplies. Communication technologies now link communities throughout the world in real time. China has more than 300 million TVs and an estimated 1.1 billion viewers seeing what lifestyles the developed nations have.[25] They will seek better lifestyles as a result—lifestyles that require more energy. With increased competition for resources, it is easy to see why the United States will not be able to increase its current share of oil supplies and, over time, may have to decrease its dependence on imported energy sources.

Oil industry experts are becoming concerned about long-term oil supplies. When the recent economic boom increased world demand for oil during 1999 and 2000, OPEC was pushed to the limit to provide the necessary supplies. At that time, only two countries were believed to have additional capacity. One of those countries, Saudi Arabia, is considered friendly to the United States but has an increasingly militant Muslim population. The other, Iraq, is an avowed enemy.

Continued increases in world oil demand could create even tighter oil markets, particularly if the large Asian economies resume above-average growth patterns. The availability of incremental oil supplies may all too soon depend entirely on the willingness and ability of OPEC's Middle Eastern members to increase production. This may sound like crying wolf, but it is a world energy reality, especially when a 1 or 2 percent shortage could lead to a doubling of prices or worse.

- "In 2000, the Persian Gulf countries (Bahrain, Iran, Iraq, Kuwait, Qatar, Saudi Arabia, and the United Arab Emirates) produced nearly 28 percent of the world's oil, while holding 65 percent of the world's oil reserves."[26]
- Saudi Arabia holds about 25 percent of known oil resources and produces 8 to 9 million barrels per day from about 1,400 wells.[27]
- OPEC holds 76.7 percent of world oil reserves.
- The United States holds 2 percent of total proven world oil reserves and produces less than 5,830,000 barrels per day from hundreds of thousands of wells.[3]
- The United States uses 25 percent of the world's oil production.

New energy sources must be developed, whether oil, natural gas, biomass, wind, geothermal, or solar. In the long term, the outlook for energy of all kinds is quite bullish. In the near term, however, increasing domestic production of natural gas must be the United States' primary focus. OPEC will continue to supply oil to satisfy world oil demand, but natural gas demand must be supplied on a regional basis. Finding domestic natural gas should be easier than finding equivalent amounts of oil. Only a fraction of the millions of wells drilled domestically have targeted natural gas as the primary objective. This means that there are likely significant domestic resources left to be found. Natural gas is the emerging energy giant and is likely to afford investors significant opportunity to profit if the investor takes care in making investments. Care starts with understanding the territory.

IT'S NOT JUST A BARREL OF OIL EQUIVALENT (BOE)

Analyzing oil energy companies usually starts with a review of pertinent Securities and Exchange Commission (SEC) financial information, other regulatory documents, or companies' annual or quarterly reports. Many of the terms used are familiar, such as P/E ratio and cash flow, whereas others, such as "proved developed producing," "probable," "WTI," and "BOE," are not so familiar and may need some explanation. There is not adequate space to define many of the energy industry's unique terms in this chapter, but it is essential that anyone investing money in the energy sector obtain a good dictionary of terms and spend a little time becoming familiar with the vernacular.

Proved developed producing (PDP) refers to oil and/or gas reserves that have been confirmed by independent engineering analysis and are currently producing. Other "proved" categories include proved behind pipe (PNP) or reserves located directly offsetting producing wells (PUDs). WTI, or West Texas Intermediate, refers to a pricing and quality classification of certain oil found in the United States. BOE is the acronym for "barrels of oil equivalent" and requires some further explanation.

BOE ratios have existed for decades and are accepted as the most practical way of summarizing an oil and gas company's production and reserve statistics. Each 6,000 cubic feet of gas is credited by the SEC as the equivalent of one barrel of oil. In Canada, however, where an increasing percentage of U.S. gas supplies are produced, both a six-to-one and ten-to-one ratio are common. Canadian analysts often apply the most appropriate ratio based on regional pricing. In the United States, SEC protocol virtually dictates the use of the six-to-one ratio.

Not only is identifying the ratio being used important, but recognizing that homogenizing oil and gas values can be a very misleading practice. This practice continues today and successfully misrepresents the values in most reporting oil and gas companies. Knowing the ratio utilized, particularly for any company with significant natural gas reserves, allows the investor to more accurately identify and value assets.

DECOUPLING NATURAL GAS AND OIL

Pricing for oil and gas is increasingly becoming decoupled. Oil and natural gas are not truly fungible commodities, meaning that they can't be freely interchanged. Therefore, the historic concept that 1,000 cubic feet (MCF) of gas is worth its Btu equivalent of oil is becoming less valid and only in situations where fuel switching is practical. Oil and gas commodity values are now independently supply/demand related. This is particularly true given the developing dependency on natural gas as a primary fuel for electric generation.

Natural gas is more closely linked to its local market than oil, and, therefore, the investor's understanding of regional pricing is important. Natural gas is also considered the environmental fuel of choice. Natural gas is most effectively transported through a pipeline system that delivers the product directly to the end user. Pipeline infrastructure has improved measurably over the past decade, making the product more available to industry and individual homeowners. In addition, changes in the regulatory environment have reduced transportation charges and removed monopolistic control over pipeline capacity. All these changes have contributed to differentiating natural gas from oil, but what hasn't changed is the accounting treatment most regulatory bodies use to describe oil and gas assets.

For example, Company A produces net to its account 1,000 MCF (1,000,000 cubic feet) of natural gas in the Sacramento Basin in California during January 2001. It receives a price of $12 per MCF, or $12,000, from Calpine for each day's production. On Company A's balance sheet, this 1,000 MCF gas is valued at the equivalent of 166.67 barrels of oil (1,000/6) or $5,000 based on a value of $30 per barrel. The result is that less that half of the value of Company A's California gas is reflected in its reserves statements. To the degree that Company A has significant gas reserves in California, its true worth will not be found in its SEC filings. The opposite would be true if natural gas were produced at $2 per MCF.

UNDERSTANDING THE TREADMILL

The preceding illustration, only one of many possible, demonstrates the need to understand the territory, and the territory is different from what most technology and service sector investors have come to be familiar with over the past two decades. As pointed out earlier, oil and gas are depleting resources. From the day production starts, there is less available for future use. Every day, exploration and production companies must hop on the treadmill and trudge up the reserve replacement hill.

Resource replacement is accomplished two ways. Companies find new resources through exploration and development activities, or they acquire someone else's resources through mergers or outright purchase. Both approaches can be effective, but doing both well is a rare capacity, particularly for small, independent oil and gas companies. Acquiring resources at attractive prices is often a function of good business acumen. Finding resources through drilling takes a much different set of skills that emphasize scientific expertise.

Understanding which treadmill a company uses to keep replacing produced reserves is important and makes a difference in how a stock is analyzed. Company B is very successful in buying its production during periods in which energy prices are low. These reserves produce terrific profits as prices rise, but the company faces a dilemma. Its staff consists predominantly of business and field operations people who must make a very difficult decision. They must either continue to buy higher and higher-priced reserves or conserve their cash while waiting for lower prices.

Company B chooses to conserve its cash. It understands the cyclical nature of commodity pricing and doesn't want to buy high and sell low. The company continues to sell production and shows very large profits that attract investors by the droves at ever-increasing stock prices. Investors see only that Company B is making a large profit, but they fail to see that the company's reserve base is rapidly eroding. As reserves deplete, production rates drop, cash flow decreases, and share prices plummet.

Company A is an exploration and development firm. It supports a staff of geologists, petroleum engineers, geophysicists, and landmen. During periods of low prices, Company A is always struggling to maintain its staff. Although the company is successful finding oil and gas, the low prices never seem to produce much net cash flow. Over the years, Company A manages to keep its head above water but never has enough cash to fully develop its best and most expensive projects. Miraculously, prices begin to rise, and Company A's exploration activities accelerate. Not only does it have more cash flow, but other exploration companies want to participate in its projects.

Some of the projects are "farmed-out" to third parties. A farm-out occurs when the working interest owner transfers the responsibility for exploration and/or development activity and costs to another entity. The terms of the farm-out may call for a cash payment to the prospect generator, but also usually provides Company A with a "back-in after payout."

In addition to farming out a number of properties, Company A decides to drill the best projects for its own account. Drilling expense skyrockets as the company successfully drills and completes one well after another. A new field is developed and pipeline connections completed, but the company's high exploration and development expenses result in substantial losses being reported. Investors see these losses and begin selling the shares, despite the fact that reserves are increasing at a rapid rate.

Each of these examples illustrates some of the difficulties in analyzing oil and gas companies. In each case, investors react exactly opposite to developing fundamentals. The first lesson to learn is that the value of a resource company resides in its resource base. If Company B, as described above, fails to replace its reserve base, its economic viability is jeopardized regardless of its current cash flow or short-term profitability. Therefore, look for the period-to-period reserve and production tables first. Companies often summarize this material in their annual reports. More detailed, three-year historic data are available in the 10-K under Item I: Business, Item 2: Properties, or in the Supplemental Information. The 10-Ks, as well as the Quarterly and Material Event filings, are available online at the SEC's EDGAR site. Information from these reports will quickly establish if the company is growing its reserve base and whether the rate of production is increasing or decreasing. This information can eliminate a number of prospective, but subpar, companies very quickly.

The next step is to take a closer look at the quality of reserves. Reserves do not represent fixed values. The location of the reserves, production characteristics, and the lifting cost per barrel (the cost to produce a barrel) are all-important factors.

Reserves are a measure of assets in the ground. Because there is no definitive way to know the amount of oil or gas that will ultimately be produced, reserve engineers qualify their estimates in several important ways. PDP reserves represent the highest level of certainty and quantify those volumes that are expected to be recovered from producing wells using existing equipment and operating methods. Flow rates and flowing tubing pressures provide the raw information for the petroleum engineer, who then calculates the amount of resource that will be recovered. Proved undeveloped reserves are also usually calculated. These reserves are known as PUDs. For reserve calculation purposes, PUDs receive a moderate discount because production characteristics are generally known, but the timing of production is uncertain. Other reserve categories are probable and possible, although the SEC does not recognize these classifications.

Even though a reserve is proved, that does not mean it has a fixed value. Oil and gas quality varies considerably. Some gas, for example, contains H_2S, a very dangerous contaminate that must be carefully removed. Production of this gas requires very expensive production casing and surface equipment. Lease operating expenses (LOEs) for this type of production are high and should be carefully noted by the investor. Some oil is highly viscous (referred to as low API gravity oil) and sells at a discount. Generally, the lower the gravity rating of an oil, the higher the production costs. API gravity is a scale established by the American Petroleum Institute and is in general use in the petroleum industry. The higher the "gravity degree" designation is, the higher the quality of oil. High-gravity oil may receive a premium and is easier to produce and deliver to market. Total lifting costs consist of lease operating expenses plus ad valorem and production taxes. Lifting costs per barrel provide a good metric to compare oil and gas company operating efficiencies.

Natural gas has other quality distinctions. Gas sells based on its purity and its BTU value. Pipeline-quality gas is generally defined as gas that contains few impurities and approximately 1,000 Btu per MCF. Gas with 1,200 Btu content would usually receive approximately a 20 percent premium. Gas may be rich in liquid hydrocarbons (condensate). If the quantity is high enough, condensates can be stripped from the gas and sold separately.

Physical characteristics of a hydrocarbon are important, but must be considered in a geographic context. Is dependable transportation available? Is the transportation market competitive? If only one natural-gas pipeline serves an area, exorbitant transportation costs could make production of the natural gas uneconomic. Remote natural gas discoveries often have to wait years before an adequate transportation infrastructure develops. Trucking gas is not economic. During the embargo years, a common complaint was that oil and gas companies owned thousands of wells capable of production that were plugged to keep the supply/demand equation tight. With the high drilling costs and high-risk profile associated with drilling any well, it is a rare company that can plug a potentially economic well. Potentially productive wells are plugged, but only when there is no way to get the product to market economically.

Most oil and gas companies produce every barrel and/or MCF as rapidly as best practices will allow. The time value of money dictates this practice, as does the reality that internally generated cash flow is the best source of capital available to most exploration companies. Generally, a company's primary market risk relates to commodity prices. Operating expenses, taxes, transportation, and fixed overhead are relatively known values. Fluctuations in spot commodity prices are unknowable. Resource companies are increasingly hedging output to eliminate some of the market risk. Therefore, investors should pay special attention to an oil and gas company's hedging policy.

ANALYTIC TOOLS AND DATA INTERPRETATION

Analyzing an oil and gas company utilizes a standard set of financial tools, but these tools are applied differently, depending on the company's ultimate focus. There are two general categories—exploration companies and integrated energy companies. For example, earnings per share, the cornerstone for most equities evaluation, is relatively unimportant for "junior" oil and gas exploration companies, but for a large energy organization (for example, ExxonMobil, BP, and Royal Dutch/Shell), earnings per share and the P/E ratio remain the most utilized tools.

The operations of integrated energy organizations start with the exploration process, known as "upstream" activities, and often encompass numerous horizontally and vertically related activities. "Downstream" activities include all activities that follow the production of oil, condensate, and natural gas beginning with transportation to the processing plant or refinery.

Production of hydrocarbons for the integrated energy company is the beginning of a manufacturing cycle. Raw materials (crude oil or natural gas) are refined or processed, and the products are distributed. For many integrated energy companies, the distribution process involves company-owned outlets. At every point in the process, margins can be adjusted by pricing. Profitability is the goal as well as the most accepted measure by which most investors judge an integrated energy company's success. Applying the same measures to a pure exploration company, however, would not be fruitful.

The world of the pure exploration company is far different. Its end product is the crude oil or natural gas produced. Exploration companies have virtually no say in determining the price at which their production is sold. If the product is oil, OPEC has the power to determine prices. If the product is natural gas, prices have been historically determined in large part by weather. The success of this type of company is measured by cash flow, reserves, and the potential to find additional reserves. Because exploration activities are very expensive, an active exploration company will rarely show large net earnings. The primary goal of most exploration companies is not to maximize retained earnings but to convert cash into identifiable and producible reserves. Table 12.1 shows sections of a financial summary for Company A, the pure exploration and development example used earlier.

SHARE DATA AND CAPITALIZATION

The Share Data and Capitalization section is relatively straightforward. Only two categories in Table 12.1 need further comment—dilution and the rather vague concept of "Enterprise value." Many small companies issue warrants, options, or convertible financial instruments, the exercise of which can have a dramatic effect on per share results. If these instruments are "in the

TABLE 12.1 Company A—Share Data and Capitalization

Share price 5/22/01	$4.63
Shares outstanding (Million)	14.3
Fully diluted shares (Million)	15.6
Public float	69%
Market capitalization ($Million)	66.3
Working capital (surplus) ($Million)	1.7
Long-term debt ($Million)	10.7
Enterprise value ($Million)	78.7

money," it is best to rely on fully diluted numbers. Knowing when these instruments expire is equally important. Even relatively active markets for publicly traded equities can be overwhelmed by sales resulting from the exercise of options and warrants.

Care must be taken when accepting values listed under catchall terms such as enterprise value. In Table 12.2, enterprise value is based on current market prices and may have only a slight relationship to underlying asset values or income.

The use of multiples is an effective way of providing a snapshot of an energy company. Unlike most other industries, the best multiple to use is cash flow per share (CFPS) and not the P/E ratio. As pointed out earlier, rapidly increasing earnings may mean that an energy company is no longer spending funds on exploration. Earnings are dramatically affected by accounting treatments. Resource-based organizations account for exploration and development activities by using either "successful efforts" or "full cost accounting." The difference between these methods is usually significant in terms of earnings results but relatively unimportant for cash flow. "Successful efforts" requires that capital expenditures incurred for exploration and development activities that do not result in identifying economically recoverable resources be charged to exploration expense. "Full cost accounting" includes all exploration efforts and results in higher depletion cost per unit of resource.

The sensitivity analysis in Table 12.3 is very helpful in analyzing possible future events. Being able to project the impact of price swings may make the difference between reporting a profit or a loss. Sensitivity analysis helps identify companies that are best positioned to take advantage of a developing economic situation.

TABLE 12.2 Multiples

Multiples	2001E	2002E
Price/CFPS (FD)	2.8×	2.8×
Price/EPS (FD)	5.6×	6.0×

TABLE 12.3 Sensitivities

Sensitivities	Changes CFPS(FD)
Gas price +0.10/MCF	$0.017
Gas production + 10 MMCF/d	$.26
WTI + $1.00 $/bbl	$.0.03
Oil production + 1,000 b/d	$0.15

RESERVE AND PRODUCTION ANALYSIS

The heart of any resource company is its reserve base and its productive capacity. Tables 12.4a and 12.4b show various reserve categories. Look for reserve growth in all categories. Depending on the source of the information, only proved categories may be available. Canadian companies generally show probable reserves, whereas U.S. companies tend to conform to SEC reporting, which does not recognize probable or possible reserves. Historic reserve and production tables are also good sources of information. Although production numbers do not directly reflect reserves, three or more years of increased production rates would suggest that new producing reserves are being added to the asset base. Table 12.5 illustrates the use of BOEs to show reserve growth over time. As noted earlier, BOEs are a convenient way of summarizing reserve statistics and are most effectively used to show period-to-period trends (see Table 2.5).

From a growth perspective, PUDs may not be as important as probable reserves. If the PUDs refer to resources that are "behind pipe," production of those reserves may have to wait years or even decades before contributing to cash flow as the currently proved producing reserves are depleted.

Probable reserves, shown in Tables 12.4a and 12.4b, reflect likely deposits. These may be proved by new drilling and are likely to be the subject of the company's most immediate efforts. Reserve additions and subsequent increases in production are likely to occur in large chunks as a new discovery is made. Remember that a 20 percent success rate for exploratory wells is considered good (see Table 12.6).

TABLE 12.4A   Reserves (1/1/2001)

	Oil & natural gas liquids (000 bbls)
Proved producing (2000)	5,389
Proved undeveloped	951
Probable	2,340
Proved + probable	8,680
Proved + half probable	7,510
Producing reserves percent	62%

TABLE 12.4B   Production Analysis

	Natural Gas (Billion cubic feet—BCF)
Proved producing (2000)	50.3
Proved undeveloped	8.9
Probable	16.2
Proved + probable	75.4
Proved + half probable	67.3
Producing reserves percent	67%

TABLE 12.5   Use of BOEs

Reserves	BOE
1998	10,500
1999	12,600
2000	16,225

TABLE 12.6   Production and Cash Flow Summary

Dec. 31	Daily Oil Production (BOPD)	Gas Production (MMCFD/d)	Cash Flow Per Share (CFPS)	Price/Cash Flow (P/CF)
1998	1,500	6.3	$0.30	5.2×
1999	1,710	9.2	$0.470	4.3×
2000	1,725	14.5	$1.19	2.3×
2001 (Est.)	1,975	19.7	$1.84	2.5×
2002 (Est.)	2,200	22.8	$1.74	2.6×

For the short- or intermediate-term investor, production data are most important, perhaps even more important than reserves. Production translates into ability to grow (see Table 12.7). Company A's "Daily Oil Production" and "Gas Production" columns in Table 12.6 clearly indicate a strong growth pattern.

Proper production assessment also includes knowing gas and liquids ratios. Table 12.7 lists these values. The production figures describe well-balanced liquids (oil and natural-gas liquids/condensate) and natural-gas production. This company would probably not be a candidate for an investor seeking a pure natural-gas play but shows excellent natural-gas production growth. The rapid increase in cash flow in 2000, as shown in Table 12.6, is likely a function of exceptionally strong prices for natural gas. The drop in price to cash flow multiples for 2000 and later suggests that investors are wary of giving too much value to the rapid increase in cash flow due to uncertainty regarding future pricing.

FINANCIAL SUMMARIES

Present value (PV) calculations help clarify a company's production and asset characteristics. Many oil and gas fields yield their resources slowly and have very long economic lives. Other fields may be in remote areas or in an off-shore development that may require years to build the production infrastructure. The value of these reserves must be adjusted to reflect the time/value of money. The Financial Accounting Standards Board (FASB) requires a standardized measure of future net cash flow (see Table 12.8). This is computed by calculating the year-end prices for net proved reserves, adjusting for costs, taxes, and a discount rate. Generally, PV values of between 8 and 15 percent are used for internal corporate purposes and 10 percent for SEC filings. Reserves that won't be produced for 10 or more years carry little value on the balance sheet.

Addition of the PV-adjusted reserve value and undeveloped land value, less working capital and long-term debt, provides the net asset value (NAV). Comparing the net asset value to its market prices shows that the company is selling for 67 percent of its NAV. Assuming there are no off-balance sheet contingencies, such as environmental issues or lawsuits, this company appears to be a good investment opportunity (see Table 12.9).

A quick review of financial results would confirm this assessment. Cash flow per share shows strong period-to-period growth. Company A is not producing earnings by limiting its exploration and development efforts. The CAPEX to cash-flow ratio suggests that management is aggressively employing its financial resources to develop additional reserves.

TABLE 12.7 Production 2000A

Oil & NGLs (Bbls/d))	1,725
Gas (MMCF/d)	14.5
Equivalent (BOE/d)	3,174
Period over period growth	21%
Liquids leverage	54%
Gas leverage	46%

TABLE 12.8 Net Asset Value ($Million, Jan. 1, 2001)

Reserves (PV @ 15% percent pre-tax)	$99.63
Undeveloped land ($75/acre)	10.72
Working capital	(1.68)
Other assets/liabilities	0.0
Long-term debt	(10.65)
Net asset value ($000)	98.02
NAV/share	$6.85
NAV/share (FD)	$6.29
Price/NAV	0.67X

TABLE 12.9 Financial Results—Current Stock Price: $4.63
($Million Except Per Share Amounts)

Oil & gas revenue	$35,680
Cash flow	$18,422
CFPS	$1.21
CFPS (Fully Diluted)	$1.18
Net Income	$7,546
EPS (basic)	$0.53
EPS (Fully Diluted)	$0.48
Capital expenditures	20,698
CAPEX/cash low	1.1X
Long-term debt	10,654

VALUATION TECHNIQUES

Most financial/reserve reports will present several additional evaluation parameters that will assist in determining how effectively an organization
employs capital and whether its shares represent fair value. A good starting

point is to look for a reserves-per-share amount. One good formula adds all categories of proved reserves and one-half probable reserves if this information is available. Remember to convert the gas reserves to BOEs at a ratio that accurately values gas relative to prices. The most acceptable ratio is six MCF for each barrel equivalent. Proved liquid reserves plus one-half probable reserves equals 7,510,000 barrels. The gas equivalent is calculated by taking 67.3 BCF (67,300,000,000) and dividing by 6,000 (6 MCF), or 11,216,666 BOEs. The 18,726,666 total is then divided by 15,600,000 (fully diluted shares). The result shows that each share represents 1.2 BOEs. Investors purchasing the shares at $4.63 per share are paying about $3.86 per BOE in the ground. This number must be compared to current oil prices and finding costs for other exploration companies. An exploration company that can find a barrel of oil or equivalent of natural gas for less than $6.00 is very efficient. Based on its reserves-per-share, Company A is a possible target for acquisition.

Another important parameter is the "reserve replacement" factor. To calculate this value, multiply the daily BOE production by the period of production (3,174 BOEs × 365 = 1,158,510 BOE produced for the year). Divide the net increase in reserves from 1999 to 2000 by this number. Reserves increased during that period by 3,625,000 barrels and production was 1,158,510 barrels. Company A's reserve replacement factor is 3.13×. The investor is looking for positive reserve replacement values. Anything above 1.2× replacement (100 percent of the reserves produced plus a 20 percent increase) is good.

Reserve life is also an important indicator and is stated in a company's financial report. This is calculated by dividing net proven reserves by last year's production rate. A very short reserve life—anything less than five or six years—would be a point of concern for a company that had been in business more than three or four years. A very long reserve life might also be of concern. Spending capital to develop reserves that cannot be produced in a reasonable amount of time might not be an efficient use of capital.

These valuation techniques represent some of the more important energy industry criteria. If utilized in the context of the current economic and energy outlook, this knowledge should be helpful in evaluating equities. There are also other investment vehicles available to which some of this information can be affectively applied, including limited partnerships, derivatives, and direct drilling participations. These types of investments, however, are very specialized, and investors are cautioned to seek professional advice before making such investments.

NOTES

[1]Norland, D. Estimates of Energy Expenditures as a Percent of the Economy. Memorandum. (2001).

[2]Huber, P. & Mills, M. "Got a computer?" *Wall Street Journal*. (September 7, 2000). Available online: **http://www.manhattan-institute.org/html/_wsj-got_a_comp.html**

[3]Hume, S. "Alternative energy will fill the void after the end of oil: Alternatives." *The Vancouver Sun*. Vancouver, Canada. (June 15, 2001).

[4]Energy Information Agency (EIA). Historical natural gas annual 1930 through 1999. Available online: **http://www.eia.doe.gov/neic/historic.htm**

[5]Kumins, L. "Natural gas prices: Overview of market factors and policy options." Congressional Research Service: Report for Congress. (January 23, 2001). Available online: **http://www.cnie.org/nle/eng-69.html**

[6]Energy Information Agency "History of natural gas annual 1930 through 1999." (2001). Available online: **http://www.eia.doe.gov/neic/historic/historic.htm**

[7]EIA. "Oil, natural gas, coal, electricity, environment profile: United States of America." (April, 2001). Available online: **http://www.eia.doe.gov/emeu/cabs/usa.html**

[8]Kumins, L. "Natural gas prices: Overview of market factors and policy options." Congressional Research Service: Report for Congress. (January 23, 2001). Available online: **http://www.cnie.org/nle/eng-69.html**

[9]Haines, L. "Sustained growth on the U.S. natural gas horizon." *Oil & Gas Investor*. (May, 2001).

[10]Cheney, D. "New National Energy Strategy." Speech given in Toronto April 30, 2001.

[11]Arledge, D. as quoted by Haines, L. "Sustained growth on the U.S. natural gas horizon." *Oil & Gas Investor*. (May, 2001).

[12]Huber, P. & Mills, M. "Got a computer?" *Wall Street Journal*. (September 7, 2000). Available online: **http://www.manhattan-institute.org/html/_wsj-got_a_comp.html**

[13]California Energy Commission Weekly natural gas report. (June 11, 2001). Available online: **http://38.144.192.166/naturalgas/update.html**

[14]EIA. "U.S. Natural gas markets: Recent trends and prospects for the future." (May, 2001) **http://www.eia.doe.gov/oiaf/servicerpt/naturalgas/index.htm**

[15]EIA. "Annual energy outlook 2001 with projections to 2020." Table 13: Natural gas supply and disposition. (December, 2000). Available online: http://www.eia.doe.gov/oiaf/aeo/index.html#preface

[16]Barrionuevo, A., Fialka, J. & Smith, R. "Federal policies, industrial shifts, produced natural-gas crunch." *Wall Street Journal.* (January 3, 2001).

[17]EIA. "U.S. crude oil, natural, gas, and natural gas liquids reserves: 1997 Annual report." (September, 1998).

[18]EIA Table 5.2. "Crude oil production and oil well productivity, 1954–1999." Annual energy review 1999. (2001).

[19]EIA. "Oil, natural gas, coal, electricity, environment profile: United States of America." (April, 2001). Available online: http://www.eia.doe.gov/emeu/cabs/usa.html

[20]EIA. "Oil, natural gas, coal, electricity, environment profile: United States of America." (April, 2001). Available online: http://www.eia.doe.gov/emeu/cabs/usa.html

[21]"New transportation fuels: Trends and developments." Global Information, Inc.

[22]Population Reference Bureau Population 2000. (2001). Available online: http://www.prb.org/pubs/wpds2000/world.htm

[23]EIA. "Country energy briefs: India." (April 26, 2001). Available online: http://www.eia.doe.gov/emeu/cabs/china.html

[24]EIA. "Country energy briefs: India." (January 25, 2001). Available online: http://www.eia.doe.gov/emeu/cabs/india.html

[25]China in brief. "Culture and art: Television." (n.d.). Available online: http://www.china.org.cn/e-china/cultureAndart/television.htm

[26]EIA. "Persian Gulf Oil and Gas Exports Fact Sheet," p.1. (June 7, 2001). Available online: http://www.eia.doe.gov/emeu/cabs/pgulf.html

[27]EIA. "Saudi Arabia energy oil information." (June 2001). Available online: http://www.eia.doe.gov/emeu/cabs/saudi.html

[28]EIA. "Oil, natural gas, coal, electricity, environment profile: United States of America." (April, 2001). Available online: http://www.eia.doe.gov/emeu/cabs/usa.html

index